FOR SUCH A *Time* AS THIS

FOR SUCH A *Time* AS THIS

TALKS FROM THE
2007 BYU WOMEN'S CONFERENCE

DESERET
BOOK

SALT LAKE CITY, UTAH

Library of Congress Cataloging-in-Publication Data

Women's Conference (2007 : Brigham Young University)
  For such a time as this : talks from the 2007 BYU Women's Conference compilation.
    p. cm.
  ISBN 978-1-59038-861-7 (hardbound : alk. paper)
  1. Mormon women—Religious life—Congresses. I. Title.
  BX8641.W73 2007a
  289.3'32082—dc22   2007047843

Printed in the United States of America
Worzalla Publishing Co., Stevens Point, WI

10 9   8   7   6   5   4   3   2   1

Contents

"For Such a Time As This"

Wendy Watson Nelson

Our theme for this year's women's conference is one with which we are all familiar. You know the story. And you know the statement: "Who knoweth whether thou art come to the kingdom for such a time as this?" (Esther 4:14). It is from the life of Queen Esther, who, at great peril to herself, stepped forward in a most crucial way to save her people. She was the right person, at the right place, at the right time, with the right preparation to do what the Lord needed her to do.

Sisters, *we* are here in mortality now, because we're supposed to be here, now! The doctrine is clear on this point. And among those things we are to do while we're here on earth is to complete the mortal assignments we were given premortally and to which we agreed. The Savior said that He came to earth to do the will of His Father who sent Him. In like manner, we are here to do the will of our Father, that same Father, who sent us.

President George Q. Cannon said it this way:

"God has chosen us out of the world and has given us a great mission. I do not entertain a doubt myself but that we were selected and fore-ordained for the mission before the world was; that we had our parts

---

Wendy Watson Nelson holds a PhD in family therapy and gerontology and was a professor of marriage and family therapy at Brigham Young University for many years. She worked as a marriage and family therapist in addition to teaching, researching, writing, and consulting in this field. She has published several books and is the wife of Elder Russell M. Nelson.

allotted to us in this mortal state of existence as our Savior had His assigned to Him."¹ The great mission to which President Cannon was referring was the charge to build up the latter-day kingdom of God on earth by taking the gospel to every nation, kindred, tongue, and people. Note that he said every one of us had our parts allotted to us.

In order to fulfill the wonderful mission for which we were sent to earth, we need to be prepared! I love the words of the angel Gabriel when he came to Daniel in an hour of great need: "O Daniel, I am now come forth to give thee skill and understanding" (Daniel 9:22).

A few months prior to my marriage, I had an experience that illustrated, in a dramatic fashion, just how vital it is that we are prepared with the skill and understanding necessary to do what the Lord needs us to do. On the first weekend of November 2005, I accompanied my dear friend Sheri Dew to Palmyra, New York, where we participated in a symposium on the Prophet Joseph Smith.

Because our obligations lasted into Saturday evening and in order to be home in time to meet our Sunday commitments, we were booked on two early-morning Sunday flights from Rochester to Cincinnati and from Cincinnati to Salt Lake City. As a result, we pulled into the Rochester airport at 4:30 a.m. We were walking towards the terminal, when suddenly— unexplainably—I tripped and fell and did what could only be described as a cartoon face-plant, right into the cement!

Sheri, who was walking ahead of me, heard my thud, turned around, and saw me face down on the pavement, which was quickly turning red from the blood pouring from a large gash in my forehead and nose. She helped me to a sitting position on the sidewalk, and we dug through our bags looking for something to slow the bleeding. We couldn't find anything and began to look for someone to help us. There were three police cars parked only a few feet away but not a policeman to be found. And it was so early in the morning that there was not one other person in sight.

I instantly knew what had to be done. I said to Sheri, "You've got to pray for me." Without hesitating, she knelt down on the pavement next to me and began to plead with the Lord. The only way I can describe that prayer is to say that she prayed with power. She petitioned the Lord to stop my fear, to stop the bleeding, to stop the pain. And she pleaded that she would know what to do to take care of me.

My fear stopped instantly! The bleeding slowed dramatically. And the pain stopped too.

The Lord honored Sheri's prayer of faith. I did, however, still have a hole in my face that desperately needed medical attention. While I sat on the curb, Sheri darted off in search of help, finally finding and persuading an ornery cabby to call the police. A few minutes later, an officer arrived, took one look at me, and called the paramedics. About five minutes later, a fire truck, with sirens blaring, and an EMT truck, filled with paramedics clad in silver fire suits, arrived.

There must have been several million dollars worth of equipment lined up and years of emergency and medical experience available to help us. But with all due respect to these professionals, on that morning it felt as though we were dealing with Dumb and Dumber! They did *not* have the skill and understanding to help me. In fact, they couldn't quite figure out how to open up the bandages. Looking back, I wonder if their clumsiness was a response to the horrifying sight of my injury.

As they fumbled with the bandages, the EMT asked if I wanted to be transported to the emergency room. Sheri instantly intervened: "No, I'm taking her home." With a flimsy bandage finally applied so I would not scare the other passengers, I walked with Sheri's help through the airport. Once at our gate, she found a store that had basic first aid supplies. My first clue about the size of the wound occurred when she applied the Neosporin. Instead of dabbing it on the wound, she squeezed it into the hole, much like you would squeeze icing onto a cake! Just how *big* was that hole? I'll never know, because she never let me see the wound.

With the injury finally protected by a bandage that covered most of my forehead and nose, I was feeling fine, and I settled back into my seat on the plane. There was no fear, no pain, no bleeding. As the plane took off, I mentioned that I had an appointment later that week with a dermatologist and perhaps I should have him take a look at the injury.

Sheri's response was careful: "Oh," she said, "you know, after all you've been through this morning, you're probably not going to feel much like going to church today. When we get to Cincinnati, why don't we call ahead and see if we can find a surgeon, a *plastic* surgeon, in Salt Lake who will see you today? We might as well take care of this as soon as we arrive home."

She said all of this very matter-of-factly. I still had no idea just how serious my circumstance was. We did as Sheri suggested, and upon landing in Salt Lake City we learned that we were to go immediately to LDS Hospital, where a superb plastic surgeon was waiting.

As he took off my bandage, his expression told the story: "Oh, yes," he said, "it's a good thing you called me today. It looks as though you left a pound of flesh on that New York sidewalk!"

An hour later I was in surgery, where it took countless stitches (the surgeon guessed that there were well over three hundred) to put my face back together. However, the surgery did not take place until after, at the instigation of Sheri, I received a priesthood blessing.

After hearing about my accident, a friend, an experienced nurse, said, "Sheri was the right person to be with you, Wendy. I might have held up my compact mirror and said, 'Just look at this hole in your face! Notice how well-exposed the nasal bone is!' But Sheri was right to never let you see it."

There were several reasons Sheri was the right person to be with me. In the very moment, at 4:30 A.M. on a dirty airport sidewalk, she had the spiritual skill and understanding to know how to petition the Father with power in the name of the Son, so that the pain would stop, the fear would stop, and the bleeding would stop. And then she knew how to hear the voice of the Lord and His directions through the Spirit to get me from the airport sidewalk to the surgical suite.

I have often wondered how differently the story might have unfolded had Sheri not been with me:

What if I'd been with someone who didn't know how to draw upon the powers of heaven?

What if I'd been with someone who had said, "Wendy, I'll pray, but I've been meaning to repent of some things to increase my purity"; or "I've been meaning to spend more time in the scriptures so I can learn to hear the voice of the Lord, through the word of the Lord"; or "I've been meaning to spend more time in the temple so I can better understand the kind of power with which I've been endowed"; or "I've been meaning to seek more diligently, *but* I've been so busy with so many other things—good things, but not things of the Spirit! So, I'm sorry, Wendy. Let's say a little prayer and see if we can get the paramedics here."

I shudder to think what might have happened that morning if I had only been able to trust in the arm of flesh, especially when so much of mine was lying on that airport sidewalk! But I don't need to shudder. I just need to be grateful that Sheri was with me. She *was* the right person.

Let me tell you three accounts of other women who were in the right place, at the right time, with the right skills and understanding.

The first story: After much time and diligent effort to help a struggling missionary, a mission president was on the verge of sending the elder home. The mission president's wife came to her husband one day and said, "I don't feel quite right about this. Are you sure this young elder should go home? I've watched him. I've looked into his face, and this is a good young man." This visionary woman entreated her husband to reconsider his decision, which he did, and the elder stayed. And the outcome? The young elder served not only his full time in the mission field—not only a worthy mission—he served a splendid mission for the Lord. The mission president's wife was the right person, in the right place, at the right time, with the right skill and understanding to see beyond the surface. She had eyes to see the young elder's true self!

Story number two: A young woman prayed every night of her marriage that she would be protected from her husband's abuse. Her husband was under the influence of pornography and other evil practices, such as lying and oppression, and he perpetrated sexual, emotional, and mental abuse upon her from their wedding night forward. Because he looked the part of a "good Latter-day Saint man," only her mother and one friend believed her when she finally reached out for help. The Spirit confirmed for each woman that something was not quite right with the young woman's situation.

Let me pause here to say that I learned as a marriage and family therapist that when a woman says there is something not quite right, there is something really wrong.

In any event, these three women—the young woman, her mother, and her friend—learned to pray with power, to access protection and direction from the Lord. The young woman was miraculously protected from any further abuse. Many times she experienced her husband being stopped in his angry, accusing, mistreating tracks by what seemed to be unseen arms. Her mother and her friend were the right people, in the right place, at the right time, with the right skill and understanding to save her.

Story number three is actually a volume of experiences of women with whom I have spoken who have found their son or daughter through adoption—fascinating against-all-odds stories of overcoming government red tape, huge fees, an illness of the child. In every case, these women— mothers who would never give up—knew through promptings of the Spirit that there was another child who was theirs. And nothing could stop them. Like Pharaoh's daughter who found Moses in the bulrushes, these mothers were at the right place, at the right time, with the right skills and understanding, to find their children and bring them home.

Each of these accounts of faithful women prompts a simple but crucial question for you and me to consider. And the question is: How do you and I acquire spiritual skills and understanding so that *we* can be in the right place, at the right time, with the right preparation to do whatever the Lord needs us to do, including all we promised premortally to do?

For a decade I've watched Sheri driven to her knees, to the scriptures, and to the temple as she has faced one overwhelming assignment and disappointment after another. On that early November morning, I was the grateful recipient of the spiritual skill and understanding it has taken her years to acquire.

May I suggest that some of the most heart-wrenching, discouraging events in our lives—from which we long to be set free—are actually designed to prepare us with the very skills and understanding the Lord needs us to have. As we draw closer to the Lord and put our total trust in Him, in His power, and in His timing, we can leave our fires of affliction more pure, more refined, and with more skills and understanding, instead of leaving having been burnt to a crisp!

Elder Neal A. Maxwell spoke of our personal challenges this way: "Unless we are filled with resolve, what will we say to the heroes and heroines of Martin's Cove and the Sweetwater? That 'we admire you, but we are reluctant to wade through our own rivers of chilling adversity'? . . . By divine appointment, 'these are [our] days' (Helaman 7:9). . . . Moreover, though we live in a failing world, we have not been sent here to fail."[2]

It is simply inconceivable that our Father would have selected us for our day, the latter part of the latter days, if He didn't have confidence that we could overcome the world and fulfill the wonderful missions for which we were sent to earth.

In 1979 President Spencer W. Kimball prophesied about our mission as the women of these last days. Many of us can repeat from memory President Kimball's prophesy:

"Much of the major growth that is coming to the Church in the last days will come because many of the good women of the world (in whom there is often such an inner sense of spirituality) will be drawn to the Church in large numbers. This will happen to the degree that the women of the Church reflect righteousness and articulateness in their lives and to the degree that [they] are seen as distinct and different—in happy ways—from the women of the world."[3] Sisters, what are we doing to become more righteous and articulate? What are we doing to show that we are different, in happy ways, from the women of the world, such that they would be drawn to us rather than annoyed by us?

And one more question: Do *you* feel a growing urgency to do all that the Lord requires of you so that you can fulfill your life mission? Every woman here was commissioned to do something, and probably many "somethings," for the Lord.

I think of a great woman—a wife, mother, and grandmother—who has recently been focused on gaining a better understanding of her life's mission. This past Christmas she called and said, "I did all the right things. We had wonderful food and scripture readings. The children performed the nativity. We sang carols and took pictures. We celebrated the Savior's birth as a family and had a marvelous time being together. But now that Christmas is over, I'm looking for more meaning in my life." What a spiritually in-tune woman! The Spirit is moving upon her spirit and letting her know that there is yet more to her mission on earth. She is like a thoroughbred ready to run. She wants to do all that she was born to do— all that she agreed premortally to do here in mortality.

Even though she is doing all kinds of "right things," her spirit can tell there is something more, or something different, she needs to be doing. As she has thought about it, she knows that missionary work has always stirred her soul. Could it be that she and her gifts for searching out missionary moments and for preaching the gospel with simplicity and power were brought to the kingdom for such a time as this?

Congratulate yourself if you are in a situation similar to my friend, looking for more meaning in your life. It may mean that your spirit is restless and knows that you were indeed born to do something different, or more, than you are presently doing. If you feel a little unsettled these days, the problem may be that you are not yet doing what you came here to do. Does it mean that you need to make a dramatic change? It may, but it may not.

Just the other day I had an unexpected conversation with a friend who has felt very restless and underused. She is a faithful, multitalented, capable woman, and yet she said, almost in despair, "I wonder if I even have a mission!" Later, she poured her heart out to the Lord, just as she has relentlessly been doing for months. However, this time she listened in a different way and received a little "corrective feedback" from the Lord. She had been looking for her mission somewhere other than the situation in which He has presently placed her. Through the whisperings of the Spirit, her mind was enlarged and her heart changed. She was flooded with ideas, ideas confirming that she was in exactly the right place for what the Lord needs her to do. No one was more surprised than she.

President Joseph F. Smith taught this about our missions on earth:

"He that sent His only-begotten Son into the world to accomplish the mission which He did, also sent every soul within the sound of my voice, and indeed every man and woman in the world, to accomplish a mission, and that mission cannot be accomplished by neglect; nor by indifference; nor can it be accomplished in ignorance. We must learn our duty; learn the requirements that the Lord has made at our hands, and understand the responsibilities that He has placed upon us."[4]

President Smith's statement prompts the question for each of us: Why are you here on earth at this particular time? For example:

- Have you been asked to shepherd strong-willed spirits and build them into talented, faithful men and women?
- Have you been asked to learn to distinguish good from evil and to bravely speak up against practices which support the adversary's agenda?
- Have you been asked to sacrifice in a particular way for the mission of another?

- Have you been sent to live in a troubled family situation in order to increase the purity in that lineage by putting a stop, once and for all, to various impurities?
- Have you been sent to teach with clarity and charity eternal truths that will help the women of the world and their families?

What is *your* part in helping the Savior with His mission, which is to bring to pass the immortality and eternal life of man? (see Moses 1:39).

Sisters, we were indeed born for such a time as this. We came trailing abilities and assignments from our premortal existence. And the truth about finding our mission is this: Because we love the Lord and have faith in Him, we *want* to be obedient to Him. We want to do whatever He asks us to do. We are willing and happy to be, as Paul described himself, "a prisoner of Jesus Christ" (Philemon 1:1). It is our obedience to the Lord that positions us to fill the measure of our creation. The more obedient we are to Him, the more we grow into our true selves, and the more we are able to do what we came here to do. Increasingly impeccable obedience is key to finding our missions.

And consecration is key to fulfilling our missions once we've found them! The only way I know to do what we've come here to do, to live up to who we are, and to worthily fulfill our premortal commitments is to consecrate all that we have, and all that we are, to the Lord. That means putting Him and His work first. That means developing our gifts and talents to build up His kingdom rather than our own. That means giving Him even our will.

What do you think would happen if we were to look at every ability and every talent, every challenge and grueling obstacle, as being given to us "for such a time as this"? Every gift and endowment from above—every opportunity, heartache, and disappointment here—teaches us, enlightens us, and makes us who we are: women better prepared to serve the Lord, however and whenever He calls.

And what happens when the only desire of our heart is to give all that we have and are back to the Lord? When we want to consecrate every gift, talent, and resource? When we want to consecrate every relationship unto Him? What happens? Marvelous things—life-changing and spirit-enlarging things.

For example, do you have a musical talent? What happens to your practicing and performances when you give that talent back to the Lord? Do you have an ability to make something out of nothing; or to teach with clarity; or to bring family history to life with stories, pictures, and music; or to make people feel welcomed and included; or to have compassion for others; or to be a peacemaker? What comes to your mind and heart about what you want to do more of, or less of, when you really think about consecrating those abilities to the Lord for His use and to build up His kingdom? When you consecrate a relationship to the Lord, what happens to your ability to give and receive love, to be patient, to put contention aside, to give the other the benefit of the doubt?

In short, what changes when you think about doing *everything* you do, *truly* devoting your life, for the building up of the Lord's kingdom?

Now, if you've been tempted to second-guess the Lord with thoughts such as, "Well, the Lord would never use me to do anything significant for His kingdom. I don't have what it takes to move His work ahead," please consider the following truth as taught by Elder Russell M. Nelson: The Lord uses the unlikely to accomplish the impossible.

If you feel like the most unlikely person to be asked to accomplish something that looks utterly impossible, look out! Consider the Prophet Joseph Smith, who described himself as "an obscure boy . . . of no consequence" (JS–H 1:22), or Elizabeth, who was far beyond childbearing age yet gave birth to John, the forerunner of the Savior (see Luke 1:5–25, 57–80).

What were *you* designated premortally to do while you are here on earth?

Can you imagine what would happen if a popular talk show host suddenly declared that he or she had discovered that there is a premortal existence? That we had received certain assignments there, which we were to complete here on earth? And that one of the major purposes of life was to find and fulfill those assignments? How excited would the women of the world be? How quickly would a major marketing blitz be launched encouraging women to find their true purpose in life, with nothing being more important than bearing, and bearing with, children!

Can you imagine the campaign to urge women not to spend one more minute on anything that didn't move them toward finding their missions? Can you imagine the television shows that might spring up showing women's efforts and successes? What would the slogans on T-shirts, mugs, posters, bumper stickers, and pop-ups on the Internet say in order to encourage women to stop whatever they were doing, however important or urgent they thought it was, and go steadily forward with faith to find their missions, even their commissions, from our *Father in Heaven?*

What would the world do if it believed what we know to be true? But the world hasn't embraced these truths and never will! That is what makes our quest to live as covenant women of God all the more complicated and adventurous! Because if we are following the Lord, we will feel increasingly out of step with the world. In fact, perhaps an early clue that there is something not quite right in our lives is if we are feeling a little *too* comfortable with the world—if we are looking and acting a little too much like the women of the world.

The Lord knows us. He loves us. He believes in us. And He is counting on us to do exactly what we said we would do. Happily, we don't have to do it alone. He stands waiting for us to seek His help. He is eager to endow those who qualify with His power. He will gift us with skill and understanding commensurate with our seeking, our purity, and our need.

Sisters, we are part of a royal army of women, sent here to gather the good women of the earth and welcome them into the Lord's kingdom. Indeed, "we have a labor to perform [now] whilst in this tabernacle of clay, that we may conquer the enemy of all righteousness" (Moroni 9:6).

I love the words of the ninth article of faith, and "for such a time as this" I hear those truths this way:

"We believe all that God has revealed [*regarding our mission as His daughters in these last days of the latter-days*], all that He does now reveal [*regarding our mission as His covenant women upon the earth*], and we believe that He will yet reveal many great and important things pertaining to [*our role as latter-day women of God in building up*] the Kingdom of God."

NOTES

1. George Q. Cannon, *Juvenile Instructor* 22 (1 May 1887): 140.
2. Neal A. Maxwell, "Encircled in the Arms of His Love," *Ensign,* November 2002, 17.
3. Spencer W. Kimball, "The Role of Righteous Women," *Ensign,* November 1979, 103–4.
4. Joseph F. Smith, in Conference Report, October 1907, 3.

WHAT TIME *IS* THIS?

Jeffrey R. Holland and Patricia T. Holland

Sister Patricia T. Holland: We have posed the title of our remarks as a question, "What Time *Is* This?" Obviously that scriptural story of Esther marks the convergence of an important woman with an important moment, an important "time." We want to take this opportunity to emphasize what *our* time is, what *this* time is, and how we, the women of the Church, can seize it, Esther-like, to turn it to advantage.

Elder Jeffrey R. Holland: First of all, may I say this is a time to be grateful and optimistic. Ours is the most blessed, the most abundant and glorious time in the history of the world. We really do mean "fulness" when we speak of the dispensation of the fulness of times. We have more blessings spread among more people in more parts of the world than ever before in the story of the human family. You have all noted that President Gordon B. Hinckley is always so positive and upbeat. He is unfailingly optimistic. Just at general conference time in April 2007 he said in one of our meetings, "Things are just going to get better and better and better." I love that spirit.

Sister Holland: And, of course, as Latter-day Saints, the way we can

---

Elder Jeffrey R. Holland was ordained an Apostle and became a member of the Quorum of the Twelve in 1994. He previously served as president of Brigham Young University and as the Church commissioner of education.

Patricia T. Holland served as a counselor in the Young Women General Presidency. She and Elder Holland have three children and twelve grandchildren.

make things "better and better" for everyone is to share our love and share the principles, covenants, and promises of the gospel of Jesus Christ. To have had the gospel restored in *our* time, for *our* benefit and that of our children and grandchildren, is the greatest of all the blessings of "our time." We have so much to share.

Elder Holland: I have often told young people that for the privilege of living in such a time they (we) have a responsibility that has never come in exactly this way to any other dispensation of Church members. We are the people in the eternal scheme of things who must prepare the Church of the Lamb for the arrival of the Lamb. No earlier people in ancient days ever had that assignment. What a tremendous responsibility! This means that before this is over we have to look like His Church members would look and act like His Church members would act. This will require all of us to move closer and closer to the heart of the gospel, to true principles of discipleship and faith, qualities of the heart and spirit. In short, it means we have to live and be, to actually demonstrate, what it is we are always so quick to say we "know" in our testimony meetings. Eventually that has to mean not so much of programs or external schedules and certainly not so much of temporal things or the distractions the world puts before us. As a people we must increasingly strive for *inner* qualities, striving for *profound faith* and *deep spirituality,* striving to live as disciples of Christ would live. That is the task for us *and* for our families in this time of "dispensational hastening."

Sister Holland: Sisters, we especially want you to hear our great desire to pass the blessings of the gospel—and especially the *love* of the gospel—on to the next generation—our children and grandchildren and yours. In that spirit may I share a very personal story with you. My great-grandmother on my mother's side of the family came from the Bern-Interlaken area of Switzerland. You may have visited there or at least seen the travel posters! Surely it is among the most beautiful locations on the face of the earth—green and majestic nature at its loveliest.

After joining the Church and emigrating to join the Saints moving west, those great-grandparents were called to settle the little community of Enterprise in southern Utah. Perhaps you have been to Enterprise, too, but I *know* you have *not* seen any travel posters of it! I do love the community of my birth and childhood memories, but it is not Switzerland! It was hot in the summer and cold in the winter, the wind blew constantly, and it was barren! What a test of faith it must have been for these Swiss ancestors to be called to an area so totally opposite to that green land of lakes and alpine beauty they had left behind.

My great-grandmother decided she would do something about it. With her two hands and a shovel, she harvested some small pine tree seedlings from the mountains not far away and planted them around the small church building that had just been erected. Then every day she would carry two buckets of water from her home nearly three blocks away, one bucket in each hand, to water those trees and keep them growing. It was arduous work for a little woman bent over with osteoporosis, but she made every drop count in a daily ritual that over time gave each tree a regular, if meager, drink of moisture.

Elder Holland: In this exercise Pat's great-grandmother often took her little ten-year-old granddaughter with her, telling stories and reminiscing about her life in Switzerland as she carried her two precious buckets of water. One day one of the brethren of the community stopped her and said, with something of a dismissive tone, "Oh, Sister Barlocker, why do you make this useless journey each day to water those scrubby little pine trees? They will never survive in this harsh climate and difficult soil, and even if they did, they will never grow to any size in your lifetime. Why don't you just give up and forget your high Swiss hopes in this matter?"

Well, little Sister Barlocker rose to the full four feet eight inches of her stature, looked this good brother in the eye, and said, "I know these trees will not grow very large in my lifetime. But if I stay with it, they *will* live and they will grow. And although I will not enjoy their beauty and their shade, this little girl will. I am doing this for her."

Sister Holland: That ten-year-old grandchild was my mother. And my mother with all of her siblings, cousins, and everyone else in Enterprise did live to see those trees reach an impressive height and to give lovely, much-needed shade from the desert sun. Then I grew up enjoying those trees, playing under their branches, and seeing them frame the church which I attended as a young woman. And now I have lived to see not only my children but also my grandchildren play, have picnics, laugh, and hold Twenty-fourth of July relay races all through and in and around those beautiful trees, which now literally tower over the community—and over the pioneer heritage—of little windblown, once-barren Enterprise, Utah.

In this homely little story my great-grandmother taught me several wonderful lessons. First, speaking of a time for gratitude, I am so grateful that she did something for her posterity that was hard and demanding, but which she knew would bless their lives and bring them happiness. And of course that wasn't just by planting lovely trees. She taught her children and her grandchildren the gospel, lived it every day of her life, and brought pure, uncompromised righteousness to us in a way that none of her posterity could ever deny. In that sense she nourished us even more faithfully than she nourished those trees!

I pray we will all live with this sense of linked generations. In a very real way my great-grandmother did what she did for me, and that helps me want to do what I do for my children and grandchildren, for generations yet to come, so they will be blessed in the gospel and have privileges in their lives that I may not see, but which they will.

Thinking about all of this, including my husband's comments about preparing the Church of the Lamb for the return of the Lamb, has given me a new insight into the scripture in Doctrine and Covenants 52 that says, "For thus saith the Lord, I will cut my work short in righteousness" (D&C 52:11). I have always thought that meant that the Lord wouldn't let wickedness go on too long, that He would "cut the last days short" rather than allow too much damage to be done. I am sure it does mean something of that, but lately I have wondered if it doesn't also mean that the work can be cut short—or finished—only if there is a clear demonstration of righteousness among the Saints, only if we are looking and acting not only like the *Church* of the Lamb but looking and acting like the *Lamb* Himself! Maybe it is a little like the change that comes when hot water turns to steam. We can sort of move along as reasonably warm water people, but until we push it to that magic one hundred degrees Centigrade we don't get the miracle of change that a burst of steam offers. Maybe this is just my own interpretation of this scripture about "cut[ting the] work short in righteousness," but if a little more righteousness can cut these last days a little shorter and bring the Savior's return a little sooner, I am all for it!

Elder Holland: One of the great truths Pat expressed in that wonderful little story of her great-grandmother is that bringing forward this day of righteousness, a day that will make the members of the Church what we ought to be, requires us to *focus on the children.*

We don't know when the Lord will "cut short" His work, but we know that the coming generations—our children and grandchildren, collectively speaking—move progressively toward it, whenever it is, and they must be as prepared for that day as we are trying to be—or even more so.

Sister Holland: I have always loved this verse from Alma, who said to *his* children: "And now, . . . this [is] the ministry unto which ye were called, to declare these glad tidings unto this people, to prepare *their minds;* . . . that they may *prepare the minds of their children* to hear the word at the time of his coming" (Alma 39:16; emphasis added). And may I say you are doing a *wonderful* job of that. As we travel around the Church we see magnificent children and youth—Primary children who carry their scriptures to Church and teenagers who can't wait to go on missions and marry in the temple. The Lord loves you for what you are doing in preparing the minds *and* the hearts of His children. And we love you too!

Elder Holland: Dear sisters, our beloved associates in this work, in "such a time as this" may I plead with you never to underestimate or undervalue your divine role both as personal, powerful contributors to the kingdom of God and as the nurturers and benefactors of His "little ones," who will yet have such a divine impact on the unfolding of this work. I fear that virtually nothing—or at least not much—that the world says to you acknowledges your divine role as women.

I am reminded that throughout the creation sequence of Genesis God viewed His work, including the creation of man, and called it "good." But for the one and only time in that creation story He then said something was "*not* good." He said it was *not* good that man should be alone. In short the Creation, even with Adam, was incomplete. Here I invoke President Gordon B. Hinckley's language: "As His final creation, the *crowning of His glorious work,* He created woman. I *like to regard Eve as His masterpiece* after all that had gone before, the final [great] work before He rested from His labors."[1] I join my testimony to President Hinckley's in that assessment. Surely it must have been at this point, with so much that was "good" having been done and having remedied the one thing that was "*not* good," He could say after Eve's arrival it was all "*very* good."

In this great eternal work women have carried the torch of faith and family from the beginning. The need for that torch to burn brightly and dispel the darkness has never been greater than "in this time." Little wonder that the Prophet Joseph said, "If you live up to your privileges, the angels cannot be restrained from being your associates."[2] The scriptures speak of women being "elect." What a powerful doctrinal and covenantal term! And who "elects" you? You do! And so does God Himself, who has all the joy and delight of a father in you as His daughter, you who pass on light and hope, pass on life itself and a glorious gospel legacy until the work is finished.

Sister Holland: In all of this, we do not want you to feel overwhelmed. If the work of true righteousness yet before us seems monumental, remember that we have monumental help. We, as women, have too often thought we are "little" people with little influence, but the Lord keeps pleading with us not to think that way, not when we are *His* divine daughters on *His* errand. After all, "the errand of angels is given to women; and this is a gift that, as sisters, we claim."[3] And as the Lord said, "Wherefore, as ye are agents, ye are on the Lord's errand; and whatever ye do according to the will of the Lord is the Lord's business" (D&C 64:29).

Women have the commission to create, to bring to fruition, and to provide development of the divinity within the children of God. With that commission comes a divine spiritual capacity that (to me) is unfathomable to our human view. Some of the words that come to my mind regarding a woman's discipleship are life, love, energy, holiness, intelligence, strength, change.

Elder Holland: Sisters, we all need to believe in ourselves as God's "agents" much, much more than we do, activating the gifts and the powers He has given us *as if He Himself were here.* On the outside we may seem to be "little people," little everyday souls with everyday problems, but we are the everyday instruments God has always used to do His work and perform His miracles from the beginning. This is that power of the Atonement to which we pay much too little attention—not only did Christ save us from our sins but He saved us from ourselves, our horrible warped opinions and negative views of ourselves. That is the miracle of being reborn and "spiritually begotten of [the Savior]," as King Benjamin said, of saying that we are "changed through faith on his name"

(Mosiah 5:7). If we say we are "changed through faith on his name," then let's act like such a change has occurred.

Sister Holland: All of us need to remember we are more divine than we are temporal, and only the adversary would have us believe otherwise. Remember we are truly spiritual beings having a short temporal experience. If we can remember that, we can more readily call upon those spiritual gifts that are ours and that have been made powerful in us through the Atonement of Christ. I read a poet recently who wrote of the "consuming fire of Christ," a divine flame that would burn away our sins and shortcomings, our sorrows and inadequacies. That is something I want to pass on to the next generation—"the consuming fire of Christ"—a fire set by our own love.

In that spirit may I say that one of my great wishes for this women's conference is that it will be a time when we stop "beating up" on ourselves and let the grace of heaven—this divine flame if you will—wash over us and make us whole—truly "holy." Remember, no matter what you have done, you can be forgiven of it, so get the process started by forgiving yourself, and let repentance lead you on to the miracle of God's forgiveness. Take hope. Look up. Be good to yourself, because your Heavenly Father surely wants to be good to you. Let's let the Spirit envelop us, make us calm, and heal our souls.

Elder Holland: Knowing women as I do and as the presiding Church officer here today, I want to say to you, "No, everything you have done is *not* wrong. No, you are *not* a failure. No, you are not personally to blame for *every* mishap in the world since the ark landed." We are all pretty hard on ourselves, but it seems to me women are harder on themselves than men will ever be. Why is that so? We ask you not to do it. Repent when or where that is necessary, but then honor that other *R—rejoice!* Make a resolve today that this is "your time" to be good to yourself. It will surprise you how much that helps you be good to all the others whom you want so much to bless in your life.

Sister Holland: Sisters, may I make an appeal that it is a time for us, especially as women, to strip ourselves of something else that seems so prevalent among women. I suppose men suffer with such things too, but it seems to be particularly evident, and particularly painful, among women. It is closely related to the things my husband just touched on. I speak of the constant feeling we seem to have that what we are or what we have is not enough. That is Satan's demonic chant sounding continually in our ears. It is not true! We are more intelligent than this. We are stronger, much stronger, than this! Constantly comparing ourselves with others leaves us feeling so weak and worthless. It taps into our pride and poisons us with jealousy. Let's start a new "chant"—that we are women of Christ, that we are spiritually strong personally, and that we will prepare the next generation for their opportunities. Let us strip ourselves of pride and vanity and envy forever.

Listen to this counsel given in ancient days. It is *very* direct concerning what we, as sisters in this Church, ought to address. Alma asks: "Behold, are ye stripped of pride? I say unto you, if ye are not ye are not prepared to meet God. . . .

"Behold, I say, is there one among you who is not stripped of envy? I say unto you that such an one is not prepared; and I would that he [and she!] should prepare quickly, for the hour is close at hand, and [she] knoweth not when the time shall come" (Alma 5:28–29).

May I stress, sisters, that this *stripping* ourselves of envy and pride is a poignant, almost painful description of what we must be willing to do. Furthermore, when we have undergone such a potentially painful "stripping" of an adverse trait, we must then help our daughters and granddaughters and the young women who come under our influence (and the men!) do the same. Heaven only knows how much the world uses envy and pride and worldly glamour in our society. We have to walk away from these things, but this will not be easy to do. We will need these gifts of heaven of which we spoke earlier, the power of God's grace and priesthood, the atoning power of the Savior, which compensates where we try and try but seem to fall short.

James knew all this. He said: "The spirit which God implanted in man [all of us] turns towards envious desires[.] And *yet the grace he gives is stronger.* Thus Scripture says, '*God opposes the arrogant and gives grace to the humble.*' Be submissive then to God. . . . *Come close to God, and he will come close to you. . . .* Humble yourselves before God and he will lift you high" (James 4:5–10, New English Bible; emphasis added).

Isn't that a tremendous thought? If we would not "lift" ourselves up with these cursed temptations of envy and pride, God would gladly step in and do the "lifting" for us! Only He can lift us where He wants us and where we really want to be. We can't get there by clawing or clamor, by cattiness or cutting others down. We certainly can't get there by vaunting ourselves up.

Furthermore, I believe with all my heart that this is a challenge we will face again and again. We should not be discouraged if the challenge returns tomorrow just when we thought we gave it such a good effort today. I say this out of the honesty, and experience, of my own heart. I struggle with these issues just as you do, and just as everyone does. So don't give up hope and don't think you are the only one who feels these things or struggles with these temptations. We all do, but every effort is a godly one, and every victory is counted for our good. And if we turn around to face the same challenge again tomorrow, so be it. We will work again, with all our heart, to strip away anything that keeps us from truly being "meek and lowly"—in all the right ways—before God. His grace *is* sufficient to help us succeed at that.

My dear sisters and friends, collectively speaking I think about you all the time. I love you. I know most of you have experienced some heartache and disappointment as well as joy and hopefulness. We have wanted our words to be encouraging to you and hoped that you would hear in them our love for you. I truly believe that "cut[ting the] work short in righteousness" requires the element of love to prevail in our lives. Love of God, love of each other, and, yes, love of ourselves. The two great commandments are still the two great commandments. These will be the ultimate marks of our discipleship. The sooner we can come to that love, the sooner we are truly Christ's people and (to my mind) the sooner He can come. If we can do this, live with true, expansive charity and unbounded love, perhaps our children will then see our example and recognize that we, their mothers and grandmothers, their aunts and sisters, their teachers and the wonderful women in this Church, are disciples of the Savior of the world—because we have "love one to another" (John 13:35). My earnest prayer is that we can receive His image in our countenance and "sing the song of redeeming love" (Alma 5:26) forever in this, His true and redeeming Church.

Elder Holland: Sisters, Pat has testified of *our* need to increase love in our discipleship. Let my testimony be the other half of hers, to testify how much *the Father* and *the Son* personify love and shower it upon our some-times meager efforts to do the same. I believe if you could grasp in some small way the vision of Their majestic love for you, it would free you to love Them and everyone else within your circle of influence in profound and powerful new ways. One of the most important verses I know of in all of scripture is the supplication Jesus gave in the great intercessory prayer prior to His suffering in Gethsemane and crucifixion on Golgotha. In that prayer, which President David O. McKay once called the greatest prayer ever uttered, the Savior said, "And this is life eternal, that they [that is, we] might know thee the only true God, and Jesus Christ, whom thou has sent" (John 17:3). I stress that phrase "*the only true God.*"

May I declare to you and all others who will hear me that one of the tragedies of our day is that the true God is not known. Tragically, much of contemporary Christianity has inherited the view of a capricious, imperi-ous, and especially angry God whose primary duty is to frighten little chil-dren and add suffering to the lives of already staggering adults. May I unequivocally and unilaterally cry out against that sacrilegious and demeaning view of a loving and compassionate Father in Heaven. I won-der if the Savior may not have known, even in His mortal years, that this would happen, thus His plea for the world to know *the true God,* the fatherly God, the forgiving and redeeming and benevolent God. To bring that understanding was *one* of the reasons Christ came to the earth.

So feeding the hungry, healing the sick, rebuking cruelty, pleading for faith—and hope and charity—this was Christ showing us the way of the Father, He who is "merciful and gracious, slow to anger, long-suffering and full of goodness."[4] In His life and especially in His death, Christ was declaring, "This is *God's* compassion I am showing you, as well as my own." It is the perfect Son's manifestation of the perfect Father's care. In Their mutual suffering and shared sorrow for the sins and heartaches of the rest of us, we see ultimate meaning in the declaration: "For God so loved the world, that he gave his only begotten Son, that whosoever believeth in him should not perish, but have everlasting life. For God sent not his Son into the world to condemn the world; but that the world through him might be saved" (John 3:16–17).

I bear personal witness this day of a living, loving God who knows our names, hears and answers prayers, and cherishes us eternally as His children. I testify that there is no spiteful or malicious motive in Him. I testify that all He does (He who never sleeps nor slumbers) is seek for ways to bless us, to help us, and to save us. I pray that you will believe that and embrace it. I pray that you will strive to see the wonder and majesty of heaven's concern and compassion for us.

I testify that Joseph Smith's vision of the Father and the Son began a chain of events that would change—and save—the world if the world would but accept the divine beings that he saw. I testify that President Gordon B. Hinckley is a true prophet of that loving God in every sense of the word, and so will his successors be until the Savior comes to rule and reign.

I promise that there are good days ahead, always, that the darkest clouds always part and the most fearful days always flee before the beneficent face of the Father, the redeeming grace of the Son, and the sweet influence of the Holy Ghost in our lives. In our time and in such a gospel as heaven has bestowed upon us, we have every reason to be happy and every cause to be filled with divine anticipation. May you trust forever in the God who gave you life and in His Beloved Son, whose Church this is and who paid the ultimate price to redeem your life and restore your soul.

NOTES

1. Gordon B. Hinckley, "Daughters of God," *Ensign,* November 1991, 99; emphasis added.

2. Joseph Smith, *History of The Church of Jesus Christ of Latter-day Saints,* 7 vols., ed. B. H. Roberts, 2d ed. rev. (Salt Lake City: The Church of Jesus Christ of Latter-day Saints, 1932–51), 4:605.

3. Emily H. Woodmansee, "As Sisters in Zion," in *Hymns of The Church of Jesus Christ of Latter-day Saints* (Salt Lake City: The Church of Jesus Christ of Latter-day Saints, 1985), no. 309.

4. Joseph Smith, *Lectures on Faith* (Salt Lake City: Deseret Book, 1985), 42.

"ARE WE ENOUGH? OF COURSE WE ARE!"

Margaret Lifferth

My mother died when I was just a young mother with five small children. I remember sitting in her living room when an employee of the newspaper arrived to help us write her obituary. I told him where she was born, where she went to school, and the community organizations that she had been a part of. After several minutes of fact finding, he looked up at me and said, "Is that all?" I was stunned. Of course that wasn't all. But how do you put into print the influence we have on each other's lives?

My mother never graduated from college. She never had significant work in the marketplace. Though she had a flair for decorating, her home was humble. She always served in a Church calling, but for many years illness had prevented her from serving in demanding leadership positions. And age and illness slowly took their toll on her physical beauty and abilities. In the eyes of the world, my mother would have been very ordinary. But to me, she was magnificent.

My mother loved and created beauty. Even though she had many discouraging days, she developed unflinching courage as she struggled with rheumatoid arthritis. She learned and lived the gospel and bore her testimony. She loved her family and friends and consistently performed the

---

Margaret Lifferth serves as the first counselor in the Primary General Presidency. A homemaker, she earned a degree from Brigham Young University. She and her husband, Dennis, are the parents of seven children.

small daily services that enrich and strengthen and influence others for good.

So, was she enough? Of course she was!

I am obviously biased. So think about the people in your life. Think about the people in your home and neighborhood who, with all their shortcomings and all of life's challenges, continue striving to do their best. They follow the prophet. They make and keep covenants. They learn and serve and grow in testimony to the best of their ability. Are they enough? If you are striving in the same ways, are you enough? Of course you are!

This women's conference takes its theme from the Old Testament story of Esther. Her story can help us understand that we must know who we really are, who we can become, and what we are to do.

At the time of Esther, the Jews had lived for many years in captivity in Babylon. Esther lived with her cousin Mordecai, who was also a Jew. He was also a gatekeeper at the king's palace.

When King Ahasuerus decided to choose a new queen, he decreed that the most beautiful women of the kingdom be presented to him. Mordecai took the beautiful Esther to the palace to be presented to the king but warned her not to reveal that she was a Jew. King Ahasuerus picked Esther to be his queen. She lived in luxury and servants tended to her every need.

But even with this great honor, all was not well with Esther, her family, or her people. King Ahasuerus had a servant named Haman who desired that all must bow down before him. Mordecai refused to bow before Haman. Haman was angry and schemed to have all the Jews in the land be killed on a certain day.

When Mordecai heard about the law, he sent a messenger to Esther asking her to plead with the king for the lives of her people. "Who knoweth," said Mordecai, "whether thou art come to the kingdom for such a time as this?" (Esther 4:14).

Esther reminded Mordecai that she would be risking her life to go to the king unbidden and that she was further risking her life to reveal that she was a Jew. But, with great faith, she asked Mordecai to have the Jews fast for three days. She and her servants would do the same, and then Esther promised, "I will go in unto the king, which is not according to the law: and if I perish, I perish" (Esther 4:16).

After three days, Esther dressed in beautiful clothes and went before the king. Sparing her life, he welcomed her and asked, "What is thy request?" She requested that the king and Haman join her for dinner for the next two nights. At the last dinner, the king asked again, "What is thy request?"

Esther then revealed that she was a Jew and that a decree had been given to kill all her people. When it was known that Haman was behind this evil plot, the king had him hanged (Esther 5, 7). Mordecai became great in the king's house, and all the Jews praised him and Queen Esther: "In every province, and in every city, whithersoever the king's commandment and his decree came, the Jews had joy and gladness, a feast and a good day" (Esther 8:17).

This story reveals the influence of one righteous woman who understood the importance of who she really was and what she was to do. How can we apply the lessons of this story in our lives?

Do we understand who we really are? When Esther first entered the king's palace, she was one beautiful woman among many. Before she was even introduced to the king, the scriptures say, she had "six months with oil of myrrh and six months with sweet odours" (Esther 2:12). Now I read that as having a twelve-month spa experience. And then came the clothes and the jewelry and the crown and the feast in her honor. There is no question that beauty plays a part in this story. But does it define who Esther really was?

Does physical beauty define who *we* really are? The world would have us think so. I am concerned that we listen too readily to the voice of the world that tells us that physical beauty equals happiness. If you are buying into that philosophy, you will never be enough. There will always be someone prettier and thinner and having a better hair day. And let me remind you that the clock is ticking. From my own experience, I can tell you that things that were once pretty and firm will eventually droop and drag, and no amount or type of cosmetics will help.

Our Church leaders are concerned for us and the pressures that we face on this issue from a very persuasive world. They worry about our priorities and the example we set for children and youth. Listen to the counsel that Elder Jeffrey R. Holland offered at a recent general conference:

"Preoccupation with self and a fixation on the physical . . . is more than social insanity; it is spiritually destructive, and it accounts for much of the unhappiness women . . . face in the modern world. And if adults are preoccupied with appearance—tucking and nipping and implanting and remodeling everything that can be remodeled—those pressures and anxieties will certainly seep through to children. At some point the problem becomes what the Book of Mormon called 'vain imaginations' [1 Nephi 12:18]. And in secular society both vanity *and* imagination run wild. One would truly need a great and spacious makeup kit to compete with beauty as portrayed in media all around us. Yet at the end of the day there would still be those 'in the attitude of mocking and pointing their fingers' as Lehi saw [see 1 Nephi 8:27], because however much one tries in the world of glamour and fashion, it will never be glamorous enough."[1]

Now, I am not talking about being careful stewards of our bodies. Neither is Elder Holland. We need to eat wisely, exercise, and be careful in our grooming and dress. But let's not be deceived into giving an unreasonable amount of our time, money, and energy to our physical appearance. It does not define who we really are.

As beautiful as Esther was, in the end, it did not define her either. In a time of great need, she understood the importance of who she really was. She was a Jew, a woman of covenant, and through prayer and fasting she sought the help of the Lord for the courage to do what she needed to do.

Today there is a great need for us, the women of the Church, to understand the importance of who *we* are and what *we* are to do. And we can also understand that because of promises and blessings given long ago, *we have already been prepared* "to come to the kingdom for such a time as this." Are we enough? Of course we are!

The scriptures record a great vision that was shown to the prophet Abraham. He was shown "the intelligences that were organized before the world was; [including] many of the noble and great" and that the earth was to be created as a place to "prove them herewith, to see if they will do all things whatsoever the Lord their God shall command them" (Abraham 3:22, 25).

In this same vision, Abraham saw an interchange between God and His eldest son, Jesus Christ. Our Father in Heaven asked who would come to earth to bless, strengthen, and ultimately save all mankind, and it was Jesus Christ who said simply, "Here am I, send me" (Abraham 3:27).

We were there. We heard those words, and because we chose the plan of our Father and supported the role of the Savior, we are here today. And I believe that because we were faithful, noble, and valiant in that support, we are here *today*, in these latter days—women of faith, blessed with gospel covenants, with a work to do.

Like Esther, we too were given an errand and "come to the kingdom for such a time as this." President Spencer W. Kimball taught that "in the world before we came here, faithful women were given certain assignments while faithful men were foreordained to certain priesthood tasks. While we do not now remember the particulars, . . . [we] are accountable for those things which long ago were expected of [us]."[2]

Foreordination is a fascinating doctrine. Can't you just imagine Heavenly Father saying, "Save her and her and her. I will need each of those women in the latter days to be a light to the world, to establish homes of safety and righteousness, and to build the kingdom of God"?

If we were foreordained to a certain time and task, we were also prepared in our premortal life. Heavenly Father simply would not send us unprepared to fulfill our responsibilities at such a critical time as these latter days. Do you remember the vision given to President Joseph F. Smith of the Savior's visit to the spirit world? It is recorded in Doctrine and Covenants 138. In that vision, President Smith saw that included among the "noble and great" ones mentioned by Abraham were "our glorious Mother Eve, with many of her faithful daughters who had lived through the ages and worshiped the true and living God" (v. 39).

And then he says this about those noble and great spirits: "Even before they were born, they, with many others, received their first lessons in the world of spirits and were prepared to come forth in the due time of the Lord to labor in his vineyard for the salvation of the souls of men" (verse 56).

Think about it. What did we learn there that prepared us to be here now, in these glorious but difficult latter days? What qualities of spirit did you bring with you already well developed?

Think about your strengths. Think about your patriarchal blessing. What gifts can you identify that have always been yours?

Several years ago, Elder M. Russell Ballard spoke to the women of the Church. He said:

"Just as the Savior stepped forward to fulfill His divine responsibilities, we have the challenge and responsibility to do likewise. . . . Imagine the impact when you make commitments such as the following:

"'Father, if You need a woman to rear children in righteousness, here am I, send me.

"'If You need a woman who will shun vulgarity and dress modestly and speak with dignity and show the world how joyous it is to keep the commandments, here am I, send me.'"[3]

Each of us could identify many women who are fulfilling their divine responsibilities. And each of us could make our own list of prepared women who could have said, "Here am I, send me."

I want to share some stories from my own experience that illustrate that we have come prepared "for such a time as this." In these stories you will not see grandiose acts of service that required days and weeks to complete. Neither will you see women who failed to act because of their circumstances or opportunities. And you certainly won't see women who constantly compared themselves with others and felt unworthy. With all the strengths we have been given, the Lord is not pleased when we are too hard on ourselves.

Can I just tell you a secret? When you are tempted to compare yourself unfavorably with others, please remember this: No one can do it all. No one does do it all. And "doing it all" is not required anyway. And that's the truth. When you recognize and develop your own strengths, you can then celebrate the strengths of others and recognize that they are a blessing to you.

You *will* see in my stories *small, daily acts of service* that strengthen and influence others for good. That is how the Lord's work is done. In fact, the Lord reminds us that "out of small things proceedeth that which is great" (D&C 64:33). So, in that context, look for well-developed spiritual gifts that were shared with others in small, daily events.

Some years ago, when my youngest son was five, he had had too much of Halloween and stories of ghosts and goblins, and he became too afraid to sleep alone in his room at night. My husband and I catered to him for several weeks, trying to make him feel more secure. One night I was a little out of patience, and I insisted that he stay in his bed alone, with the light on, and try to go to sleep. All was quiet for a few minutes, and then he started to cry. I waited a minute, and soon it was quiet again. After about ten minutes, I decided to check things out. His older sister was doing her homework on the floor by his bed and had told him that she would stay until he fell asleep. And then my young son said, "But Mom, I'm not scared anymore anyway. My sister said a prayer with me and asked Heavenly Father to help me not be afraid, and now there are angels all around my bed protecting me."

Wouldn't you agree that spiritual gifts are easy to see in children? Can't you just imagine this child as a mature spirit saying, "Father, if you need someone with simple faith and loving empathy, here am I, send me."

Spiritual gifts are also easy to see in mothers. I have a friend with an inactive son. In fact, he has faced prison, divorce, and financial instability for many years. Every week for years, she has brought his three young children to church. They sit on the front row, and I have watched her help these children learn how to sit still, fold their arms for prayer, and show reverence and respect as she brings the light of the gospel into their lives. Just recently, she learned that her son has decided to come home to work on a new beginning. She and his children will be waiting with open arms.

I can easily imagine her saying, "Father, if you need someone to face disappointment with hope and patience and diligence, here am I, send me."

Faithful visiting teachers and neighbors also prove that we are enough and that we have come prepared. A sister in our ward broke her back in a tubing accident a couple of years ago. She had to be absolutely down for over four months, and she had a family of active teenagers. The sisters in the ward took meals, drove the children to lessons, and helped with housework. But her visiting teacher may have provided the most important service. She visited several times a week and was prepared to study and teach the Sunday School lesson with her bedridden neighbor. Together they shared scriptures and testimony, and a load was lightened.

Was she the one to say, "If you need a woman to learn and teach and bear testimony, here am I, send me"?

When I was a young bride, my husband and I moved to the Midwest, where my husband entered graduate school. We attended a small branch, and I went to Relief Society every Thursday night. Those sisters became my family away from home. One summer, when we were home for a visit, I found an old box of family histories; some were handwritten, and none were organized. I told my mother I would take them with me and type them up so they could be copied and distributed to family members. This was before word processors, and our little typewriter wasn't good enough. The "a" key always hit above the line. I called to rent a typewriter, but it was too expensive.

A sister in the branch said I could come to her home and use her electric typewriter to do the job. This was a big project, and I worked on it every afternoon. After about ten days, I could see that the typewriter was going to need a new ribbon soon. Again I was worried about the cost (we were such poor students), but I didn't say anything. The next time I went to her home to work on the histories, the typewriter had a new ribbon. The histories were finished for Christmas, and I returned the originals. A few years later my mother died, and the house was sold. Those original histories have never surfaced again. No one knows where they are. My Relief Society sister doesn't know to this day that the simple acts of offering her typewriter and buying a new ribbon has preserved those precious records for generations to come.

This friend could easily have said, "If you need someone to discern and fulfill the needs of those around me with quiet charity, here am I, send me."

One more. My mother-in-law recently passed away from bone cancer. For several years she had chemotherapy treatments every week. At one of those treatments the doctor came and sat by her to see how she was doing. He asked how she was tolerating the treatments and how he could help. She took the chance to tell him of her gratitude for her life and of her faith that all would be well regardless of the outcome of the disease. He asked her if she would write an article for the patient newsletter expressing her optimism and hope. She did so. At a later treatment, a nurse visited with her, telling her that she had just been given some money to put on a seminar for the oncology nurses and would my mother-in-law be the speaker?

I have rarely seen such an example of courage, and if she had the opportunity, I am quite sure she could have said, "Father, if you need someone to face adversity with dignity and cheerful optimism and thus give those around me great hope in Thy plan for us, here am I, send me."

Now, it's easy to see in each of these stories sisters using the divine power that is in each of us to strengthen and bless others. Can you also see in these stories the heavy burdens of mortality—fear, financial stress, wayward children, and illness?

Knowing that we struggle with the trials of mortality while we also desire to do the Lord's work helps us be patient with ourselves and realistic about the demands on our time and energy.

Are we enough? Or as the obituary writer from the newspaper asked, "Is that all?" As we build the kingdom of God in whatever venue we find ourselves, we may look pretty ordinary to the world.

But scriptures, prophets, patriarchal blessings, and the sweet personal whisperings of the Spirit confirm to our minds and hearts who we really are. We are among the "noble and great" daughters of God saved for this latter day to establish the kingdom of God throughout the earth. We are prepared with testimony, the gift of the Holy Ghost, covenants, and well-developed personal spiritual strengths.

Most important, if we, like Esther, seek the help of the Savior through fasting and prayer, we can draw upon His grace, or the enabling power of His Atonement. He will strengthen and magnify us and our works. He will help us be better and accomplish more than we ever could on our own.

Indeed, when we are on His errand, He promises: "There will I be also, for I will go before your face. I will be on your right hand and on your left, and my Spirit shall be in your hearts, and mine angels round about you, to bear you up" (D&C 84:88).

May it be confirmed in our hearts who we really are and that we have been prepared to "come to the kingdom for such a time as this."

NOTES

1. Jeffrey R. Holland, "To Young Women," *Ensign*, November 2005, 30; emphasis in original.
2. Spencer W. Kimball, "The Role of Righteous Women," *Ensign*, November 1979, 102.
3. M. Russell Ballard, "Women of Righteousness," *Ensign*, April 2002, 70.

FAITH TO BELIEVE WHEN DREAMS HAVE TO WAIT

Ardeth Kapp

The theme of the conference this year, "Thou art come to the kingdom for such a time as this" (Esther 4:14), invites thoughtful reflection for each one of us—maybe a remembering. Bishop Keith McMullin of the Presiding Bishopric, in a training session some time ago, suggested that we might go out some clear moonlit night, look up into the starry sky, and contemplate, "Why me, why now, and why here?" When you do this, some interesting pondering will take place. Maybe just one question will be enough to prompt an answer. What am I to be doing here?

At this remarkable time in the history of the Church and the world, it is, in fact, in the best of times and the worst of times that we each have a vital part to play as a result of our being reserved to come forth at this time. The Lord is counting on each one of us to rise to all the possibilities within our sphere of influence to make a difference. I smiled the other day when I read a child's comment in the "Family Circus" cartoon. He asked his mother, "Do caterpillars know they are going to become butterflies, or does God want to surprise them?"

There is no question in my mind that each of us has come to the kingdom at this particular time with greater possibilities than we realize. Yes, with wings to fly! In many ways we will be called upon even as Esther to

---

Ardeth Kapp, a best-selling author and popular speaker, served as the Young Women General President and accompanied her husband when he was president of the Canada Vancouver Mission. She has also served as matron of the Cardston Alberta Temple.

develop those attributes of courage, dedication, selflessness, and unwavering faith if we are to save our people and especially our children from the escalating evils of our day.

I want to share some eternal truths and speak of the joy of our journey—the journey in which we come to understand the doctrine, gain faith to believe, and become aware of the grand opportunities and responsibilities that are available to us in our time and place. As we gain an eternal perspective, trusting in the Lord's time line, we live with a sense of anticipation. Anticipation is what you feel in your heart, your mind, the back of your neck, your arms, and your whole soul when you know that something is forthcoming when you commit to the Lord, the provider of your fondest dreams. You become future-oriented and full of faith, dedication, and commitment as you begin to see the big picture and your part in it.

As you are aware, the title for this session comes from a powerful and inspiring address given by Sister Sheri Dew while she was serving as a counselor in the Relief Society General Presidency. I wish to quote from Sister Dew's powerful address. She shared doctrinal insights inviting wonderful, thought-provoking truths:

"When we understand the magnitude of motherhood, it becomes clear why prophets have been so protective of woman's most sacred role. While we tend to equate motherhood solely with maternity, in the Lord's language, the word *mother* has layers of meaning. Of all the words they could have chosen to define her role and her essence, both God the Father and Adam called Eve 'the mother of all living' (Moses 4:26)—and they did so *before* she ever bore a child. Like Eve, our motherhood . . . is more than bearing children, though it is certainly that. It is the essence of who we are as women. It defines our very identity, our divine stature and nature, and the unique traits our Father gave us."[1]

With unwavering faith in the Lord's promises, we can taste the joy even while we ache for blessings delayed. With faith in Christ's promises, you can turn ache into hope and be filled with peace while finding many, many ways to let your mother heart find fulfillment as you work to nurture the children of God, no matter who gave them birth.

I have not lived so long that I have forgotten the challenges of living in a Mormon culture with the knowledge that everything important is focused on the family. It is at the very heart of our mortal life. Families become our identity, the focus of our attention, the purpose of our existence, and the basis for our values and our happiness. And we without children in this life do not ever want to lose the desire for children, yes, the yearning for children of our own—except maybe for just a moment on an early Saturday morning after six of the most precious children under age twelve who call you grandma wave goodbye. It is after several days of wonderful time together exploring and enjoying Grandma's house, with never-ending activities inside and out, including breakfast, lunch, and dinner. But when they leave, you are reluctant to wipe the finger marks off the windows. Just evidence that they were there warms your home and your heart in a special way.

Oh yes, Mother's Day will come every year. There will be weddings (you didn't have to pay for) and missionary farewells and Christmas cards from friends whose families have more and more posterity every year. Then there is the inevitable question that is asked early in the conversation when meeting members of the Church for the first time: How many children do you have?

Years ago it was uncomfortable to address those questions, but not anymore. I just say with a smile, "Not any children yet." Considering my obvious age they return the smile, maybe thinking I'm still hoping like Elizabeth did, after her many prayers in her old age.

We who have not been blessed with children in this life can wallow in self-pity, or we can experience birth pains as we struggle to open the passageway to eternal life for ourselves and others. President David O. McKay gave a perspective that is simply beautiful: "The noblest aim in life is to strive . . . to make other lives better and happier."[2]

My husband and I have come to realize you need not possess children to love them. Loving is not synonymous with possessing and possessing is not necessarily loving. The world is filled with people who need to be loved, guided, taught, lifted, and inspired.

One day in years past when I had set our dinner table with two plates only, in my mind I could see my sister Shirley setting her dinner table with thirteen plates for eleven children and a mom and a dad. I could see on the kitchen cupboard her well-worn scriptures, which she used to guide her in her mothering responsibilities. These are the times when you have a question burning deep within. Why? Why the difference? I have come to know that these are also the times when answers come in unexpected ways. I like to think of my scriptures as my letters from home. On a day when I was feeling like a caterpillar, unaware of the promise of the future butterfly, I opened my scriptures and read what felt to me like a personal letter from a loving Father in Heaven.

The message comes from Paul's writings to the Corinthians. Consider the opportunity to be in partnership with God as Paul counsels: "Blessed be God, even the Father of our Lord Jesus Christ, the Father of mercies, and the God of all comfort; who comforteth us in all our tribulation, that we may be able to comfort them which are in any trouble, by the comfort wherewith we ourselves are comforted of God" (2 Corinthians 1:3–4). How validating it is when from your own experience you can comfort a brother or sister in times of their disappointment, discouragement, heartache, or tragedy. You might say, "I think I have some idea of how you feel," and then, guided by the Spirit, proceed to help bear one another's burdens, as we agreed to do in our baptismal covenant.

Do we have the faith to believe all the Lord has promised, that no blessing will be denied when we choose to stay on the path and follow Him, reaching out to others along the way? I have been inspired by the words of Elder Neal A. Maxwell: "So often our sisters [and I would add brothers] comfort others when their own needs are greater than those being comforted. That quality is like the generosity of Jesus on the cross. Empathy during agony is a portion of divinity! . . . They do not withhold their blessings simply because some blessings are [for now, at least,] withheld from them."[3]

Knowing that this life is not the beginning, or the end, and that we have a great plan of eternal happiness, we can learn to live in anticipation as we enjoy the opportunities that are before us each day of our lives. There are many voices in the world today that attack the sacred role of motherhood and minimize the profound influence of good women. These same voices negatively impact the strength of the family unit and the attention given to children. We who do not have the responsibility of motherhood at this time in our lives can be a strong force for good as we assume some responsibility to articulate our values and defend the role of mothers and the importance of children and family, because we know the plan and what the future holds. I'm not suggesting that we see the entire plan. In this life, we grow line upon line as we seek answers to life's questions. Maybe we even remember in some cases things we have known for eons of time.

One of the powerful messages that provides daily guidance comes from Proverbs: "Trust in the Lord with all thine heart; and lean not unto thine own understanding. In all thy ways acknowledge him, and he shall direct thy paths" (Proverbs 3:5–6). When we truly trust in our Father in Heaven, knowing of His unconditional love for us individually, and seek to be guided by the Spirit, we can feel the power of the Comforter in our hearts and feel peace as many opportunities to be an instrument in the Lord's hands open up.

There are times when we are allowed to be in partnership with the Lord in answer to someone's earnest prayer. When we take the opportunity to let our influence, our voice, and our values be known in a world that is shouting conflicting messages, we are on the Lord's errand.

I'm reminded of an occasion when my sister Sharon heard of a brokenhearted mother who had just lost two of her children in a terrible motorcycle accident. She felt prompted immediately to go to this sister's home. She went empty-handed, no brownies or pie, just a heart full of compassion with the feet of an angel and a message of hope. The sister opened the door. Sharon asked what she might do to help. This heartbroken sister just shook her head as they embraced each other. Sharon felt prompted to ask if they might pray together. They knelt by the couch and offered a prayer. As you know, there is great power in prayer. Later the sister testified to Sharon that the Lord had comforted her broken heart at that very moment; she said it was the best help she had received. On that occasion there were three involved in the healing, as is so often the case when we reach out in love and service.

"In 1916 the *Relief Society Magazine* published a series of articles entitled 'Mothers in Israel.' One prominent woman honored was Sister Eliza R. Snow. Though childless, she was called a 'mother of mothers in Israel' and praised for her leadership among women, for her intelligence, and for her faithful support of the Church and its leaders."[4]

"President Joseph Fielding Smith said: 'To be a mother in Israel in the full gospel sense is the highest reward that can come into the life of a woman' [*Relief Society Magazine* 57 (Dec. 1970): 883]. It is a promise open

to all faithful sisters who love and serve the Lord and keep his commandments, including those who do not have the opportunity to bear children
in this life."[5]

We should never feel like one sister expressed, saying she feels over-
looked, that she doesn't belong, like being skipped over on the playground
when the motherhood team was being chosen. We have each been chosen
at this time in our current status to be a part of the motherhood team to
help protect, defend, and guard the home and family in our troubled
society.

I've often said, "We can all rejoice in the sacred calling of motherhood. To give birth is only one part of this sacred mission, the miracle of
life. But to help another gain eternal life is a privilege that is neither
denied to nor delayed for any worthy woman. And to be a mother in Israel
may be within reach of every righteous woman even now."[6]

Make no mistake, we each have a vital part to play at this critical time
in the history of this Church. The Lord is counting on us—every one of
us. On occasion we may feel like another mother, who expressed a feeling
of being a bit overwhelmed when she said, "I know God will never give
me more than I can handle, though I sometimes wish He didn't trust me
to handle so much." These are the words of Mother Teresa. She spoke
them when she was asked about taking on the insurmountable task of
ministering to the dying souls on the streets of Calcutta.

The challenges of our day are not limited to the streets of Calcutta.
The enemy is real and the Lord's chosen are the target. We must be strong
in defending our values, as we agreed to be in our pre-earth life experience.

I am reminded of the insight I gained when asked by our Church leaders to participate in a religious coalition with a common cause in
Washington, D.C., a number of years ago while I was serving as the Young
Women General President. There were women from all walks of life—
different cultures, educational backgrounds, experiences, language, and
more. After the opening prayer, one woman spontaneously stood before
the group and stressed the importance of us all singing off the same song
sheet if we are going to make a difference in fighting the battle that could
threaten our values and the very foundation that makes America great.
She then shared her perspective on the power of unity. "One woman can

be helpful," she said, "ten women influential, one hundred women powerful, and one thousand women invincible." There is a great power in unity whether you have children or not. We must all take a stand in defense of our values centered on the family.

During the three years that my husband and I served in the Cardston Alberta Temple, we had opportunities to have our eyes opened and our understanding increased as never before. Today I have a deeper understanding, with more of an eternal perspective, regarding the great plan of happiness and the ultimate purpose of our earthly journey, with or without children. It is through the covenants made in the house of the Lord that we learn more about who we are and who we are to become. It is in the temple that we find our greatest source of light and knowledge and hope and promises as we seek answers to difficult questions, are taught by the Spirit, and learn to walk by faith.

I have wondered, could the commandment to multiply and replenish the earth be a responsibility in which we all can participate in one way or another as we strive to fill the measure of our creation?

By definition, to multiply is to increase in numbers or enlarge or make something increase by a considerable amount. To replenish is to nourish, to fill somebody or something with needed energy or nourishment. I testify from personal experience that we can all take part in multiplying and replenishing as we use the gifts and talents the Lord has given us to help build the kingdom at this time and place.

Recently I received a little note from a young woman who lives in Kingman, Arizona. She wrote, "Thank you so much for your speech! I'm not very active right now. Your talk gave me the little push I needed." And one more: "Thanks for helping me remember how much worth I have and how much the Lord loves me. Thank you." I don't know what these sisters heard, but they felt the Spirit. They looked at life and themselves differently. Would that not qualify as helping to multiply and replenish the heart of a young woman?

The impact of our motherly influence cannot be overestimated. We don't need a podium to bear testimony and express love. In fact, some of the Savior's most powerful and effective teaching was done one-on-one. Usually the most memorable lessons come at unexpected times, often in our homes.

A few weeks ago, when I thought I was very busy, my husband answered the doorbell to find two little boys in our neighborhood who come to our door frequently to visit. I greeted them as they walked right past me on their way to the cookie drawer, where they made their selections. With one cookie in each hand, they headed for the library, selected from a whole shelf of children's books one of their favorite stories, called *Dinner Time*. They followed their established pattern, placed the book in the center of my desk, opened it, and took their places standing on each side of the desk, waiting for me to sit down between them. Had it been the little girls who come by, they would have gathered around the big chair on the floor at my feet. The boys didn't seem at all sensitive to the urgency I felt for the things I had on my agenda that day. When the little visit was over and I ushered them to the door, one of the boys put his arm around his friend's shoulder and said in a tone loud enough for me to hear, "She's like a grandma."

Those sweet words brought back an echo from more than fifty years ago, when on another day, a little boy knocked on my door. He was new in the area and asked if my children could come out and play. When I painfully looked into his bright eyes and explained that I didn't have any children, he asked the question I had not dared to put into words. "If you're not a mother, what are you?" That day I closed the door and repeated his question over and over: If you're not a mother, what are you?

I wish I could talk to that little boy, who would be a grown man by now, because I am prepared to give him an answer. I would tell him of the joy of the journey when I was taught by the Spirit that we can all be mothers. I believe it is in our mothering moments, when we are nurturing others, that we feel the joy that helps clarify our true identity and our divine nature.

The visiting teaching message in the March 2007 *Ensign* posed this soul-searching question: "How can the Spirit magnify me to be an instrument in the Lord's hands?"[7] The answer included this inspiring insight, applicable to each one of us today, from Sister Eliza R. Snow, who served as a Relief Society General President in the early history of the Church:

"When you are filled with the Spirit of God, . . . that [Spirit] satisfies and fills up every longing of the human heart, and fills up every vacuum. When I am filled with that spirit, my soul is satisfied. . . . The Spirit of God

will impart instruction to your minds, and you will impart it to each other.
. . . Remember that you are Saints of God; and that you have important
works to perform in Zion."[8] There are many Eliza R. Snows among us here
today. And you are instruments in God's hands in ever so many ways.

We, with or without children, can identify with the desire expressed in
the last verse of the hymn "O My Father," written by Eliza R. Snow:

> *When I leave this frail existence,*
> *When I lay this mortal by,*
> *Father, Mother, may I meet you*
> *In your royal courts on high?*
> *Then, at length, when I've completed*
> *All you sent me forth to do,*
> *With your mutual approbation*
> *Let me come and dwell with you.*[9]

By way of personal testimony, I would like to share with you one of
my most tender mother experiences that continues to warm my heart
every day.

I was in Arizona, where my niece Shelly had just given birth to her
fourth child, giving her four precious little boys. I got to be grandma that
weekend because Shelly's mom, Sharon, was away on an assignment for
the Church to some far-off place. At about one o'clock on a Wednesday
afternoon, the three little boys were waiting anxiously for the moment
when their mom, dad, and new baby brother would arrive home from the
hospital.

To help pass the time, we sat at the kitchen table with rocks and
paints I had brought with me in hopes of providing a fun learning activity.
With their very creative minds, they were busily painting bugs and bees
and butterflies and many unidentifiable objects when the front door
opened. Mom and dad and a baby brother were immediately surrounded
by excited brothers anxious to take their turn holding this precious little
spirit that had just begun his mortal journey. As Trevor looked into the
eyes of his little brother, I had the strong impression they had known each
other before. It was a precious moment. When each had taken his turn,
it was time to let their mom take over, and the boys returned to their rock
painting.

After only a minute Josh, with brush in hand, looked at me in all seriousness and asked, "Nana Ardie, how many birthdays do you have left?" With a smile, I said, "I don't know, Josh. Why do you ask?" He laid his brush down, put his arms around me, and said, "Because I love you, and I don't want you to ever die." "Josh," I said, "I have something wonderful to tell you." I then explained to him that because Jesus came to earth and did everything His Father had asked Him to do while He was here, He made it possible for us not to worry about birthdays. I explained that when I went back to Utah, we would keep thinking about each other and loving each other and looking forward to when we would be together again. That is how it is when we run out of birthdays. As though he understood more than I had said, he eagerly picked up his brush and went back to his painting.

If the children had been a bit older, I would have expanded on the lesson. I would have picked up the largest rock on the table and I would have testified in the words of Helaman to his sons:

"And now, my sons, remember, remember that it is upon the rock of our Redeemer, who is Christ, the Son of God, that ye must build your foundation; that when the devil shall send forth his mighty winds, yea, his shafts in the whirlwind, yea, when all his hail and his mighty storm shall beat upon you, it shall have no power over you to drag you down to the gulf of misery and endless wo, because of the rock upon which ye are built, which is a sure foundation, a foundation whereon if men build they cannot fall" (Helaman 5:12).

I truly believe with all of my heart that we are in partnership with the Lord when we strive to know His will and endeavor to carry it out. As we honor our covenants and take upon us Christ's name and keep His commandments, we can always have His Spirit to be with us to comfort, guide, encourage, and help us remember. Remember that there is a divine plan, and we each have a significant part to play in filling the purpose of our earth-life mission. It is through our covenants made in the temple that we gain an eternal perspective of the very purpose of life and live with greater anticipation of all the blessings our Father has promised, even to becoming joint heirs with Jesus Christ. With the mothering skills that we practice here, we will be better prepared for increased responsibilities when some of us will be raising our children during the Millennium, when Satan is bound.

My beloved sisters, we are not alone. We have been called at this time to help build the kingdom. With faith to believe, "Shall we not go on in so great a cause?" (D&C 128:22). I testify that as we honor our covenants that bind us to the Lord, we have power to fill the measure of our creation, live with anticipation, and enjoy the journey.

NOTES

1. Sheri Dew, "Are We Not All Mothers?" *Ensign*, November 2001, 96; emphasis in original.
2. David O. McKay, in Conference Report, April 1961, 131.
3. Neal A. Maxwell, "The Women of God," *Ensign*, May 1978, 10–11.
4. *Encyclopedia of Mormonism*, edited by Daniel H. Ludlow (New York: Macmillan, 1992), 2:964.
5. *Encyclopedia of Mormonism*, 2:964.
6. Ardeth Greene Kapp, *My Neighbor, My Sister, My Friend* (Salt Lake City: Deseret Book, 1990), 136.
7. "Become an Instrument in the Hands of God by Listening to and Following the Promptings of the Spirit," *Ensign*, March 2007, 57.
8. Eliza R. Snow, in *Women's Exponent*, September 15, 1873, 62; as quoted in "Become an Instrument in the Hands of God by Listening to and Following the Promptings of the Spirit," *Ensign*, March 2007, 57.
9. Eliza R. Snow, "O My Father," in *Hymns of The Church of Jesus Christ of Latter-day Saints* (Salt Lake City: The Church of Jesus Christ of Latter-day Saints, 1985), no. 292.

"TOUCH OUR EYES THAT WE MAY SEE"

Cheryl Fogg

Recently our neighbor, an eleven-year-old girl, came over with a little gift in her hand for us. I invited her in for a visit. As she was leaving, I said, "Thank you, Olivia, for thinking of us." Her response was, "Well, every ward needs some nice *old* people." (I don't remember getting old!)

I know something about each of you. *You* are getting old, a year at a time. Every time I have a birthday, you do too. It is a blessing to have birthdays (even if the candles do cost more than the cake). One year my little grandson called to wish me a happy birthday. He asked me how old I was, and I told him sixty-five. He was quiet for a moment, and then he asked, "Did you start at one?"

"Sunrise, sunset—*swiftly* fly the years."[1] Can we keep a positive attitude about getting older? Can we welcome a new wrinkle? (I call *mine* character lines. Other people get wrinkles.) Even if we don't look as young as we used to, we older sisters still feel young inside. Our spirits continue to be young.

Is there an upside to aging? In some ways, we get better with age. Our priorities improve; many things that used to matter don't matter anymore; and we see that our real treasures are the gospel, family, and friends. As disciples of Christ, our faith in the Lord deepens because we have seen

---

Cheryl Fogg, a graduate of the University of Utah, is a mother, grandmother, and musician. She has served with her husband as a humanitarian missionary in fifteen countries, including Cambodia, Albania, Burma, Nigeria, and Vietnam.

what He has done in our lives, and even though our eyes may dim, we see life from a wiser perspective. The upside to aging is that our spiritual vision improves as we mature and our spirit learns to follow the will of the Lord.

I love this Primary song I learned when I was a little girl:

> *Father, let thy light divine*
> *Shine on us, we pray.*
> *Touch our eyes that we may see;*
> *Teach us to obey.*[2]

As a child, I wondered what it meant to "touch our eyes that we may see," as my eyes could see. Only as I matured did I learn how, through my obedience and faith in Him, the Lord can touch my eyes with increased spiritual vision. He wants us to see who we really are. He wants us to see spiritual realities not visible to the natural eye. He wants us to see how we must live to be worthy to return to God's presence. Above all, we must see that Jesus Christ is our Savior! Knowing this will help us see our purposes here.

Our purposes? I now see that they are not *our* purposes, but the *Lord's* purposes for us. These purposes are, first, to come unto Christ, to follow Him, to submit to His will for us, and then, to lift and help others improve their lives and come to Christ.

President Gordon B. Hinckley has said: "Each of you has the responsibility of standing as a witness of the everlasting truth of the gospel of Jesus Christ. Your responsibility is to open the eyes of *others* 'and to turn them from darkness to light, and from the power of Satan unto God.'"[3]

My husband is an eye surgeon and has restored sight to many people through eye surgery. In 1988, there was a widow in Poland, Mrs. Brazuza, who did stitchery for a living. She found herself going blind. She went to a doctor in Poland, who did cataract surgery on one eye, but it was unsuccessful. That eye would never see again. As she was praying about how she could save her other eye, she met a friend of ours visiting in Poland, who told her of my husband. Mrs. Brazuza decided to travel to Fresno, California, to have Dr. Fogg operate on her eye. In great faith, she sold all her furniture to pay for her flight. When the doctors heard of this, they and the hospital did the surgery without charge. This cataract surgery was successful. She could now see clearly. She was so ecstatic that she couldn't quit hugging her doctor and everyone around.

What would *you* give to have the Savior touch your eyes that you may see? Just as Mrs. Brazuza sacrificed all her belongings to have her physical sight restored, wouldn't we give all that we possess to have Christ touch our eyes with spiritual sight? As we mature in obedience and faith, He will touch our eyes that we will see our lives, our challenges, our possibilities, our families, and our blessings with enlightened spiritual vision.

Recently, my eyes were opened when I was on the coast in Mexico. Early in the morning while I was yet in bed, I could see that the sky was getting a bit lighter, so I hurried outside where I could watch the sun rise over the ocean. The sky was heavy with clouds, some very dark, that began to turn into beautiful pinks, fuchsias, and golds as they gradually reflected more and more of the coming sun. This incredible crimson light continued to spread in every direction as it grew in brilliance, until the risen sun dispelled darkness from the entire sky.

As I watched the sunrise, I thought of the effect the Savior has had on my life through the years. Troubles may cloud my vision and darken my perspective, but if I patiently keep my eyes on the Son of God—the Light of the World—I see the darkness dissipate and the dark clouds of my life eventually change into beautiful blessings.

C. S. Lewis said, "I believe in Christianity, as I believe that the Sun has risen, not only because I see it, but because *by* it I see everything else."[4]

Trials bring us to Christ. Like many of you, I have had trials in my life. As I share with you some of my tests and what I have learned, think back to a time when you saw your life through the lens of the Savior. Maybe that time is now. He has the power to turn your darkest difficulties to light, if you truly come unto Him and submit to His will.

Our daughter, Kimberly, has dealt with learning disabilities all her life, never learning to read above a basic level or to drive. As a child, she spent many frustrating hours working with tutors, doing patterning exercises, and traveling many miles to specialists that we hoped would have some answers. Kim's story is one of struggle, for her and for us. When I would seek the Lord's help, I was reminded to "trust in the Lord with all thine heart; and lean not unto thine own understanding. In all thy ways, acknowledge him, and he shall direct thy paths" (Proverbs 3:5–6).

Over the years, challenges such as Kim's have taught me to trust the Savior more completely, as I have seen Him direct her paths and mine. I am so grateful that the Lord has blessed Kim with a good husband and a meaningful job as a teacher's aide for handicapped children in Utah's School for the Deaf and Blind.

Another difficult trial for me was the illness of our youngest child. We were devastated when our little Gregory was diagnosed with leukemia at age three. For years we watched him bravely submit to needles, tests, radiation, and chemotherapy treatments. It is so painful to see a loved one suffer. How we rejoiced when the disease finally went into remission. But, after his relapse at age seven, our only hope was a bone-marrow transplant. The matching donor was his oldest sister, Linda, the mother of two little children.

As Greg entered the hospital this time, realizing the risk he was taking, he drew a picture, asking, "Why me?" During the long and sometimes terrifying transplant, I was usually alone with Greg in isolation at UCLA Hospital, more than four hours from our home. I took great comfort in the scriptures.

For instance, Doctrine and Covenants 68:6 says: "Wherefore, be of good cheer, and do not fear, for I the Lord am with you, and will stand by you; and ye shall bear record of me, even Jesus Christ, that I am the Son of the living God, that I was, that I am, and that I am to come."

I often felt the Savior with us, standing by us and bringing peace. While angel friends cared for my family at home, unseen angels attended us in our hospital room. Some of the most sacred experiences of my life took place while I stayed night and day with my little son.

The bone-marrow transplant was successful. After six weeks we happily took Greg home, but a week later he was back in UCLA Hospital with complications. For the previous four years, we had constantly prayed with great faith that Gregory would be healed. The Lord *had* answered our prayers by giving him many good days and sweet miracles. But now, heartbroken to take a sick boy back to the hospital, we began to realize that the Lord needed us to *listen*—listen more carefully and truly submit to His will.

One sobering day in the hospital, my husband and I went to the outside stairway, where we could pray. With great faith as we prayed, we told the Lord that we didn't want our little son to suffer but to fulfill the Lord's plan for him—that he was His child first. We now truly submitted our little son to God's will. Within the hour, Gregory was taken home to his Father in Heaven.

Words cannot express the warm, sweet, and tender spirit in that hospital room. As all six of our children had traveled hundreds of miles to be with us at Greg's bedside that day, our entire family knelt together around Greg's body in the hospital bed and thanked Heavenly Father for this precious little boy's life and his impact on our family. We felt encircled in the arms of our Savior's love, as He sustained us and comforted us in our great loss.

With this life-changing experience, the eyes of my understanding were opened to our Father in Heaven's magnificent love for His children. With Greg's death, Christ's Atonement became so personal and priceless! How I love the Savior and appreciate His great Atonement. Because of Him, we will have our son again. What a joyful and glorious day that will be.

I learned how precious life is and how priceless our children are. I learned that we must more fully and unconditionally love and cherish the people in our lives and tell them often of our love and of God's love for them.

Even though this trial was *very* difficult for all of us, Greg's illness affected our family in profound ways. I saw the increased love of my children for each other. For instance, after my daughter had undergone the surgery to harvest her bone marrow for Greg, she was in her hospital room recovering. I went in to her and said, "Thank you so much, Linda, for donating your bone marrow to Greg—for giving your little brother a chance to live." Her sincere reply was, "Mother, if he needed my leg, I would give it to him."

Two years later, our faith was once again tested as our three-year-old granddaughter, Linda's daughter, was also diagnosed with leukemia. My cry to the Lord was, "How can we go through this again? What have we not learned from this? Help us understand." There were more years of chemotherapy and painful tests, more fasting and prayer to hold on to little Brittany. Gradually, we yielded our hearts and submitted her to the

Lord's will. This time, the Lord's will was for Brittany to live. Despite the destruction that the toxic chemotherapy inflicted on her little body, Brittany is now a young mother of two little boys, her motherhood a miracle in itself.

I learned that as we mature in obedience and faith and learn to submit to the Lord's will, our spiritual vision improves. We then see more clearly that God is over all and knows all, especially what is best for us. His eternal plan for each of us is perfect.

I have seen families with tough trials be strengthened or shattered. For instance, I met a couple in the hospital who also had a child with cancer. They were so overwhelmed by this experience that it was beyond their ability to cope, and their marriage ended in divorce. I learned that how we respond to such trials is determined by our faith in the Lord and our spiritual vision and understanding.

Watching our little ones suffer with this life-threatening illness, *we* were tested to the edge of *our* faith. While there were some things we didn't understand, we chose to deepen our faith and respond with more commitment to the Lord.

Through my experiences with Mrs. Brazuza, watching the sunrise, our children's trials, and seeing how my faith grew to be able to submit our children's lives to the Lord's will, I have seen His hand. As I have come unto Christ and learned to submit to His will, I have matured in my commitment to Him. The Lord has often touched my eyes with enlightened spiritual vision. For this I am so grateful.

"Because I have been given much, I, too, must give."[5] After we have come unto Christ and have felt His touch, we see meaning in our lives. Then, we see those around us who need this same touch by which to see, and we wish to bring this joy to them.

We see that our first responsibility is our family. As I have seen how precious our children are and how wicked the world has become, I see that we need to do all we can as mothers, grandmothers, aunts, and friends in bringing our children to Christ. We must prepare them for their life's trials and for Satan's attacks on their faith, which are happening now.

What can we teach our children that will fortify them against the threats to their faith that will come? We must witness of Christ and teach them the doctrines of the kingdom that will strengthen and save them.

Have we not come for such a time as this? Elder Henry B. Eyring said, "The words you speak today may be the ones they remember. And today will soon be gone."[6]

In our family, we have annual family reunions. You probably do this also. If you don't, please consider this for your family. Our reunions make such a wonderful difference. We gather our family together for a week every year to play together, pray together, and have lots of crazy fun. Our family is like fudge: mostly sweet, with a few nuts.

Because my incredible, almost-perfect grandchildren all live far away, I see that I need to spend more time with them than the reunion allows if I am to really know them and influence them. I came up with a plan I call EFG, which stands for Especially for Grandkids. If you are an aunt, you can do this as well, and you can call it Especially for Goodkids. We invite them by age groups for a week each summer, without their parents. We do fun activities, from skits to skating, and have lots of music. EFG gives us an opportunity to teach our grandchildren about us, our convictions, and our family heritage. We encourage them to set goals and be strong in the faith. How we enjoy these special grandchildren. Someone has jokingly advised: Never have children, only grandchildren.

In addition to our families, there is much to be done to help others in need. There is no greater joy than seeing how our efforts can help others improve their lives and prayerfully lead them to Christ. We can be productive kingdom builders, even after age fifty-five.

Will we offer the Lord our lives in His service? There is an urgent need for senior missionaries, both for full-time missions and for Church-service missions. All of us are needed for family history work, temple work, and volunteering in our communities. My friend Edna Decker, now 104 years old, is still a faithful visiting teacher. We can be diligently engaged in good works no matter what our age.

My husband and I are now serving as missionaries on the Church Humanitarian Vision Project. For more than two years, we have traveled to fifteen developing countries to help the blind get their sight restored. We have traveled to countries such as Nigeria, Moldova, Albania, and Nepal. We visit eye surgeons, hospitals, and ministers of health. We assess what *they* need to enable *them* to restore vision to their blind and poor. We then return home to have the Church send such vitally needed eye equipment as surgical microscopes, slit lamps, and supplies for eye surgery. We also locate LDS eye surgeons who will leave their practice to go to one of these countries to share their skills. These people are so very grateful for this help.

Everywhere we go, there are such great needs. Everywhere we go, we see the hand of the Lord in this work. And in every country, we see doors open to us. We are put together with the right people at the right time to accomplish the Lord's purpose of restoring sight to the blind. We marvel and ask, Just how does this happen? Of course, we realize that the Savior wants to bless all His children, all over the world. It is so rewarding to know that everywhere we go, more of the blind will have the beautiful blessing of sight.

As we travel throughout the world, we are humbled to see so many of God's children suffering because of hunger, poverty, and blindness. Our eyes have been opened again and again to our great blessings of living here in this wonderful land of clean water, freedom, and plenty.

President Thomas S. Monson said: "Those who have felt the touch of the Master's hand somehow cannot explain the change which comes into their lives. There is a desire to live better, to serve faithfully, to walk humbly, and to be more like the Savior. Having received their spiritual eyesight and glimpsed the promises of eternity, they echo the words of the blind man to whom Jesus restored sight: 'One thing I know, that, whereas I was blind, now I see.'"[7]

How many more birthdays will we have? We don't know. But join me in celebrating with more than candles and cupcakes. Let us celebrate each year by coming to Christ with more obedience and more faith and trust in His will. Let us celebrate by giving more loving service to help others improve their lives and find the eternal joy of coming to Christ. As we do this, we will be blessed with increased spiritual vision by which to see the path back to our Father.

God lives. Jesus Christ is the Son of the Living God, our Savior. He knows and loves each of us and will stand by us in our trials. Through His infinite Atonement, so vast and yet so personal, He will touch our eyes that we will see.

NOTES

1. Sheldon Harnick, "Sunrise, Sunset," in Jerry Bock, *Fiddler on the Roof* (New York: Pocket Books, 1966); emphasis added.

2. Matilda Watts Cahoon, "The Light Divine," in *Hymns of The Church of Jesus Christ of Latter-day Saints* (Salt Lake City: The Church of Jesus Christ of Latter-day Saints, 1985), no. 305; emphasis added.

3. Gordon B. Hinckley, "Inspirational Thoughts," *Ensign*, February 2007, 6; emphasis added. Originally from a meeting held in Nairobi, Kenya, 4 August 2005.

4. C. S. Lewis, "Is Theology Poetry?" in *The Weight of Glory and Other Addresses* (San Francisco: HarperSanFrancisco, 2001), 140.

5. Grace Noll Crowell, "Because I Have Been Given Much," in *Hymns*, no. 219.

6. Henry B. Eyring, "The Power of Teaching Doctrine," *Ensign*, May 1999, 74.

7. Thomas S. Monson, "Anxiously Engaged," *Ensign*, November 2004, 58.

How Do We Increase
Our Faith?

Cecil O. Samuelson

Our women's conference theme reminds us that living in this day and age, and perhaps even where we live, is not an accident. Further, as we have been reminded regularly by President Gordon B. Hinckley, this is a wonderful time to be alive, arguably the best time in the history of the world and certainly the best time in the history of the Church. Problems and challenges abound among and around us, yet we are blessed in significant and unprecedented ways.

President Hinckley has also expressed, "Of all our needs, I think the greatest is an increase in faith."[1] I'm confident that none of us would dispute this assertion as we reflect on the obstacles and difficulties we each face. Likewise, it seems apparent to me that well-founded and grounded faith, like other cardinal virtues, is something that is never excessive or in too rich supply. The real question for most of us who accept that increased faith is both desirable and necessary is, How do we gain more meaningful, sustaining, and life-changing faith?

As with most things of real worth or value, there are no significant shortcuts. The Apostle Paul's experience on the road to Damascus was

Cecil O. Samuelson is the president of Brigham Young University and a member of the First Quorum of the Seventy of The Church of Jesus Christ of Latter-day Saints. In addition to his career as a physician, he served at the University of Utah as a professor of medicine, dean of the School of Medicine, and vice president of health sciences. At the time of his call to full-time Church service, he was senior vice president of Intermountain Health Care. He and his wife, Sharon, have five children and seven grandchildren.

dramatic and life changing. Although the book of Acts gives two detailed accounts of his unexpected conversion (see Acts 9; 22), we do not know the antecedent events or efforts that qualified him for this remarkable intervention by the Savior.

In the same vein, we may think the Prophet Joseph's First Vision experience was a similar, spontaneous event that occurred without special preparation or effort. Happily, we have the evidence and understanding that this was by no means the case (see Joseph Smith–History). In fact, by careful study of Joseph's early life, we recognize that sustained and arduous effort made by this very young man led him to the Sacred Grove and the world-changing events that occurred there. He listened, learned and was "quick to observe," much like another very precocious young boy, Mormon (see Mormon 1:2).

While the lad Joseph Smith was impressed and touched by the religious fervor in his surrounding environs, he also quickly perceived the conflict and inconsistencies evident in the competing claims and assertions of the various existing churches. Although he was respectful of the views of others, he also recognized his personal responsibility to consider and search out answers for himself. He did not take these matters lightly. In fact, he admitted to significant distress and angst. Let me turn to his words: "In the midst of this war of words and tumult of opinions, I often said to myself: What is to be done? Who of all these parties are right; or, are they all wrong together? If any one of them be right, which is it, and how shall I know it?" (JS–H 1:10).

Because most of us are so familiar with his account and history, it may be tempting to rush ahead rather than to consider carefully the circumstances and the process. First, we should acknowledge with gratitude that young Joseph was taught by his parents, before the Restoration of the gospel, to believe and have faith in God the Father and Jesus Christ. Further, we know he was already somewhat knowledgeable about the Bible and had an understanding that important answers and guidance are available in the scriptures. Without this background and the sustaining experiences of his physically impoverished but spiritually rich youth, it is highly unlikely that Joseph would have pursued the course that he followed. Let us return to his account: "While I was laboring under the extreme difficulties caused by the contests of these parties of religionists, I was one day reading in the Epistle of James" (JS–H 1:11).

Note that he did not say "while I was casually considering my religious responsibilities because I had nothing else to do or think about." No, he admitted that he was working and thinking very hard about these issues and carefully studying to find answers. While we don't have all the data, my guess is that this was not the first time he had read from the New Testament nor perhaps was this the first time he had read the words of James. These are the words he read: "If any of you lack wisdom, let him ask of God, that giveth to all men liberally, and upbraideth not; and it shall be given him" (James 1:5).

Again, we return to Joseph's narrative: "Never did any passage of scripture come with more power to the heart of man than this did at this time to mine. It seemed to enter with great force into every feeling of my heart. I reflected on it again and again, knowing that if any person needed wisdom from God, I did; for how to act I did not know, and unless I could get more wisdom than I then had, I would never know; for the teachers of religion of the different sects understood the same passages of scripture so differently as to destroy all confidence in settling the question by an appeal to the Bible" (JS–H 1:12).

Think of how all of this must have weighed on this young man for an extended period of time. Sometime during this process of stretching and learning, he came to understand that while helpful and even essential, the scriptures were not enough in themselves. More was needed. The additional requirements included not only prayer, but faith of sufficient strength to pursue the answer sought and then the resolve and commitment to follow through on all the implications of the answers or instruction given.

Joseph's stretching was not only an essential prelude to the First Vision but was also an inescapable necessity for his role in the Restoration of the gospel, with the coming forth of the Book of Mormon, the organization of the Church, the building of temples, the establishment of missionary work, and all that we take for granted today in the Lord's kingdom. Not only did these things transpire "line upon line, precept upon precept" (D&C 98:12; 128:21), but each step of the way was arduous and difficult and Joseph often encountered detours.

As it was with the Prophet Joseph, so it is with us. I have come to believe that if life always seems to be perfect, we are likely missing some very important and essential lessons and experiences! I also believe that as wonderful as some days are, few if any of us ever go long without finding something we wished were different or easier.

With the permission of my wife and family, let me use a personal example which I believe in the microcosm of our circumstance illustrates the principle with both its attendant challenges and blessings. I hasten to add that what I share is not likely to be generally transferable to others with similar problems but is only an example of how our faith was strengthened and great blessings resulted from disappointments that we never expected nor welcomed. Knowing what we do today, I also gratefully acknowledge that we would not change our experiences even though they were tremendously challenging at the time. I believe it is an affirmation of the doctrine taught by President Spencer W. Kimball that "faith precedes the miracle"[2] and also affirmed by Moroni in his treatise on faith (see Ether 12).

When Sharon and I married over forty years ago, we were united in our desire for a family, preferably a large one. Both of us had had close to idyllic family lives in the homes in which we grew up. Neither was perfect except in the truly important things, but our parents loved each other and their children, and the feelings were reciprocated. While we were aware that our favorable circumstances were not consistent with the experiences of everyone else, it frankly did not occur to us that we would ever have challenges in achieving the family for which we aspired.

We were not unduly concerned that our first baby did not arrive until we were just beginning the fourth year of our marriage. I was still in school with many years of education and training yet ahead, and we thought, if we thought at all, that perhaps this was just a temporary blessing to a financially struggling young couple. Shortly after, however, we became aware of a medical challenge and the need for Sharon to endure several surgical procedures over the next few years. We were thus thrilled when our second child was born a little over five years after the first. We were advised that if we wanted further children, given the medical situation we were facing, it would be good to have them as soon as possible. We were grateful to have another pregnancy before too long. Sadly, that turned out to be an ectopic pregnancy that not only threatened Sharon's life but led us to the understanding that further pregnancies were highly unlikely.

While we were grateful for our two sons, we were saddened that our assumptions about our family size required this major adjustment. In addition to our own distress, however, was the tenderness in dealing with the feelings of our oldest son. At the time his brother was born, he had, with the firm faith that a five-year-old can demonstrate, prayed for a brother *and* a sister. When he only got a little brother, as much as our firstborn loved him, he began to question why Heavenly Father had not answered his prayer. It turned out he was as naive about such things as were his parents, and I'm afraid our answers to him were not fully satisfactory in his young mind.

While we prayed about these things, we also understood that we had great blessings already and did not dispute with nor doubt the Lord. We asked a few timid questions about adoption, but were told by well-meaning and fair people to be happy with what we had and remember the many who had no children at all. Frankly, we had to agree that we had no business competing with them for the woefully short supply of babies available for adoption.

One day in early 1977, while fulfilling a new Church assignment, we were informed by an associate that it might be possible to adopt a set of twins that were to be born shortly in Guatemala. The birth mother was not able to keep them and was hoping that they might have a bright future with a family who would love them and care for them in ways she was not able to do.

Our two sons were then nine and four years old, and they were included in our family council about this frankly daunting and unexpected opportunity. Going through the process of study and faith and remembering the persistent prayer of a young boy for a baby brother and a baby sister, we determined that the twins, a little boy and a little girl, needed to become part of our family. Not knowing any better at the time, we did not find it unusual to have the legal and administrative details completed and have them home with us in the United States within two months of their birth.

Almost five years after the twins joined our family, we had the blessing of another baby, but this time she came in the usual way and proved again that doctors often are not as smart as they think they are!

As we fast forward in time thirty years, the twins, together with their three siblings, have all married very well and are starting their own families. Each has at least one child, albeit that several of them, in different ways, also have trouble getting babies to arrive in a timely fashion when they place the order for them.

We are very proud of our five children, their wonderful spouses, and particularly our seven exceptional grandchildren. But that is not the reason for this long, personal account. My purpose in sharing these details is to bear testimony of the blessings that come through the stretching of our faith. Many of these blessings—now recognized and appreciated, but years ago not expected nor anticipated—would not have been ours without the challenges and disappointments, the tears and the trials. In fact, our lives have been so much better, fuller, and richer than we could have imagined in our early married life as we fantasized about our perfect future. We can now bear testimony to that wonderful principle articulated by Moroni: "Faith is things which are hoped for and not seen; wherefore, dispute not because ye see not, for ye receive no witness until after the trial of your faith" (Ether 12:6).

As we all know, faith in the Lord Jesus Christ is the first of the first principles because it is the foundation on which all other principles are built. President Hinckley has counseled that we need to increase our faith and, I believe by implication, gain a greater understanding of what our faith really is.

There are many definitions of faith. As we strive to strengthen our faith, we need to be sure exactly what we are magnifying. I like the definition in the eleventh chapter of Hebrews: "Now faith is the substance of things hoped for, the evidence of things not seen" (Hebrews 11:1). Alma and other prophets give similar definitions (see Alma 32).

I worry that, on occasion, we may confuse our faith with certain knowledge. Certain knowledge about fundamental things is eventually essential but cannot occur without first developing and strengthening our faith. Likewise, just as knowledge does not come without effort, so is the situation with faith.

President Hinckley has made reference to the account of the ruler of the synagogue who fell at Jesus' feet and pled with the Savior in his daughter's behalf. You remember the words: "My little daughter lieth at the point of death: I pray thee, come and lay thy hands on her, that she may be healed; and she shall live" (Mark 5:23). As we know, Jesus went with him and the crowd followed along. On the way to the child's sick bed, the poor woman who had been bleeding or hemorrhaging for twelve years, with no help or cure from all the physicians she had seen, pushed through the crowd and touched the Lord's garment because her faith was such that she believed that that act alone would result in healing her, an event that did transpire.

Jesus felt "that virtue had gone out of him" (see Mark 5:30) and stopped, turned, and asked who had touched him. Because they were in a crowd, the disciples and others were perplexed because they were surrounded by a "multitude" and likely had been touched, brushed, or jostled by many people. At any rate, the woman confessed and Jesus told her that her faith had made her whole or well (see Mark 5:31–34).

We don't know how long this interruption or delay took, but while this miracle was being accomplished and the attendant lessons were taught to strengthen the faith of the afflicted woman and the disciples, a messenger from the synagogue ruler's house arrived. He announced that the little girl, so loved by her father, had died and suggested that it would not be beneficial to trouble the Master further (see Mark 5:35). Let's return to Mark's account: "As soon as Jesus heard the word that was spoken, he saith unto the ruler of the synagogue, Be not afraid, only believe" (Mark 5:36).

We know the rest of the story. Jesus, along with Peter, James, and John, accompanied the sorrowful father to the home, corrected the loving but faithless household, and took the girl by the hand and commanded her to arise, which she did. He then commanded the witnesses to confidentiality with respect to these events and finally, ever practical even in the context of performing miracles, the Savior instructed that she should be given something to eat (see Mark 5:37–43).

President Hinckley has shared the experience of his early missionary days. We have heard him describe his discouragement and his father's advice to forget himself and go to work. That is great advice for all of us as well. I think he was not surprised at his father's counsel. On the day

President Hinckley left for his mission, his father gave him a card with these words written on it: "Be not afraid, only believe."[3]

Our faith is essential to, and our fears are antithetical to, our faith. That is why we should always read the verse in James that follows the one Joseph quoted.

"If any of you lack wisdom, let him ask of God, that giveth to all men liberally, and upbraideth not; and it shall be given him.

"But let him ask in faith, nothing wavering. For he that wavereth is like a wave of the sea driven with the wind and tossed" (James 1:5–6).

Think of another example involving faith and water. Peter walked on the water because he had faith, and he sank into the water when he wavered or his faith failed him (see Matthew 14:28–30). As with many of the Savior's miracles, we likely do not understand all of His purposes and all of the lessons that might be learned from this event on the Sea of Galilee. It does seem useful and appropriate as we try to "liken all scriptures" to ourselves (see 1 Nephi 19:23) to think of this experience in our own context rather than as an example of Peter's momentary weakness.

Like the disciples, while we yearn to have Jesus or His representative, the Holy Ghost, with us at all times, we too often have periods of separation. Almost always, in our day, such separation is a result of our individual actions or neglect. At any rate, Jesus had sent the disciples away in a ship as He went to pray in solitude. A windy storm came up on the Sea of Galilee, as it frequently does, and those on the boat were uncomfortable. As they scanned the horizon, they saw Jesus walking on the sea and they were understandably surprised and concerned. Let's pick up the account from Matthew:

"But straightway Jesus spake unto them, saying, Be of good cheer; it is I; be not afraid.

"And Peter answered him and said, Lord, if it be thou, bid me come unto thee on the water.

"And he [meaning Jesus] said, Come. And when Peter was come down out of the ship, he walked on the water, to go to Jesus.

"But when he saw the wind boisterous, he was afraid; and beginning to sink, he cried, saying, Lord, save me.

"And immediately Jesus stretched forth his hand, and caught him, and said unto him, O thou of little faith, wherefore didst thou doubt?

"And when they were come into the ship, the wind ceased" (Matthew 14:27–32).

We know that this event was not only instructive for Peter but also for those with him. We understand that this experience strengthened the faith and testimony of all in the ship. Frankly, I wince whenever I hear someone be a little critical of Peter as his faith wavered and he began to sink. I've wondered if I would have been one of those never inclined to leave the boat in the first place.

It is clear that this was just one of the many tutorials that helped shape the courageous, confident, and ever-faithful leader Peter became as he presided over the Church in the years to follow. I suspect that the others present were also strengthened and prepared for their future responsibilities.

How might we apply these lessons to ourselves? Just as Jesus said to the grieving father from the synagogue, he might have also said to Peter and his crew, as well as to us, "Be not afraid, only believe." As He did with the young girl and with the Apostle Peter, Jesus stretched forth His hand. He will help us in ways most appropriate to our circumstances just as He and His Father did for the young Prophet Joseph Smith. None of those helped had perfect faith, but all had some faith and were doing the best that they knew how to do. That applies to us as well.

How does Jesus reach out to us? It may be in ways described in the scriptures, and it is often through the ministrations of the Holy Ghost, who He promised would be given as a "Comforter" to the faithful when the Savior Himself would not be present (see John 14). Another frequent example of His reaching out to us comes through the tender service rendered to us by others, including His servants. Think of the actions of the Apostle Peter in later years and how he likely learned to do what he was doing:

"Now Peter and John went up together into the temple at the hour of prayer, being the ninth hour.

"And a certain man lame from his mother's womb was carried, whom they laid daily at the gate of the temple which is called Beautiful, to ask alms of them that entered into the temple;

"Who seeing Peter and John about to go into the temple asked an alms.

"And Peter, fastening his eyes upon him with John, said, Look on us.

"And he gave heed unto them, expecting to receive something of them.

"Then Peter said, Silver and gold have I none; but such as I have give I thee: In the name of Jesus Christ of Nazareth rise up and walk.

"And he took him by the right hand, and lifted him up: and immediately his feet and ankle bones received strength" (Acts 3:1–7).

All of this gives us added understanding of what the resurrected Jesus meant as He instructed His disciples in the Western Hemisphere as to their responsibilities. He said:

"Therefore, what manner of men [and women] ought ye to be? Verily I say unto you, even as I am" (3 Nephi 27:27). Likewise, as He prepared to "go unto the Father," He invoked this blessing and this promise which apply to all of us as well in our own lives and challenges:

"Whatsoever things ye shall ask the Father in my name shall be given unto you.

"Therefore, ask, and ye shall receive; knock, and it shall be opened unto you; for he [or she] that asketh, receiveth; and unto him [or her] that knocketh, it shall be opened" (3 Nephi 27:28–29).

It is in following Jesus and the pattern He has given for proper and faithful living that we find the secrets of increasing the faith that we so vitally need. It is in serving others and following the Savior's prescriptions that we increase both our faith and the faith of others. It is in so doing that we realize that the Lord knows best what we really need and that our lives, including the unexpected twists and turns, are in His loving hands.

It is my witness that He lives and that our Father in Heaven knows us better than we know ourselves. He hears our prayers and answers them, not necessarily to our immediate preferences, but to our ultimate benefit because of the Atonement and intercession of His Beloved Son, Jesus Christ, in whose name we pray and whose example we seek to emulate.

NOTES

1. Gordon B. Hinckley, "'Lord, Increase Our Faith,'" *Ensign*, November 1987, 51.
2. Spencer W. Kimball, *Faith Precedes the Miracle: Based on Discourses of Spencer W. Kimball* (Salt Lake City: Deseret Book, 1973).
3. Gordon B. Hinckley, in Conference Report, October 1969, 114.

SHOW FAITH, NOT FEAR

Cheryl C. Lant

This life experience is a wonderful, exciting time. It is given to us by a loving Father that we might "have joy" (2 Nephi 2:25). Life is full of many things bright and beautiful and things that bring us challenges and difficulties. Many of our experiences—both the wonderful and the hard—come to us simply because they are part of this earth life. Some things that we experience are brought upon us by others. These can be blessings we receive through no effort of our own or challenges inflicted when we have no choice in the matter. And some of our experiences are of our own making as we use our agency.

All of our experiences, both the positive and the negative, if used wisely, can bring us closer to Heavenly Father in this life and closer to an eternal relationship with Him. All of them are part of His plan of happiness. This means that as we partake of the good things life has to offer, we can find great joy and fulfillment. It also means that as we have to face the hard things, we have choices to make. We can choose to turn away from the Father in fear, anger, weariness, bitterness, rebellion, or discouragement, or we can choose to embrace all of what life brings with a determination to stay close to our Father in Heaven. We can choose to be

---

Cheryl C. Lant serves as the Primary General President. She and her husband, John, founded a private school called Learning Dynamics Academic Preschool. They are the parents of nine children.

strong as we endure and trust in His love and in His Atonement. We can choose to follow Him in faith.

Our beloved prophet, President Gordon B. Hinckley, is a wonderful example of a man of faith. President Thomas S. Monson said of him, "He is a man of vision who does not take counsel from his fears."[1] When you think of all that President Hinckley is responsible for, and who he is responsible to, it's not hard to imagine that fear, doubt, and feelings of being overwhelmed might creep into his mind and heart. But always we see him as an example of optimism, love, encouragement, strength, and hard work. Rather than taking counsel from his fears, he never lets them enter. He does not give them equal time in thought and energy. He is proactive and diligent in his service to the Lord. We see him as a man of faith.

Living in faith is the opposite of taking counsel from our fears. Let's talk for a few minutes about this first principle of the gospel—faith. The Bible Dictionary says, "Faith is to hope for things which are not seen, but which are true." And "to have faith is to have confidence in something or someone."[2] Our question might be: Who and what should we have faith in? Of course, first and foremost we must have faith in the Lord Jesus Christ and in His Atonement. In *Preach My Gospel,* the wonderful book that our missionaries are now using, we read this beautiful explanation: "When you have faith in Christ, you believe in Him as the Son of God, the Only Begotten of the Father in the Flesh. You accept Him as your Savior and Redeemer and follow His teachings. You believe that your sins can be forgiven through His Atonement. Faith in Him means that you trust Him and are confident that He loves you."[3]

Faith must be our foundation. Our very salvation depends on whether we have faith in Jesus Christ as our Savior. We must seek through study and prayer to know this truth. We must accept His Atonement into our own lives as we work to overcome our weaknesses. We must accept His forgiveness and forgive ourselves. But the last sentence of this statement is the part that I believe can take each of us from having a basic testimony of the Savior and His Atonement to hoping and then trusting that it really will work for me—and that He loves me enough to know me, to help me, and to forgive my sins, no matter how large or small. Listen to this sentence again: "Faith in Him means that you trust Him and are confident that He loves you." This kind of faith makes it possible for us to face life and all of its complexities, both positive and negative.

So, let's talk about real life for a moment—my life, your life. Do you ever find yourself wondering if you have enough faith? Do you ever feel that life is just too hard? Do you ever begin to get discouraged, to worry and doubt? I think all of us can answer yes to one or all of these questions. But I do not believe that this necessarily means that we don't have any faith. This is because developing faith is a process. It is because we are learning and growing every day of our lives. It is because our faith increases over time and with use. It is because as our faith is tested, we may struggle.

Let me give you an example. Years ago, one of our sons was diagnosed with cancer. At first I was downright fearful. Then I began to worry like crazy. I worried about his life because the prognosis was not good. I worried about his little family. I worried about his finances. I worried about his future. I worried about everything. At first, this worry and fear made me physically sick. I became ineffective in my duties and responsibilities as a wife and mother.

However, this fear and worry took me to my knees and to the scriptures. I sought for direction, comfort, and strength. I began to feel the stirrings of faith. I found that the scriptures became a living thing for me. Every time I opened them, I found something that brought peace to my soul. I found that my prayers became more heartfelt than ever before. I prayed for faith sufficient to accept His will. I determined what I needed to do in my life to become more worthy to receive the blessings I sought. I learned where I could turn for peace.

Through this experience, I also found that while one day my faith would be strong, the next day, when a negative test result would come, my faith would be shaken. Each experience would send me to my knees again, to the scriptures again, to the Lord again. I learned that to have faith is a process—an ongoing process. We have to always work at it. But I also learned that the Lord does love us; He is in charge. He will always answer our prayers for our best good. This does not mean the answer will always be yes, or that the answer will come now. Accepting this can strengthen our faith.

Can we not suppose that this is the very design of heaven? We have to endure trials, we have to submit our will to our Heavenly Father, and we have to trust and labor with our weaknesses in order to become strong— to become like Him, to come to Him. Each experience we have that tests our faith, if we pass it well, accepting the will of the Lord, will strengthen us in preparation for the next such experience. Elder Richard G. Scott talked about this concept in April 2003 general conference:

"'The Lord . . . doth bless and prosper those who put their trust in him.' (Helaman 12:1.) . . .

". . . Every time you *try your faith*, that is, act in worthiness on an impression, you will receive the confirming evidence of the Spirit. Those feelings will fortify your faith. As you repeat that pattern, your faith will become stronger. . . . As you walk to the boundary of your understanding into the twilight of uncertainty, exercising faith, you will be led to find solutions you would not obtain otherwise."[4]

I have found this to be true. Each time a trial comes, I have to go through the process of building up my faith. But as each new experience strengthens me, I seem to be able to start with a stronger foundation of knowledge and faith.

There are some other principles concerning faith that I would like to mention. One is that faith is a principle of power. The power of God is accessed by faith. It is the power to endure, the power to overcome, the power to accept the Lord's will.

We have all heard of the faith of a mustard seed having the power to move mountains. Well, what are the mountains in our lives? Maybe you have a really big mountain in your life right now. Maybe you just have lots of little molehills. Our lives as women in the Church are so full and rich, and yet full of stress. I remember looking down the bench in sacrament meeting one Sunday and seeing my children struggling to behave appropriately. Their dad was the bishop and was on the stand. The speaker was talking about the blessings of having families. I was exhausted, and I thought to myself, "My greatest blessings are my greatest trials!"

Wherever you are in your life, as a mother, wife, sister, daughter, friend—woman—there are things that will be better met if they are met with faith. Jesus taught, "If ye have faith as a grain of mustard seed, ye shall say unto this mountain [or this molehill], Remove hence to yonder place; and it shall remove; and nothing shall be impossible unto you"

(Matthew 17:20). Our molehills, conquered with faith, prepare us for moving the mountains in our lives.

Another principle of faith is that it must lead to action. We read in James 2:17–18: "Even so faith, if it hath not works, is dead, being alone. Yea, a man may say, Thou hast faith, and I have works: shew me thy faith without thy works, and I will shew thee my faith by my works." Some of the actions of faith are repentance, obedience, and dedicated service. Our faith is manifest through diligence and work. Just professing that we have faith is not enough. Faith is not an abstract principle. It is living, breathing, acting. Our faith has to be in motion for the Lord's blessings to come. We must pray as if everything depends on the Lord, and then get up and work as if everything depends on us.

When I was called to be the Primary General President, President Hinckley told me that he wanted me to take care of all the children of the world. Then he asked me if I thought I could do that! Well, you can imagine what fear that put in my heart. But he didn't leave it there. He opened the door to faith as he instructed me to rely on the Lord and to just work at it. Fear brings inertia into our lives and then a gradual decline of our testimony and faith. To have faith is to face forward, take positive action, find peace, and feel the confidence of the Spirit as we go to work.

Faith also means to endure. There are some things in our lives that we cannot change. Our hearts must be open to the Lord and we must be willing to accept some of the challenges that come, even as we have faith in future blessings. Let me give you an example. My dear mother lost her sweetheart, my father, more than four years ago. He had suffered from Parkinson's disease. She spent her strength as she nursed him and cared for him with great love and with great faith in the plan of our Father in Heaven. When Dad died, I wondered how Mom would go on. He had been her whole life. It was then that her faith really became clear to me. She has been lonely, yes, and there have been hard days, but she has never really felt the despair of deep grief because she knows where he is, what he is doing, and that they will be reunited again. She does get anxious to join him, but she is sweet and peaceful and happy while she is here, blessing all who know her with her faith. She endures, but more than that she rejoices in knowing what the waiting will bring. She simply waits upon the Lord.

Now, how can we come to the point that we can demonstrate that kind of faith? It begins by believing, by opening our hearts to the Lord. We must trust in the Lord. In Alma 36:3 we read: "Whosoever shall put their trust in God shall be supported in their trials, and their troubles, and their afflictions, and shall be lifted up at the last day." As was mentioned before, faith is the opposite of fear. We must get rid of our fears. We read in Doctrine and Covenants 6:36: "Look unto me in every thought; doubt not, fear not." Joseph Smith said it this way: "Where doubt and uncertainty are there faith is not, nor can it be. For doubt and faith do not exist in the same person at the same time; so that persons whose minds are under doubts and fears cannot have unshaken confidence; and where unshaken confidence is not there faith is weak; . . . and they will grow weary in their minds, and the adversary will have power over them."[5] That is an interesting concept. Without faith we become weak and weary, beaten down by all the challenges in our lives. It is at that point that Satan begins to gain power over us. It is so important that we turn to the Lord for His help before we get to this point, recognizing where our strength comes from.

Next, we must recognize that when we pray to our Heavenly Father for blessings we need, having faith that He can help us is not enough. We must qualify ourselves by becoming worthy to receive the blessings we seek. As President Harold B. Lee taught: "If you want the blessing, don't just kneel down and pray about it. Prepare yourselves in every conceivable way you can in order to make yourselves worthy to receive the blessing you seek."[6] This means really looking at our lives and making choices about what is most important. Are the things we are spending our time doing bringing us closer to Jesus Christ, or are they merely taking up space and time?

Many of our choices in this life are between good and good. Sometimes we have to accept that we cannot do everything. We have to set priorities. We must make sure we are choosing wisely, using an eternal perspective. Elder David A. Bednar said: "If we put essential things first in our lives—things such as dedicated discipleship, honoring covenants, and keeping the commandments—then we will be blessed with inspiration and strong judgment as we pursue the path that leads us back to our heavenly home. If we put essential things first, we 'cannot go amiss' (D&C 80:3)."[7]

This seems to instruct us as to what we need to choose to do, but it also implies that as we make good choices, we will see more clearly what choices we need to make in the future.

Then we must seek to have the Holy Ghost with us and learn to hear His quiet, gentle whisperings. The still, small voice brings thoughts, inclinations, and impressions into our minds and confirms them in our hearts. If we are watchful, we will be able to tell when it is the Holy Ghost because of the good that will come of it. As we learn to listen and discern the voice of the Holy Ghost, we must act on what we receive.

As we turn to the scriptures, we see all of these things illustrated in the life of young Nephi when he was given something really hard to do. He was asked to go back to Jerusalem and get the records. It was a long way. It would take a long time and a lot of effort. It was dangerous, and there was no guarantee that they would be successful. And to make matters worse, his two older brothers were against going. But what was Nephi's response? He said something that we can all quote: "I will go and do the things which the Lord hath commanded, for I know that the Lord giveth no commandments unto the children of men, save he shall prepare a way for them that they may accomplish the thing which he commandeth them" (1 Nephi 3:7). Here is a declaration of great faith. But the part of this story that I love best comes in the next chapter. "And I was led by the Spirit, not knowing beforehand the things which I should do. Nevertheless I went forth" (1 Nephi 4:6–7). Nephi's faith in the Lord, his willingness to listen to the Spirit, and his courage to do what he was asked to do qualified him in the sight of the Lord. Things were not always easy for him—in fact, we don't know of much that was easy for him. We know that he was a man of faith.

We too can rely on the Lord to guide us. We may not be able to see the end from the beginning, but we can follow the impressions of the Spirit, and eventually we will see what it is that the Lord had in mind for us all along. We can go forth.

Lastly, I would like to mention having faith in the Lord's timing. So much of the time, when I petition the Lord, I want it right now. When this doesn't happen or when the answers aren't exactly what I thought they should be, I must remember that the Lord requires us to have patience along with faith. We often must wait for the Lord's promised blessings to be fulfilled. This act of waiting is a trial to our faith in and of itself. It can strengthen us, or it can throw us right back into the cycle of doubt and fear. If we do not understand some of the ways that the Lord answers our prayers, our faith may be shaken. He may answer yes. He may give us answers a little at a time over a long period of time. He may say no, or we may feel as though we are not getting any answer at all. We must just have the faith that the Lord knows what is best for us. He wants what is best for us.

Sometimes, with our limited vision, we are not able to understand. As our faith in Him grows, we can come to realize that we do not always need to understand. Our understanding does not change a thing. We can put our hand in His, not taking counsel from our fears, and move forward in our lives, with freedom born of faith and confidence in the Lord Jesus Christ. President Hinckley said: "When I discuss faith, I do not mean it in an abstract sense. I mean it as a living, vital force with recognition of God as our Father and Jesus Christ as our Savior. When we accept this basic premise, there will come an acceptance of their teachings and an obedience which will bring peace and joy in this life and exaltation in the life to come."[8]

I am grateful for our beloved prophet, who teaches and testifies of our Heavenly Father and His Son, Jesus Christ. I know that Jesus Christ is our Savior, that He lives, He loves us, and He waits for us to come to Him in faith. I know that faith is a real, vital force in our lives and that as we live in faith rather than in fear, we can be happy, we can serve others, we can become what our Father in Heaven would have us become. I know that it is through faith that we can return to Them.

NOTES

1. Thomas S. Monson, quoted in "News of the Church," *Ensign*, June 2005, 74–75.
2. Bible Dictionary, s.v. "faith."
3. *Preach My Gospel* (Salt Lake City: The Church of Jesus Christ of Latter-day Saints, 2004), 116.
4. Richard G. Scott, "The Sustaining Power of Faith in Times of Uncertainty and Testing," *Ensign*, May 2003, 76–77; emphasis in original.
5. Joseph Smith, *Lectures on Faith* (Salt Lake City: Deseret Book, 1985), 71.

6. Harold B. Lee, *The Teachings of Harold B. Lee: Eleventh President of The Church of Jesus Christ of Latter-day Saints,* ed. Clyde J. Williams (Salt Lake City: Bookcraft, 1996), 129.

7. David A. Bednar, "A Reservoir of Living Water," CES Fireside for Young Adults, 4 February 2007.

8. Gordon B. Hinckley, "With All Thy Getting Get Understanding," *Ensign,* August 1988, 5.

GROWING IN THE GOSPEL: INCREASING OUR FAITH

Helen S. K. Goo

In the fall of 1960 an eighteen-year-old young man by the name of Roger Romrell from Idaho Falls, upon the persuasion of his parents, enrolled at Brigham Young University as a freshman. Once on campus he made new friends and a new commitment to Church and family. During this time he began to think about serving a mission. However, he was not sure if he should go as soon as he turned nineteen. That October his parents came to attend general conference. Roger met them in Salt Lake City and went to conference with them.

At the end of the conference, as Roger and his mother were standing at the back of the Tabernacle waiting for his father, they watched the General Authorities walk past as they exited the Tabernacle. It was especially thrilling to see the prophet, David O. McKay. As Roger stood there a thought came to his mind: If he could shake hands with the prophet, it would be an acknowledgement that he should do all he could to serve a mission. President McKay was so loved that there was a very large crowd of Saints waiting to see him. Some of those in the front rows were able to shake his hand. Roger was standing a couple of rows back, but as President McKay was about to get into his waiting car, he turned around, reached his hand over the crowd, and shook Roger's hand.

Helen S. K. Goo has served in various Church auxiliaries. She also served with her husband when he presided over the Hong Kong Mission. Sister Goo is a mother and grandmother.

On December 13, 1960, Roger received his mission call to the Southern Far East Mission with headquarters in Hong Kong. Little did Roger know that his decision to serve a mission would have great impact on my life. In faraway China when I was about eight years old, my parents left in a hurry for Hong Kong to escape the communist invasion of our city. I was left behind with my aunt, who was my mother's youngest sister.

A year later my parents met a woman who was taking her daughter back to China to live while she would return to Hong Kong to work. My parents asked the woman if she would bring me to Hong Kong using her daughter's passport, and the woman accepted the assignment and a sum of money for this favor.

I remember my aunt telling me about this woman. She helped me to memorize the name of the little girl and instructed me that I would be using that name when I crossed the border to Hong Kong to be reunited with my family. It was a joyous occasion when I finally arrived in Hong Kong to live with my family.

When I was twelve, I met the missionaries through a classmate, Anna. My mother was a member of a Lutheran congregation, and I was then attending a Lutheran school. I often attended church with my mother, but I never felt I belonged. One day as Anna and I were walking home from school we saw two young American men walking toward us. Surprisingly, Anna greeted them. Because I came from China, where I was taught that Americans were evil people, I stood aside and didn't want to have anything to do with these *Quai Lows,* or foreign devils. But Anna brought them to me, and they shook my hand and spoke to me in Cantonese. They proceeded to tell me about a prophet named Joseph Smith. I had been taught that the Bible was the only scripture, and since the name Joseph Smith could not be found in the Bible, I rejected their message.

One night two missionaries knocked on our door and asked for me. Surprisingly, my mother allowed them in. One of the elders told me that from the record he could see that I had gone through several sets of missionaries, and he wanted to know what my problem was. I told him that I could not accept Joseph Smith as a prophet, and he asked if I had read the Book of Mormon and prayed about it. I said no, and he challenged me to do so to find out if it was true. I wanted to get rid of them, and so I promised them that I would study and pray about it. That night as I got into bed to sleep, I thought of my promise to them. I got up and started to read the Book of Mormon.

Afterwards, I knelt down to pray sincerely to the Lord, asking if this was true. Nothing spectacular happened, but I did feel a sense of peace and serenity. As I continued to study and pray I became a very active nonmember of the branch. I was asked to help with the Primary every Saturday by rounding up the children and taking them on the bus to church to attend Primary. I would save my daily allowance from my breakfast and lunch so that I had money to help pay the bus fare for some of them. The chapel soon became my second home.

After a while, my mother began to resent the Church for occupying so much of my time. Her ministers took advantage of her discontent to tell her falsehoods about Mormonism. This upset her even more, and she started to restrict my Church activities. In those days church was held in two sessions, Sunday School in the morning and sacrament meeting in the afternoon. I was allowed to go to one but not both. It was very difficult for me because I was a translator in Sunday School and the chorister for sacrament meeting. I just had to go to both. From then on I had to be extra good around the house. On Sundays I would get up very early and do all the chores in order to put my mother in a position where she really could not refuse to let me go to church. After Sunday School I would just stay in the chapel and wait for sacrament meeting in the afternoon. I knew that if I went home, my mother would not let me go out again. From that time on, whenever my mother was upset with me, I would find the door locked upon my return from church and there would not be any dinner. My Church friends would buy me some bread to eat while I waited outside the door until my father let me in.

As I was going through this difficult time, my desire to be baptized increased each day. After I listened to the eighteen discussions I knew I wanted to be a member of the true church. When the missionaries challenged me to be baptized, I told them I had to wait because I knew my parents would not sign the permission form.

A short time later I overheard my parents making plans to go to Macau to visit an aging aunt. An idea came to mind, and the next day I told the missionaries that I could be baptized on Saturday. The night before my baptism I packed my little wicker school basket with a towel and a change of clothes. Well, like many things in life, this event did not work out as smoothly as planned. My parents surprised us and returned home a day earlier, on Friday night. I was determined to go ahead with my baptism. The next morning I told my parents that I was going swimming. I met Anna at the bus stop and we took the bus to the mission home where the baptism would take place in the swimming pool. When the missionaries asked for my permission slip, I told them that my parents had gone to Macau. Seeing that I was such a faithful and earnest nonmember, they believed me. On August 1, 1958, I was baptized a member of The Church of Jesus Christ of Latter-day Saints. Following the baptism and receiving the gift of the Holy Ghost, I realized that I should be honest with my parents. I waited until my mother had gone to bed and then told my father about it. Being an understanding man, he told me that he knew how much I loved the Church, and his only request was that I would not do anything to bring shame to the family name.

I am one of those blessed with great enthusiasm for almost everything in life, and missionary work was no exception. I felt I could save the world. My enthusiasm caused me a great many trials in my life. The Lutheran school I was attending became very concerned over the lack of attendance in their own Sunday School meetings. Upon further investigations they discovered that Anna and I had been taking our classmates to our church to Sunday School and to MIA. They decided to take action against us.

On Easter Sunday 1960, following the mandatory Sabbath worship for all the students, the principal announced that Anna and I were to come to his office immediately after the meeting. To our astonishment we were advised that we were being expelled from school. No explanation, no consultation with parents; we were just expelled. We were devastated. We had disgraced our families.

When I notified the branch president he called the mission office, and President Taylor sent missionaries to see the principal. Eventually they were told that Anna and I were expelled because we were communists. When evening came and my father was alone, I told him what had happened to me in school. My father was disappointed with me but told me not to let my mom know and he went about securing a tutor for both

Anna and me. We would meet at the chapel each day for our lessons until my father secured a slot for me in another high school. Eventually my mother found out, and I was punished for disobeying her.

Life was not good for me at home. I felt a sense of hopelessness among my relatives, who regarded me as an outcast. At the age of sixteen I was set apart as Primary president, and that kept me happy in my life. Each day I faced my life with faith in my Heavenly Father, knowing truly that I was His daughter and that He loved me. That knowledge alone has helped me to feel my worth and to live each day with hope for a brighter future. As the sacrament meeting chorister I worked with the pianist, Elder Roger Romrell from Idaho Falls. He could play only eight hymns, and every Sunday we sang those eight hymns. Elder Romrell was a very compassionate person and perceptive to my situation. He asked if I would like to go to Idaho to live with his family and finish my education. He said he had five brothers and they had always wanted a sister.

At the age of seventeen, in September 1962, I left Hong Kong. Many of my Primary children came to the airport, and they presented me with a doll. I clutched the doll, left behind a difficult situation, and went on to begin a new life in the hands of my Heavenly Father. I am grateful for my simple faith that comes from knowing in my heart that Heavenly Father will watch over me. I am not saying that I was not afraid. I cried almost all the way from Hong Kong to Tokyo.

At long last I arrived in the Idaho Falls airport. There the Romrells, along with Sister Long, who had served her mission in Hong Kong, met me at the airport and embraced me with love. I felt instantly that I was part of their family. On the way to their home I asked if I could see the Idaho Falls temple. When I saw the holy temple I felt so much peace and happiness in my heart. I knew I belonged to the true church of God.

In the spring of 1964, when I was a senior at Idaho Falls High School, Dad Romrell was a member of the stake presidency and often had meetings with the Church leaders. During one of his meetings in Salt Lake City, Elder Gordon B. Hinckley asked what my plans were after high school. Dad Romrell told him that I was going to enroll in Ricks College. Elder Hinckley replied, "No, I want Helen to go to the Church College of Hawaii, where she will meet and marry her own."

When Dad Romrell returned home and told me what Elder Hinckley had said, I told him, "I will go to the Church College of Hawaii." The summer after my freshman year in college I met a young man of Chinese ancestry, Charles Goo, who was born and raised in Hawaii. He was attending Brigham Young University and was the home teacher for my friends from Idaho Falls. They told him to look me up when he came home for the summer.

Shortly after we met he was called to serve his mission in Hong Kong. We corresponded for two and a half years, and after his mission we were married in the Hawaii Temple. I am grateful for his faith and his commitment to the gospel. Because of that I have had the privilege of supporting him in many Church callings. Serving side by side with my husband has given me opportunities to grow in the gospel. Through these choice experiences I have gained greater love for my Heavenly Father, His Son Jesus Christ, and my brothers and sisters throughout the world. We raised five wonderful children, three daughters and two sons, and each one of them has served a mission. Four of them are married and are married in the temple to worthy individuals. They are the crowning joy in our lives, along with our eight grandchildren. I am thankful to now-President Hinckley for his love and concern for me. Because I listened and followed his counsel, my life has been blessed.

When we choose to exercise our faith, we can become instruments in God's hands to bring about His purposes and to bless His children. Roger Romrell exercised his faith in Heavenly Father. A living prophet who was in tune with the Spirit reached out to shake Roger's hand, and I became the beneficiary of that act of faith. I was able to come to America to live and practice my religion without persecution. During my years in Idaho Falls, I learned from Mom Romrell's example as a supportive wife to a busy Church leader, and later in my life I found the same joy in supporting a busy husband in his Church assignments. It was not a coincidence that I was led to live with the Romrells. It was by divine intervention that I went there to live and to learn what a Latter-day Saint family is all about. I am grateful for a loving Heavenly Father who knew what training I would need to better prepare for my future. Faith allows miracles like this to happen.

Our living prophet, President Hinckley, desires that we increase in faith. These are the words spoken from his heart to our Heavenly Father on our behalf: "Father, increase our faith. Of all our needs, I think the greatest is an increase in faith. And so, dear Father, increase our faith in Thee, and in Thy Beloved Son, in Thy great eternal work, in ourselves as Thy children, and in our capacity to go and do according to Thy will, and Thy precepts."[1]

As I read his prayer, I can see in my mind's eye our beloved prophet kneeling down by his bed and pouring out his heart to God to implore Him to bless us with an increase in faith. It brings tears to my eyes just to feel that great love President Hinckley has for us. Our prophet knows an increase in faith is needed in our lives as we face the uncertainty of our future in these troubled times. Let us honor our prophet and strive to increase our faith in God and His Son, Jesus Christ.

What Is Faith?

The Prophet Joseph Smith taught that faith is "the first principle in revealed religion, and the foundation of all righteousness." He explained that faith "is the assurance which men have of the existence of things which they have not seen, and the principle of action in all intelligent beings."[2] President Hinckley observed: "When I discuss faith, I do not mean it in an abstract sense. I mean it as a living, vital force with recognition of God as our Father and Jesus Christ as our Savior. When we accept this basic premise, there will come an acceptance of their teachings and an obedience which will bring peace and joy in this life and exaltation in the life to come."[3] *Faith* in the Chinese language is made up of two characters. The first character is *Shun,* which means believe. The second character is *Sum,* which is the heart. In other words, faith comes from a believing heart. We often hear people say, "If your heart is in it you will do fine, but if your heart is not in it you won't succeed."

A believing heart is the motivating force that leads us to do good and live virtuous lives. It is extremely important that we nurture our hearts with knowledge of the divinity of our Father in Heaven and the Savior, Jesus Christ. Sisters, we must check our hearts regularly and ask ourselves these questions:

• Do I know that Heavenly Father and Jesus Christ live and that They love me?

- Do I know that Jesus Christ died and atoned for my sins?
- Do I know that I am a daughter of God?
- Do I know that God is at the helm and that He knows what is best for His children?
- Do I listen to and obey the counsel of our living prophet?
- Do I live the gospel to the best of my ability?

If our answers are not affirmative, it is time to humble ourselves and follow these guidelines in the book of Helaman: "Nevertheless they did fast and pray oft, and did wax stronger and stronger in their humility, and firmer and firmer in the faith of Christ, unto the filling their souls with joy and consolation, yea, even to the purifying and the sanctification of their hearts, which sanctification cometh because of their yielding their hearts unto God" (Helaman 3:35).

We can reclaim our faith and work toward our eternal progression. The plan of salvation begins with faith and continues by increasing in faith. Every blessing that comes into our lives is the result of exercising our faith in God the Father and His Son, Jesus Christ.

One of my favorite Book of Mormon stories is the account of the two thousand young warriors. These young men told Helaman that they had been taught by their mothers that if they did not doubt, God would deliver them. They also added that they did not doubt their mothers knew it (see Alma 56:45–48). I have often wondered what manner of women their mothers were. What did they do to raise their sons with such faith and courage? So great was their faith that it brought down the power of heaven for their protection. I don't have all the answers, but I am certain that these women were of great faith and taught by their examples. I imagine that if they were living today, they would show faith in all the programs of the Church, such as Primary, Young Women, and Young Men, by supporting their children in their activities. They would know the scouting program in order to encourage and support their sons to achieve the highest rank of Eagle Scout. They would learn the duties of the offices in the priesthood and see to it that their sons perform their duties with exactness as they advance in the priesthood.

If they had daughters, I think they would learn the Young Women values with them and align their teachings at home with these values. I am sure they would see to it that they have family prayer daily, family home evening weekly, and scripture study daily as well. I imagine they would bear their personal testimonies to their children regularly. I am sure they would teach compassion to their children by the many hours of service they perform with joyful hearts.

These faithful converted Lamanite mothers did a marvelous job of instilling faith in their sons, and we salute them for their great achievement. Now it is our turn as we have come for such a time as this. We too will dedicate our lives in bringing up generations of youth who will be worthy sons and daughters of God. As we live our lives with faith in our hearts, our children will recognize our faith, and they will not doubt that we know God lives and Jesus is His Son and this is His true Church.

Quite a few years ago, a member of our ward, Sister Baker, had a brain tumor. It was announced in church that our ward would fast and pray for her on Monday as she went into surgery. That afternoon at family dinner, we discussed fasting as a family on Monday. Our youngest son, LeGrand, had not fasted for twenty-four hours before, but he too wanted to fast and pray for Sister Baker. On Monday he told his teacher that he wasn't going to eat lunch, and he stayed in the classroom to read while his classmates went to lunch. A couple of months later, when Sister Baker stood in sacrament meeting to announce that she was completely healed and to thank the members for their faith on her behalf, our son LeGrand was so excited that upon his return from church, he announced that his prayers and fasting helped Sister Baker to get all better. How grateful I am that my children have had many wonderful faith-promoting experiences in their young lives as their anchors. I believe these experiences helped them develop their faith in God and in themselves.

As daughters of God, we can exercise our faith by calling on our loving Heavenly Father for special blessings. If our desires are in harmony with His will, He will grant us the desires of our hearts. By the same token, we exercise our faith in accepting God's will and trusting that He knows what is best for us. When I was a young mother with three daughters, I wanted to have sons who would carry the family name in the Church. One day as I was reading in 1 Samuel a thought came to me. *Hannah wanted a son, and she asked God for a son. I also would like to have sons, and I can do what Hannah did and ask the Lord for sons.* At the time my husband and I were temple workers for the Cantonese-speaking sessions. One day as I was about to leave the temple I knelt down in the locker room and petitioned my Heavenly Father to bless me with sons, and I promised Him that I would name my first son after the living prophet, Spencer W. Kimball. I also promised my Father in Heaven that I would teach my sons to dedicate their lives to serving God and keeping His commandments. The following year, Spencer Milton Yan Loong Goo was born. Seven years later, LeGrand Charles Yan Ming Goo was born. I am grateful for a loving Heavenly Father who granted me the righteous desires of my heart. Now the Goo name will remain faithful and strong in the Church for many generations to come.

I truly believe that with God nothing is impossible. We are the ones who put limits on His miracles because we lack faith in our hearts that He is the all-powerful God. "For if there be no faith among the children of men God can do no miracle among them; wherefore, he showed not himself until after their faith" (Ether 12:12). Faith precedes miracles.

I live in a magical place in the middle of the Pacific Ocean on an island called Oahu. Our little village is situated on the North Shore. Many mornings when my husband and I go for our morning walks through our community, we are amazed at its serene beauty and peace. Laie was the *Pu'uhonua*, which means a place of refuge. The Aliis, who were the chiefs, had decreed that any criminal who could make his way to Laie would be saved. It was a barren land, with no water. It was doubtful that anyone could survive there for long.

The early Saints came and endured many hardships. Some were contemplating leaving. When Joseph F. Smith was serving his third mission, he made this prophetic statement: "My brothers and sisters, do not leave this land, for this place has been chosen by the Lord as a gathering place for the Saints of the Church of Jesus Christ of Latter-day Saints in Hawaii. . . . Do not complain because of the many trials which come to you, because of the barrenness of the land, the lack of water, the scarcity of foods to which you are accustomed, and the poverty as well. Be patient, for the day is coming when this land will become a most beautiful land. Water shall spring forth in abundance, and upon the barren land you now see, the Saints will build homes, taro will be planted, and there will be plenty to eat and drink. . . .

"And upon this place the glory of the Lord will rest, to bless the Saints who believe in Him and His commandments."[4] With faith in their hearts the Saints remained in Laie. Soon after, true to the prophecy, wells were discovered. A pristine source of pure water from an aquifer deep beneath the ground was found. The Laie we see today is the result of the dedication and endurance in faith of the Hawaiian pioneers.

Later on, labor missionaries from all over the Pacific Islands, as well as the mainland United States, came with faith in their hearts to help build the temple, the Church College of Hawaii, and the Polynesian Cultural Center. These three entities bless our lives in countless ways while they stand as a witness to the world that we worship a living God and His Son, Jesus Christ.

Today we see evidence of that same faith in Laie. We have in our midst many senior missionaries and volunteers who have left their children and grandchildren to serve the Lord. They come from all walks of life, armed with years of experience to serve and to mentor in the university, the Polynesian Cultural Center, and the temple. With faith in their hearts, they go forth to do good among the children of God. And because of their faith and diligence, the Lord remembers their families and loved ones at home, and He extends His blessings to them as well. They are building a legacy of faith for their posterity and for all of us by their great examples.

To increase our faith simply means to place more trust in God and His Son, Jesus Christ. It means to work harder and do more than what we are doing in service to God and His children. It means listening to the promptings of the Spirit and following those promptings and doing something about them. Our faith will increase when we live up to our Heavenly Father's expectations of us. Increasing our faith will purify our hearts, sanctify our souls, and bring us closer to our Heavenly Father and Jesus Christ.

We may not be called to save a nation as Esther did, but one thing is certain: we are not here by chance but by the will of God. If we are faithful, we have a tremendous role to play in building Zion and preparing for the Second Coming of our Savior. I am grateful for the missionaries who came to Hong Kong with faith in their hearts to bring the gospel of Jesus Christ to the Chinese people. I am thankful to the Romrells for their love for me and for nurturing me in the gospel in my early years in the Church.

I consider my membership in this Church the most significant blessing in my life. It is the fountain from which all my blessings flow. I testify that President Hinckley is a prophet of God and that Heavenly Father and His Son, Jesus Christ, live.

NOTES

1. Gordon B. Hinckley, "'Lord, Increase Our Faith,'" *Ensign*, November 1987, 54.
2. Joseph Smith, *Lectures on Faith* (Salt Lake City: Deseret Book, 1985), 1.
3. Gordon B. Hinckley, "With All Thy Getting Get Understanding," *Ensign*, August 1988, 5.
4. R. Lanier Britsch, *Unto the Islands of the Sea: A History of the Latter-day Saints in the Pacific* (Salt Lake City: Deseret Book, 1986), 142. Brother Britsch commented: "It is probable that Saints at Laie were discouraged about the Laie plantation during the time when President Smith was among them. Some writers and speakers have implied that the continued existence of the Laie settlement was in serious question. (See David W. Cummings, *Centennial History of Laie*, 1965.) There is no evidence in the records of the mission or of the missionaries at that time that this might have been so.

    "On the other hand, there is little reason to doubt that President Smith made this statement. According to Castle H. Murphy, who was in Hawaii when President Smith visited there on several occasions after the turn of the century and with whom this writer has conversed, such statements as these are in harmony with the kinds of things he said in Murphy's presence.

    "The principal problem with the document quoted above is that it was written after the fact by a woman who was young at the time it was spoken. She stated that though she was young when President Smith made the prophecy, her memory of the event was reinforced by the retelling of it by her grandparents. Although her testimony tends to lend authenticity to the fact that he did make the prophecy, it also leads one to question the exactness of the statements she remembered after so many years" (*Unto the Islands of the Sea*, 144 n. 34).

Faith, an Anchor for the Soul

Brad Wilcox and Wendee Wilcox

In Ether 12:4 we read: "Wherefore, whoso believeth in God might with surety hope for a better world, yea, even a place at the right hand of God, which hope cometh of faith, maketh an anchor to the souls of men, which would make them sure and steadfast, always abounding in good works, being led to glorify God."

Steadfastness and good works come from hope and faith, but not just any faith. Many people who are not members of the Church believe in God. They even like to swap stories over the Internet about God and angels. Still, in many cases their faith doesn't affect or change them. They rarely make any choice in their lives differently because of their professed faith than they would if they had no faith at all. Faith is not an anchor to them. That helps us better understand what Joseph Smith taught in *Lectures on Faith*. He said that true faith is more than knowing there is a God. It is knowing God—knowing His attributes and His relationship to us. We must know He has a plan for us and that we are living in accordance with that plan.[1] Many people believe there is a higher power, but without knowing Him, they are limited in accessing that higher power to

Brad Wilcox is an associate professor of teacher education at Brigham Young University and a popular author and speaker. He recently returned from serving as president of the Chile Santiago East Mission. He and his wife, Debi, are the parents of four children.

Wendee Wilcox, daughter of Brad Wilcox, is a junior at Brigham Young University majoring in home and family living. She holds a degree in cosmetology.

help them improve. Elder Richard G. Scott of the Quorum of the Twelve Apostles has said: "You must understand and use the power of the interaction of faith and character. God uses your faith to mold your character. . . . In turn, fortified character expands your ability to exercise faith."[2] That is the life-changing cycle that many have yet to discover.

Christians have faith in Jesus Christ but not a true faith as Joseph Smith described. Millions of Christians in this world follow Christ and many do so with all sincerity of heart. But it is one thing to follow Christ, and another thing entirely to be led by Him. Latter-day Saints are the only Christians on this globe who are led by Christ the same way He has always led His people, through living prophets and apostles. That sets our faith apart. Just as Joseph Smith defined a true faith in God, so we testify that a true faith in Christ is more than just knowing about Him, as do many in the world, or even believing He is divine, as do many Christians. We must know His Atonement is real. We must use it to be transformed, and we must realize it is a continuous force in our lives.

THE ATONEMENT IS REAL

We remember a man in Chile who asked, "Who needs a Savior?" Obviously, he had no understanding of the Fall and its effects. He certainly didn't understand the precariousness and limited duration of his present state. Perhaps this man had not yet felt the sting of death. But he will. Perhaps he had justified and rationalized his sins for so long that he didn't feel the sting of guilt, remorse, and shame. But he will. Sooner or later, someone close to him will die, and he will know what it is like to feel as if part of his soul is being buried right along with the body of his loved one. On that day, he will hurt. He will need a Savior. Sooner or later, he will run out of escape routes and have to face himself in the mirror, knowing full well that his sinful, selfish choices have affected others as well as himself. On that day, he will hurt. He will need a Savior.

But the blessings of the Atonement are not limited to freedom from death and sin. It is also there when we feel down, overwhelmed, afraid, and alone. The Atonement is there when we face sickness, pain, or the consequences of the choices of others. It is even there when we make mistakes—not intentional sins, just stupid mistakes. When we hurt, we need a Savior.

John the Baptist cried, "Prepare ye the way of the Lord. . . . Every valley shall be filled, and every mountain and hill shall be brought low" (Luke 3:4–5). That is what Jesus does for us. If the knuckles of my hand represent the valleys and mountains of my life, it is Jesus who offers to hold our hand through both the highs and the lows. He makes the mountains manageable and fills the valleys.

The word *atonement* is from the ancient Hebrew word *Kaphar,* which means to cover. Isn't it interesting that when Adam and Eve discovered their nakedness in the Garden of Eden, God sent Jesus to make coats of skins to cover them? Coats of skins don't grow on trees. They had to be made from an animal, which means an animal had to be killed. Perhaps that was the very first animal sacrifice. Because of that sacrifice, Adam and Eve were covered. In the same way, through Jesus' sacrifice, we are also covered.

When Adam and Eve left the garden, the only things they could take to remind them of that place were the coats of skins. The one thing we take with us out of the temple to remind us of *that* heavenly place is a similar covering. We are always surprised when we hear women say they don't like their garment or that they don't think it is feminine enough. The garment reminds us of covenants, protects us, and even promotes modesty. However, to us it is much more. The garment is a powerful and personal symbol of the Atonement—a constant reminder both night and day that because of Jesus, we are covered.

THE ATONEMENT IS TRANSFORMING

But is it enough to know that the Savior sacrificed for us, that His Atonement is real? Many Christians know of these realities without fully understanding their complete purpose. Jesus did not come only to save us, but also to redeem us. Most of our lives we have thought the two terms were synonymous, but that is not the case. The second question in the temple recommend interview is: Do you have a testimony of the Atonement of Christ and His role as Savior *and Redeemer?* The words describe two separate roles, and having a testimony of both roles is essential.

By definition, a redeemer is one who buys or wins back, one who frees us from captivity or debt by the payment of ransom, one who returns or restores us to our original position. However, since our family's mission in Chile we have come to appreciate an additional definition: A redeemer is one who changes us for the better. If our whole goal is just to be in God's presence again, then why did we leave it in the first place? In the premortal existence we were already with God, but we were also painfully aware that we were not like Him physically or spiritually. We wanted to be like our Heavenly Parents and knew it was going to take a lot more than just dressing up in their clothes the way little children do. We needed to fill their shoes and not just clomp around in them. The goal is not just being with God, but being like God. It is common to hear people say, "God loves us and wants us back." But that is only partially right. Christ's redemption doesn't just put us back where we were. It makes us better. God loves us so much He doesn't just want us back. He wants us better. Some are old enough to remember the TV show *The Six-Million-Dollar Man*. (He would cost a lot more today!) At the beginning of the show a voice would say, "We can rebuild him. We can make him better than before." That's what Jesus does for us.

At Easter we sing the hymn "He Is Risen!" by Cecil Frances Alexander. The text speaks of Christ's saving role—His victory over death and how He has freed us from sin. But notice how the third verse also speaks of Christ's redeeming role. It says:

> *He is risen! He is risen!*
> *He hath opened heaven's gate.*
> *We are free from sin's dark prison,*
> *Risen to a holier state.*[3]

John W. Welch has taught that the parable of the Good Samaritan can be viewed as an allegory of the fall and redemption of mankind. A certain man (Adam) fell and was left for dead. Finally a Samaritan—he that was hated of men (Christ)—saved him. But, the Samaritan didn't just bind his wounds and restore him to the health he had enjoyed previously. He also took him to an inn and paid additional funds to take care of him.

Based on this allegory, Christ's redemption does not stop with restoring us to life. It also provides a better quality of life (see Luke 10:25–35).[4]

Once, after a lesson about how Jesus had suffered for all of us, a young man said, "I never asked Jesus to do that for me. If anyone has to suffer for my sins, I will do it for myself." This young man was ignorant of the amount and degree of suffering we are talking about. In Doctrine and Covenants 19:18 the Lord says, "Which suffering caused myself, even God, the greatest of all, to tremble because of pain, and to bleed at every pore, and to suffer both body and spirit."

But along with not understanding the extent of the suffering, this boy was also ignorant of just what suffering can and cannot do. Doctrine and Covenants 19:17 makes it clear that those who do not repent and accept Jesus' Atonement "must suffer even as [he did]." So will that cocky teenager be able to suffer for his own sins and then waltz into the celestial kingdom and live with God and his family eternally? Will he be beaten "with a few stripes and at last . . . be saved in the kingdom of God"? (2 Nephi 28:8). No. The Book of Mormon makes it clear that such an idea is false, vain, and foolish (see 2 Nephi 28:9). While one can meet the demands of justice by suffering for his own sins, such suffering will not change him. Just as a criminal can pay his debt to justice by doing time in prison and walk out no different, suffering alone does not guarantee change. Real change can only come through Jesus.

We must accept Christ, not because it will save us some pain down the road, but because it is the only way we can become new creatures (see 2 Corinthians 5:17; Mosiah 3:19). No one walks into the celestial kingdom simply because a debt is paid, whether it is paid by Jesus or by ourselves. The justified must still be sanctified. Those who dwell with God are those who have come to be like Him through fulfilling what He asks. He who met the conditions of justice now turns and meets us with a few conditions of His own. What He asks of us does not pay justice, but helps us change. Christ asks faith, repentance, ordinances, and covenants—not to pay justice, but to allow the Spirit to begin to change and sanctify us.

We once imagined the final judgment as a time when people would be begging Jesus to let them stay in His presence and He would have to say, "Sorry. You missed it by two points." Then the individuals would beg Jesus to reconsider. Now we imagine the scene quite differently. Instead of unworthy persons saying, "Let me stay. Let me stay," we think they will be saying, "Let me leave. Let me leave." The unworthy will choose to leave Christ's presence because they will not be comfortable. No one will have to be kicked out. Sadly enough, they will leave on their own.

We've heard our current mortal condition described in many ways. Some say we are in a hole. Others say we are in debt or that we are lost. Whatever the analogy, Jesus doesn't just save us by lifting us out of the hole. He redeems us by lifting us to a much higher plane. He doesn't just save us by paying the debt. He redeems us by paying us in addition. He doesn't just save us by finding the lost. He redeems us by guiding us home. Jesus not only opened to us the possibility of returning to God's presence, but also of returning with His image in our countenances. Redemption is more than paying justice and bringing everyone back to God. It is mercifully giving us the opportunity of being comfortable there. Not only can we go home, but we can also feel at home.

THE ATONEMENT IS CONTINUOUS

The Atonement is real, and through repentance and sanctification it is transforming. But that transforming change is a process that takes time—a long time. The Atonement is a continuous force in our lives. Perfection is the ultimate goal, but we get lots of chances to reach it.

Our friend Brett Sanders once pointed out a lesson to be learned when a new priest is blessing the sacrament. He is nervous and messes up when reading the prayer. He knows the prayers have to be perfect and that expectation can't be lowered. So what happens when the priest makes a mistake? He looks at the bishop, who nods his head, and the priest simply begins again. What if he stumbles a second time or a third? Does he finally just give up, or is there a trap door that opens and he falls through? No. He just starts again. How many times? As many times as it takes to get it right.

When Brad was serving as the bishop of a Brigham Young University ward, a young man came to him to confess. He unloaded everything he had ever done wrong since elementary school. Brad heard what he had never had the courage to tell another bishop, stake president, mission president, or parent. Although the sins were not of major proportions, they needed to be confessed and should have been taken care of years earlier. Imagine the young man's relief and joy as he finally let go of all he had been carrying so needlessly, privately, and personally for so long. Brad prayed and reviewed some scriptures with him. They discussed the role of confession in the repentance process and set goals for the future. When that young man left Brad's office, he almost floated out of the room.

The following Sunday Brad looked for him in church but didn't see him. The next week he wasn't there either. Brad called his apartment and left messages. Finally Brad went over. The young man answered the door but didn't invite Brad in. The boy's countenance was dark and his eyes hollow. His comments were negative and sarcastic, revealing his depressed mood. Brad asked if he could come in and talk with him.

The young man said, "Like that will make any difference?" His words were cold and hard. "Just face it, Bishop, the Church isn't true. No one can even prove there is a God. It's all just a joke, so don't waste your time."

Wow! From floating on air to the pit of despair, and all in a matter of days. Brad's first reaction was to become angry. This boy had no call to be so rude. Brad also wanted to defend the truthfulness of the Church and the existence of God, but then he had one of those bishop moments. Instead of raising his voice or quoting scripture, Brad simply said, "You messed up again, didn't you?"

The young returned missionary's darkened expression melted and he began to cry. Between sobs he motioned Brad into his empty apartment and they sat together on the couch. The young man said, "Bishop, I'm sorry. I just feel so bad. I finally repented. I was finally clean. I finally put it all behind me. I finally used the Atonement and felt so good. Then I blew it all over again. Now, my former sins have returned and I feel like the worst person in the world."

"So the Church is true and there is a God after all?" Brad asked.

"Of course," he said sheepishly.

"So you just need another chance?"

"But that's the problem. D&C 58:43: 'By this may ye know if a man repenteth of his sins—behold, he will confess them and forsake them.' I confessed. I didn't forsake. So I didn't really repent. It's over."

"Tell me about the Savior's grace, then."

He said, "Oh, you know 2 Nephi 25:23: We are saved by grace 'after all we can do.' We do our best and then Christ makes up the difference. But I did that and it didn't work. I still went out and did the same old dumb thing. I blew it. Nothing changed."

Brad said, "Hold on. What do you mean Christ makes up the difference? Christ doesn't just make up the difference. He makes all the difference. He requires us to repent, but not as part of paying justice—only as part of helping us to change."

The young man said, "I thought it was like buying a bike. I pay all I can and then Jesus pays the rest."

Brad said, "I love Brother Robinson's parable. He has helped us all see that there are two essential parts that must be completed,[5] but I think of it more like this: Jesus already bought the whole bike. The few coins he asks from me are not so much to help pay for the bike, but rather to help me value it and appreciate it."

The returned missionary said, "Either way, it doesn't matter since I just crashed the bike. So much for grace!"

Brad said, "Wait. What do you mean, *so much for grace?* You think this is just a one-shot deal? Don't you realize that Jesus has a whole garage full of bikes? Knowing that Christ makes the difference doesn't mean much unless we also realize how often He does it. The miracle of the Atonement is that He will forgive our sins (plural), and that is not just multiple sins, but also multiple times we commit the same sin."

Of course we don't condone sin. Joseph Smith taught clearly that "repentance is a thing that cannot be trifled with every day."[6] Still, the same Jesus who forgives those who "know not what they do" (Luke 23:34) will also forgive those of us who know exactly what we do and just can't seem to stop (see Romans 3:23).

Brad said to the returned missionary, "Christ commanded us to forgive others seventy times seven times (see Matthew 18:22). And we don't think He is going to forgive us more than once?"

The young man's face began to show hints of a smile. "You're saying there is still hope for me?"

"Now you are beginning to understand grace," Brad said.

In 1 Corinthians 15:19 we read that there is always hope in Christ. Elder Neal A. Maxwell called the gospel inexhaustible.[7] Perhaps that is a good word for the Atonement as well—the inexhaustible Atonement. We hear many words associated with the Atonement. We hear it is infinite, eternal, everlasting, perfect, divine, incomprehensible, inexplicable, and even personal and individual. However, there is another word that must be more closely associated with the Atonement if we are ever going to be able to maintain hope in this world full of addictions. And that word is *continuous*—the continuous Atonement.

Preach My Gospel explains, "Ideally, repenting of a specific sin should be necessary only once. However, if the sin is repeated, repentance is available as a means of healing (see Mosiah 26:30; Moroni 6:8; D&C 1:31–32).

"Repentance may involve an emotional and physical process."[8]

So next time a priest in your ward has to begin the sacrament prayers again—next time he has to start over—just remember that is what the sacrament is all about. That's what the Atonement is all about—the continuous Atonement.

Verbal expressions of belief or faith can't save us. True faith always results in faithfulness. True faith in Jesus Christ is trust in, confidence in, and reliance upon the Atonement. We must know it is real, that its purpose is to transform us, and that it will be there as long as that perfecting process takes. It is continuous. With that testimony, we, like the returned missionary, can surely hope for a better world, yea even a place at the right hand of God. That is the hope and true faith that becomes an anchor to our souls.

When we or those we love are stuck in cycles of compulsive behavior, and we say, "I'll never do it again" and then we do it and we say, "I'll never do it again" and then we do it and we say, "This is so stupid. I will never do it again" and then we do it—there is always hope.

We don't have to pretend there is no God or desperately try to find reasons why the Church is not true in order to avoid change. We don't have to seek out others who are struggling so we feel justified, or hate those who aren't struggling so we can feel better. We don't have to hate ourselves. We just have to let faith be an anchor for our souls and begin again. How many times? As many times as it takes. We can have true faith because we have a Savior who covers us, a Redeemer who transforms us, and a Good Shepherd who is willing to go in search of us again and again—continuously.

NOTES

1. See Joseph Smith, *Lectures on Faith* (Salt Lake City: Deseret Book, 1985), 38–44.

2. Richard G. Scott, "Living Right," *Ensign*, January 2007, 10, 12.

3. Cecil Frances Alexander, "He Is Risen!" in *Hymns of The Church of Jesus Christ of Latter-day Saints* (Salt Lake City: The Church of Jesus Christ of Latter-day Saints, 1985), no. 199.

4. See John W. Welch, "The Good Samaritan: Forgotten Symbols," *Ensign*, February 2007, 41–47.

5. See Stephen E. Robinson, *Believing Christ: The Parable of the Bicycle and Other Good News* (Salt Lake City: Deseret Book, 1992), 30–32.

6. Joseph Smith, *Teachings of the Prophet Joseph Smith*, sel. Joseph Fielding Smith (Salt Lake City: Deseret Book, 1976), 148.

7. Neal A. Maxwell, "The Inexhaustible Gospel," *Speeches: 1991–92 Devotionals and Firesides* (Provo, Utah: Brigham Young University, 1992), 136; or see Bruce C. Hafen, *A Disciple's Life: The Biography of Neal A. Maxwell* (Salt Lake City: Deseret Book, 2002), 345.

8. *Preach My Gospel* (Salt Lake City: The Church of Jesus Christ of Latter-day Saints, 2004), 187.

DEVELOPING THE FAITH TO OVERCOME FEAR

Brian K. Evans

Several months ago, we received a letter from our son Keith, who is serving in the Washington Seattle Mission. He wrote:

"Unfortunately, this letter has to be the bearer of some bad news. Saturday night, Elder Abel [his companion] collapsed in the bathroom. I gave him a blessing and . . . that night we visited the fireside for departing missionaries. When Sister Pinegar saw how peaked and pale he looked, she immediately sent him to the mission doctor. When we met up again that night, Elder Abel filled me in: 'He says I'm incredibly healthy; I'm just anemic. They want me to see another doctor tomorrow.' Upon [my] return to Bellevue, I learned that Elder Abel had been put in the hospital. [The] president talked to me and informed me that Elder Abel would be discharged in a few hours and would be spending the night at the Pinegars. I went and collected some things he would need for his overnight stay. When I got to the president's home, I waited until Elder Abel and [the] president arrived. As I was about to leave I said, 'Well, Elder Rice (the elder I was with) and I are gonna go find some people for you and [me] to teach.' There was a funny silence, and [the] president said, 'Why don't you two head in here, and Elder Abel can talk to you.' I

Brian K. Evans is the chief financial officer and administrative vice president of Brigham Young University. He has worked for twenty-six years as a professional consultant and university administrator. Brother Evans has served in numerous Church callings and is a husband, father, and grandfather.

realized something was wrong, and as Elder Abel and I walked into an adjacent bedroom I said, 'That doesn't sound good, buddy. What's going on?' I turned to Elder Abel, and after a second he said, 'I have leukemia.' His eyes got red, [and] then mine got red. We both sat down. 'What does that mean, Elder Abel?' He started to cry, which I have never seen him close to doing, 'It means I'm going home Sunday.' I've never seen anyone cry more bitter tears than when he was explaining that his mission was about to end. We talked and laughed and cried our eyes out for about half an hour."

Our family was shocked and saddened by the news of Keith's companion. We prayed for Elder Abel and pondered how even those who are most worthy—indeed those who are wholly devoted to the service of the Savior—are not immune from the vagaries of mortality.

It is apparent that each of us will face significant challenges in this life. Elder Marvin J. Ashton said about these challenges:

"It would seem that no one escapes some uncertainty, insecurity, doubt, and even fear. This mortal existence is invariably challenging and unpredictable. An honest person who is acquainted with the characteristics of life cannot ever be completely confident that his circumstances will not change unexpectedly."[1] Indeed, if you consider the faithful people you know who face significant challenges, you will probably realize that the list is rather long. Even those who seem to live a charmed life are not immune. It reminds me of a new bishop who sat on the stand during his first week of service and thought, "Wow, no one in our ward has any problems!" After several months, he scanned the same congregation and observed, "Wow, every person in our ward has problems!"

Since we will all face doubt and fear from time to time, how can we learn to develop faith that is stronger than fear and to trust in Him who understands all things and knows the beginning from the end?

President Thomas S. Monson once said of President Gordon B. Hinckley, "He is a man of vision who does not take counsel from his fears."[2] Note that President Monson didn't say, "President Hinckley has no fears." He said, "President Hinckley does not take counsel from his fears." There is a difference. Lt. John Putnam, who died at the age of twenty-three during World War II, said, "Courage is not the lack of fear but the ability to face it."[3] Sadly, fear has become a common commodity in our modern age. Purveyors of entertainment use fear to attract patrons. Movies, books, video games, amusement park rides, and extreme sports promise an adrenalin rush by causing patrons to confront their most fundamental fears, including the fear of death. Fear sells products and it can decide elections. Indeed, fear has become a potent military and political weapon. The primary objective of the terrorist, after all, is to spread fear in the population.

There is nothing that will tear the fabric of society more quickly in a crisis than fear and panic. No one understood this better than Franklin Delano Roosevelt, who famously observed in his first inaugural address: "The only thing we have to fear is fear itself—nameless, unreasoning, unjustified, terror which paralyzes needed efforts to convert retreat into advance."[4] Many from that era agree that President Roosevelt's greatest contribution may have been that he gave people courage and hope.

In our lives, it is possible for us to be overcome by our fears:

- I might lose my job.
- What if my children are not faithful?
- There is a convicted felon living in my neighborhood.
- My spouse could leave me.
- My son has been called up for military service.
- I have an incurable disease; I will never get better.

The list could go on and on. Those who take counsel from their fears are prone to agonize and worry. They may suffer the physical and psychological effects of anxiety or feel paralyzed by their situation, as though there were nothing they could do to change the inevitable outcome. Some may require medical treatment or counseling to deal with these feelings, which can be intense and overwhelming.

May I suggest some things that can be done when we have feelings of fear and uncertainty?

First, remember that God is over all. He numbers all the hairs of our heads. He is in charge. Elder Hugh B. Brown taught this great lesson in his famous story of the currant bush. As he pruned a currant bush in his garden, he imagined the protestations from the bush as it was cut back. "'How could you do this to me? I was making such wonderful growth.'" He mentally reminded the bush that pruning would make it stronger:

"'Look, little currant bush, I *am* the gardener here, and I know what I want you to be.'" Years later, when Elder Brown considered his own life and the ways he felt he had been unfairly cut back, he exclaimed, "'How could you do this to me, God? . . . There is nothing that I could have done—that I should have done—that I haven't done.'. . .

"And then I heard a voice. . . . It was my own voice, and the voice said, 'I am the gardener here. I know what I want you to do.'"

Said Elder Brown of this experience:

"I wanted to tell you that oft-repeated story because there are many of you who are going to have some very difficult experiences: disappointment, heartbreak, bereavement, defeat. You are going to be tested and tried to prove what you are made of. I just want you to know that if you don't get what you think you ought to get, remember, 'God is the gardener here. He knows what he wants you to be.'"[5]

In 1981, I had just completed a graduate degree and was anxious to put my newfound knowledge to good use. In other words, I needed a job. We had two small children at the time and were surviving thanks to the kindness of my in-laws. Although I was diligent in seeking employment, months passed with no offers. The economy was poor, and competition for work was intense. Faced with this challenge, I began, for the first time, to take counsel from doubt and fear. I imagined a worst-case scenario where no one would hire me. I might become the first unemployable MBA graduate in history. What would I do? How would I provide for my family? Naturally, there was fervent prayer and abundant humility. Ultimately, I came to the knowledge that Heavenly Father was aware of our situation and that everything would work out.

Within a few more weeks, and through a miraculous series of events, I was able to secure a position with a fine firm and begin my career. Because of my experience, I never took anything at work for granted. I was glad to have a great job. I worked hard and was appreciative of the opportunity I had been given. This incident provided the foundation for a career that has been personally rewarding and provided sufficient income for our family.

Second, pray for Christ's strength and courage. Mormon's great teaching on charity shows the pattern whereby we can be partakers of all Christlike attributes. He states: "Wherefore, my beloved brethren, pray unto the Father with all the energy of heart, that ye may be filled with this [substitute faith and courage for] love, which he hath bestowed upon all who are true followers of his Son, Jesus Christ; that ye may become the sons of God; that when he shall appear, we shall be like him" (Moroni 7:48).

Remember, the Savior has felt the same feelings you are feeling. As He faced His greatest challenge, He exclaimed, "Father, if thou be willing, remove this cup from me: nevertheless not my will, but thine, be done. And there appeared an angel from heaven, strengthening him" (Luke 22:42–43).

Elder Neal A. Maxwell said, comparing our own experiences to those of the Savior, "As we confront our own lesser trials and tribulations, we too can plead with the Father, just as Jesus did, that we 'might not . . . shrink'—meaning to retreat or recoil (D&C 19:18). Not shrinking is much more important than surviving! Moreover, partaking of a bitter cup without becoming bitter is likewise part of the emulation of Jesus."[6]

Years ago in the mission field in Chile, where I served, we sometimes used a first contact approach called "harvesting the field." This involved knocking on a door, asking for the head of the household, and stating, "We are representatives of the Lord Jesus Christ. He has sent us here to leave His peace and blessing in your home. May we come in and do that?" When we were allowed in, we would say, "This blessing is for the entire family. Would you mind gathering the family together?" After the family assembled we would again explain, "We represent Jesus Christ, and He has sent us here to leave His peace and blessing in your home." Then came the hard part. We would kneel and ask the family, "Will you kneel with us as we do this?" There we were, on our knees in a stranger's home, looking up and inviting them to join us in prayer. If we hesitated when we knelt, there was usually uncomfortable giggling or laughter and the response, "No thanks, perhaps another time." If we didn't hesitate, and we demonstrated our resolve, there was a good chance the family would kneel with us. Then a prayer for the family and a priesthood blessing would be pronounced. Many times, this was a powerful spiritual experience that paved the way for teaching the gospel.

I have never had a more intimidating experience as a missionary than when we were "harvesting the field." This made street contacting feel like child's play. As you might expect, spiritual preparation before this approach was critical. We prayed earnestly for the strength of the Lord and to be filled with His courage.

On one occasion, after an evening of "harvesting" with one of the assistants to the president, we were filled with the joy of several powerful experiences. He said, "Elder Evans, that was incredible! I've never done that before." I was surprised. I assumed he was an old hand at these things. As we talked, we realized that without an endowment of courage from the Lord, this experience would never have been possible.

It also illustrates to me that fear need not be connected to a specific problem or crisis. It can just as easily arise from a challenging Church calling or other significant responsibility.

Third, exercise faith. Since fear and faith cannot coexist, we must take action to have faith replace fear. Otherwise, fear is likely to linger like an unwelcome guest. Endless consideration of the question Why did this happen to me? is unlikely to be constructive or instructive. Be proactive as you go about your daily activities. Be prayerful and decide on a course of action. Seek the Spirit to confirm your decisions as described in Doctrine and Covenants 9. Remain positive and be grateful for the blessings you enjoy.

Elder Robert D. Hales taught: "I have come to understand how useless it is to dwell on the *whys, what ifs,* and *if onlys* for which there likely will be given no answers in mortality. To receive the Lord's comfort, we must exercise faith. The questions Why me? Why our family? Why now? are usually unanswerable questions. These questions detract from our spirituality and can destroy our faith. We need to spend our time and energy building our faith by turning to the Lord and asking for strength to overcome the pains and trials of this world and to endure to the end for greater understanding."[7]

Let me tell you about a wonderful couple I home teach. Dan and Linda are an inspiration. I enjoy visiting them, as I am strengthened and uplifted each time we meet.

About three years ago, Dan was diagnosed with cancer. After the initial shock of the news, Dan and Linda sought priesthood blessings.

They were counseled to seek knowledge about the situation and were promised that they would know what actions to take. They were also promised that they would have peace. Immediately they began an extensive study of Dan's disease. A regimen of diet and exercise was started, consistent with the principles of the Word of Wisdom. Linda participated along with Dan, and both experienced the benefits of increased energy. They both look great and Dan has never felt better. Throughout this continuing challenge, Dan and Linda have remained optimistic and proactive. They take counsel from their doctors but keep the ultimate responsibility for Dan's treatment for themselves.

Most important, this experience has strengthened their relationship with one another and with the Lord. They study the scriptures regularly, pray individually and as a couple, attend the temple, serve faithfully in ward callings, and minister to the needs of those around them. Their attitude is positive. They enjoy the peace of the Spirit.

Let me return to the story of Elder Abel. He is undergoing chemotherapy and is reported to be responding well. Of him, my son Keith wrote:

"Elder Abel [has] been an inspiration to the whole mission. His optimism is just incredible. He's maintained such a positive outlook throughout all this. Isn't it funny how it's usually the person to whom the problem comes that's the strong one, while everyone else falls to pieces? If anyone can get through something like this, Elder Abel can."

Keith's experience with Elder Abel also teaches us a powerful lesson. Just as we must learn to deal with personal challenges, we may also be deeply affected by the challenges faced by our loved ones. Keith was emotionally drained and fearful for his missionary companion. He found it necessary to acknowledge Heavenly Father's omnipotence, seek the Savior, and exercise faith in Elder Abel's behalf.

Keith also has his own personal way of considering eternal principles—he sketches. Often his drawings are of heroic persons from the scriptures, such as Nephi, Captain Moroni, or the Apostle Peter. Some of the other elders in the mission have asked Keith to sketch their favorite scriptural story or person. As I was preparing for this conference, I happened to be flipping through Keith's letters home, which often contain a copy of his latest sketch.

THE LIVING CHRIST

When I came to this drawing, patterned after the well-known *Christus* statue, I was appreciative of the thoughts, desires, and personal insights that must have gone into its creation. My mind was turned to the teachings of the Savior that have personally given me comfort in times of fear and uncertainty.

One day several years ago, while I was minding my own business and enjoying life, I became dizzy and had trouble standing. After a series of medical tests over several months, I was diagnosed with Meniere's disease, a disorder of the inner ear, which causes hearing loss, constant ringing, and attacks of vertigo. These attacks come without warning and create the sensation that the world is spinning. You might say that Meniere's patients believe that the world revolves around them. These attacks can be frightening and usually involve nausea, vomiting, and partial incapacity. The unpredictable nature of the disease has caused sufferers to describe themselves as feeling like a time bomb waiting to go off. When I was first diagnosed and learned the implications of my situation, I feared that I would become deaf and be unable to work or drive a car. During some attacks, which can last for hours, the thought has occurred to me, "What if the vertigo never stops?" During these times, this scripture has come to my mind: "Peace I leave with you, my peace I give unto you: not as the world giveth, give I unto you. Let not your heart be troubled, neither let it be afraid" (John 14:27).

Sometimes during an attack, I have found myself repeating this verse over and over. From my experience with Meniere's disease, I have learned that faith dispels fear and that the fruit of faith is peace. Peace comes from the Holy Ghost. I am not cured. I could have an attack at any time. But I am not afraid. I know that God is over all, I seek the strength of the Savior, and I choose to be proactive and exercise faith. I have enjoyed blessings and spiritual experiences that would not have been available except for this challenge. I am not suggesting that we should pray for a problem so that we can grow, but I do believe we can become better people through the challenges we face.

President James E. Faust taught: "Let us not take counsel from our fears. May we remember always to be of good cheer, put our faith in God, and live worthy for Him to direct us. We are each entitled to receive personal inspiration to guide us through our mortal probation. May we so live that our hearts are open at all times to the whisperings and comfort of the Spirit."[8]

May we be blessed to face the challenges of fear and uncertainty in our lives.

NOTES

1. Marvin J. Ashton, "'Strengthen the Feeble Knees,'" *Ensign*, November 1991, 71.
2. Thomas S. Monson, quoted in "News of the Church," *Ensign*, June 2005, 74–75.
3. Retrieved December 2007 from phobialist.com/fears.html.
4. Franklin Delano Roosevelt, *The Public Papers and Addresses of Franklin D. Roosevelt, 1933* (New York: Russell and Russell, 1938), 11.
5. Hugh B. Brown, "The Currant Bush," *New Era*, January 1973, 14.
6. Neal A. Maxwell, "'Applying the Atoning Blood of Christ,'" *Ensign*, November 1997, 22.
7. Robert D. Hales, "Healing Soul and Body," *Ensign*, November 1998, 14–15; emphasis in original.
8. James E. Faust, "Be Not Afraid," *Ensign*, October 2002, 6.

THE GRAND PURPOSE OF
RELIEF SOCIETY

Julie B. Beck

I have a testimony of this great latter-day work of the restored gospel, and I have been blessed by being part of it. I have a testimony of my Heavenly Father and his son Jesus Christ. I have felt that power in my life. Years ago I made covenants with the Lord that He could use me where He needed me to build His kingdom. Over the years I have accepted calls to serve in Primary, Scouting, Relief Society, Young Women, and missionary work. Each call has brought growth and experience. It is a privilege to serve Him and to accept a call from His ordained prophet on the earth.

When President Gordon B. Hinckley called me to be the Relief Society General President, he asked me, "How much do you know about Relief Society?"

Well, I entered Relief Society when I was eighteen, so I have had many years of experience and a great love for Relief Society. I know that Relief Society was organized to function under the direction of the priesthood for "the relief of the poor, the destitute, the widow and the orphan, and for the exercise of all benevolent purposes"[1] and "not only to relieve the poor, but to save souls."[2]

The original work of the Relief Society focused toward the temple. Faithful women wanted to organize to hasten the work of building a

Julie B. Beck serves as the Relief Society General President. She has also served as first counselor in the Young Women General Presidency. Sister Beck and her husband, Ramon, have three children and ten grandchildren.

temple so they could make covenants with the Lord Jesus Christ and form eternal families. That great work continues today. In January 2004, President Hinckley said, "I am convinced there is no other organization anywhere to match the Relief Society of this Church. It has a membership of more than five million women across the earth. If they will be united and speak with one voice, their strength will be incalculable."[3]

I will discuss relief, the need for relief, and how we can unite in this great relief effort. The words *relief* and *relieve* come from the Latin word *levare*, which means "to lift up, lighten." It means a raising up. "The notion is to raise (someone) out of trouble."[4]

OUR CHALLENGE

In Mark 13:8, the Savior tells about our day: "For nation shall rise against nation, and kingdom against kingdom: and there shall be earthquakes in divers places, and there shall be famines and troubles: these are the beginnings of sorrows." Is this a day of trouble? Yes, we are troubled on every side.

This is a day of many natural calamites. There are storms, tempests, earthquakes, droughts, fires, and floods. There seems to be no place on earth that is not vulnerable to the natural elements. There are also wars, conflicts, unrest, and horrible violence that in recent years has become random and unexplainable.

In the 2004 Worldwide Leadership Training Meeting, President James E. Faust spoke about the confusion, disorder, and "breakdown of the moral fabric of society that confronts the sacred family institutions." He spoke about how marriage rates have declined, cohabitation is widely accepted, divorce is increasing, and children are less valued, as evidenced by high abortion rates and smaller families.[5]

We know that good families are busy and distracted. Keeping up with the activities and pressures of life has eroded family time. It is increasingly difficult for families to gather to strengthen one another at mealtimes, in prayer, scripture study, family home evening, and other essential family-building activities.

We see that the world and its influences are eating away at worthiness and the ability of the Lord's children to feel the Spirit. For instance, pornography is rampant and in the homes of Latter-day Saints. Media and its messages are pervasive in our lives. Those messages confuse gender, which eats away at our eternal identities and roles. Media also pressures us to buy and accumulate more and more things, which increases our debt burdens.

All of this destroys our sense of peace and wears on our spirits. I do not know of a time in the history of the world when a full-scale relief effort was more needed. Because we are disciples of Jesus Christ and we have made covenants with Him, we have committed to be part of that relief effort. By being organized into this society, we are now enlisted in a relief effort that has no comparison on the face of the earth.

President Hinckley said: "We must not give up. We must not become discouraged. We must never surrender to the forces of evil. . . .

"We call upon the women of the Church to stand together for righteousness. They must begin in their own homes. They can teach it in their classes. They can voice it in their communities.

"They must be the teachers and the guardians of their daughters. Those daughters must be taught in the Primary and in the classes of the Young Women of the values of The Church of Jesus Christ of Latter-day Saints. When you save a girl, you save generations. She will grow in strength and righteousness. She will marry in the house of the Lord. She will teach her children the ways of truth. They will walk in her paths and will similarly teach their children. Wonderful grandmothers will be there to lend encouragement.

"I see this as the one bright shining hope in a world that is marching toward self-destruction."[6] President Hinckley has described our relief challenge.

THE RELIEF EFFORT

So, how do we participate in this relief effort? We do it by first strengthening our own homes and families and then by helping to strengthen the homes and families in our wards and stakes. We start in our own lives and our own homes and branch out from there to give relief and save souls. I will share with you some ways we do that.

We offer relief by studying and teaching correct doctrine and principles. We are all teachers, and we are always teaching. In every encounter, in formal and informal situations, we are teachers. As we teach in our homes, as we teach in Primary classes, as we teach and lead young women, as we serve in Relief Society, we teach by our words and by our examples. Our words matter. We must firmly believe what we teach. That means we must spend time in the scriptures and know the doctrine. We then must be able to defend and teach that doctrine.

We teach by what we do. There is nothing that teaches as powerfully as our examples. When we share what we believe about the gospel, we provide relief to those in spiritual destitution and we save souls. We look for opportunities to teach what we believe. That means if we are riding in cars with our children, we should focus on them and what we can teach them. We teach while we do dishes and when we are together anywhere with our families or friends. We pray to know what to ask and what to teach. But please understand that every lesson, every testimony, and every encounter is a teaching opportunity.

We are part of the relief effort as we pray and seek for missionary experiences. That is as simple as inviting friends to attend something you normally do as a member of the Church—a meeting, a family home evening, a family activity, or a ward activity. Just invite a friend to go with you. There are too many of our Heavenly Father's children who need the relief of saving ordinances. You can provide relief by contributing to mission funds and by saving for a mission for yourself. Those are obvious ways we can be part of the work, but it is easy to overlook the power that is in our own homes and wards to proclaim the gospel. Every one of us has family members or friends who, for one reason or another, have lost their way and have stopped participating in the blessings of the gospel. Are you praying for a missionary opportunity with them? Sometimes families pray for others to be the one to influence and help their child. Are you the one they are praying for?

As women, we offer relief by lifting and blessing the youth of the rising generation. This relief work is usually done by youth leaders and parents, but everyone must help with this. Think of the people who heard King Benjamin and were so enthusiastic about his message. Then what happened? There were many of the rising generation who did not believe. Why didn't they believe? They were too young to hear and understand that message. But every single adult around them heard it and committed to living the gospel. Whose responsibility and opportunity was it to pass that belief along? Everyone's!

Have you ever thought that every single teenager in your ward is an investigator until they have their own conversion? You are part of the relief effort for them. Do you know their names? Are you interested in their progress? Do you know who their parents are? Is what you are wearing and saying and doing in your personal life strengthening their faith? Will they know what a disciple of Christ looks like because of what you do? Are you bearing your testimony in sacrament meeting and other places in such a way that they will be touched by what you know? Are you helping them prepare for missions? Is there something you can do to help them get their own testimony?

Look around you in your wards and families. Who is destitute in spirit? Our work is to save souls and provide relief. Do your neighbors have a husband and father in their home? How can you help fill the gaps for those who do not? If you got on your knees and asked how to provide relief to someone, the ideas would flood into your mind. You will not have time to reach and provide relief to all, but it would be wonderful to try! Just ask each day, "Who needs my help?" You won't have any trouble knowing whom to help and how to help them.

You can provide relief to relatives who have died without a knowledge of the gospel. This way of saving souls is one of the principal reasons the gospel was restored. Families must be linked, and every child of God must have the opportunity to receive saving ordinances. Are you part of this relief effort? Do you have a current temple recommend? Do you attend the temple? Have you read or written a history of a relative? Have you written your own? Do you record your experiences and testimony so that others who follow you can know what you know? Do you know how to use a family history program? Do your children know how? Your children are your greatest asset. They know and love technology. When they work with you in this work, your family will be stronger and your children will be defended and protected because it is a work involving the Spirit.

We can provide relief from the onslaught of media coming into our homes by using it appropriately. Parents need to be wise in the amount of media that comes in and restrict its influences. This includes everything from games to movies to music to telephones. Technology is a marvelous miracle, but it is a tool, not a way of life. Our young people text message each other; they chat online and download podcasts. They go to the computer to do research instead of reading a book. One of the downsides about so much technology is that we are all being exposed to things that can desensitize us to the Spirit. Our spirits need relief from the constant noise and images and messages of the world. Our homes will be stronger if we have some relief from so much information.

We can provide relief by teaching social skills. Much of what is out there in technology is designed to be antisocial. Why do we need some relief from this? Because when we raise a generation of children who do not have well-developed social skills, they are less confident in social situations and are less likely to form eternal families. We are in the business of saving souls. We can help with this.

We are experiencing a storm of pornography that is weakening our homes and families. We need to take an active part in providing relief from this tidal wave of filth. Never assume it is not happening in your family. We can learn much from Captain Moroni in the Book of Mormon when we examine his tactics against a determined enemy. He gathered into centers of strength; he built walls and pickets and trenches to defend his center of strength. Are our homes those centers, and are the people in your family safe there? Are they safe in the homes of their friends? The Church has provided some great helps to defend us against this. Please use them.

Another place to seek relief is in the area of debt. Have you been working to get out of debt? Have you reached a point where you do not need to accumulate more things? We all need relief from rampant consumerism. This is a priority of the prophets, and it will strengthen our families if we heed their counsel. This is an important way to strengthen our families and homes and provide relief.

CONCLUSION

There is a great need for a full-scale relief effort, and you are now enrolled in this effort. I hope you have noticed that I have not given you any special assignments. This is not about new programs or creating guilt.

None of these things are new to you. I do hope they put a focus on the good things you are already doing. This is about being part of a society that provides relief. In the days of Nauvoo, this relief centered on the temple and getting a temple built in their midst. They needed a temple so they could have the saving ordinances and covenants for themselves and their ancestors and the rising generation. The focus should still be the same. It is still about providing relief from worldly influences and making sure that each and every sister, each and every child in the rising generation, is prepared to make and keep temple covenants. That happens as we first build a desire for the temple in our hearts and in the hearts of the rising generation, and then we also provide that relief to our ancestors who have died without hearing the gospel by providing saving ordinances for them.

Each sister—married, single, old, or young—is needed in this relief effort. In Primary we prepare and teach children to make and keep covenants. In Young Men and Young Women we prepare our youth to make and keep sacred covenants. In Relief Society we support and encourage those efforts and help ensure that every family and every sister can also make and keep those covenants. That is what we are about. This is our goal—saving souls.

The blessing and byproduct we receive for working together in this great relief effort is the sociality and friendships we form that help support us in life's challenges. Our testimonies of the Lord Jesus Christ grow as a byproduct of our relief efforts because we are acquiring His qualities in our lives. Pray to know how you can personally be part of this relief effort, and the personalized ideas will come to you. Pray in your homes and families and in your service capacities in the Church about how to provide relief from the storms of this world. The Spirit will direct you in appropriate ways. This is how you become part of a worldwide relief effort.

Sisters, I love you. This Church is full of beautiful, magnificent women, poised to make a difference in the world. What a blessing and exciting opportunity we have. I hope we can see ourselves as a strong and powerful force for good. We must commit to lift, to raise up, and to exercise ourselves in benevolent purposes. This society was organized under the priesthood to provide relief. I have absolute confidence that we can work together to provide that relief.

I leave you my testimony of this restored gospel. It is the work of our Heavenly Father and His son, Jesus Christ. It is led by a living prophet, who guides and directs this work on His behalf. President Hinckley has a vision and charge for the sisters of this Church, and he expects that we will each do our very best to accomplish that charge. I commit to work with you in this great worldwide relief effort.

NOTES

1. Joseph Smith, *History of the Church of Jesus Christ of Latter-day Saints*, 7 vols., ed. B. H. Roberts, 2d ed. rev. (Salt Lake City: The Church of Jesus Christ of Latter-day Saints, 1932–51), 5:25.
2. Smith, *History of the Church*, 4:567.
3. Gordon B. Hinckley, "Standing Strong and Immovable," Worldwide Leadership Training Meeting, 10 January 2004, 20.
4. Douglas Harper, *Online Etymology Dictionary* (www.etymonline.com), 2006.
5. James E. Faust, "Challenges Facing the Family," Worldwide Leadership Training Meeting, 10 January 2004, 1–2.
6. Hinckley, "Standing Strong and Immovable," 20.

THE ERRAND OF ANGELS

Barbara Thompson

Being on the Brigham Young University campus has brought back so many wonderful memories. It was here at BYU where I first attended Relief Society. This is where I had my first visiting teaching assignment and received my first visiting teachers.

One Relief Society memory that stands out for me was our ward cookbook. Everyone was asked to contribute some recipes. I had put it off until the last night, the night they were due. Our Relief Society president came over and put on a little pressure to turn in some recipes. My roommates and I sat down and got busy on the assignment. My roommates delved into their mother's recipes books, but I didn't have mine with me. So I was forced to make mine up. My homemade recipes had real ingredients in them, but I totally made up the amounts of sugar, salt, and flavoring that should go into the recipes. And now, I want to sincerely apologize to anyone who may have tried those recipes—especially the Ice Box Dessert. I thought it really looked good, but I can't imagine how it tasted. I'm sorry if any of you wasted time or money on it.

I would also like to apologize to our dorm parents for sometimes forgetting the rules and especially for having that fake candle-passing and

Barbara Thompson is the second counselor in the Relief Society General Presidency. She holds degrees from Brigham Young University and the University of Utah. She was recently the executive director of an international organization for abused and neglected children.

pretending that one of our dorm sisters was engaged when she really wasn't. I realized afterwards that my roommates and I did not give proper respect to this time-honored tradition. And for those who needed counseling to recover from that event, I'm really sorry.

I would like to say I have made significant changes for the better since that time, but that might be exaggerating. However, lately I have been trying a lot harder.

A little over one month ago I was busy at work in my office of a charitable organization for abused and neglected children when my bishop called. He is rather a kidder, and it took him some time to finally convince me that I needed to call President James E. Faust's office right away. Immediately fear gripped my heart. I knew I hadn't done anything bad enough to get excommunicated by a member of the First Presidency. I tried to convince myself that maybe he was calling me to be on the Days of '47 Parade Committee—I love parades—but somehow I knew it wasn't that. I finally knew it was Relief Society.

I left the office and cried all the way home and for several hours after that as I had a bright recollection of all the people I had offended, been cross with, been impatient with, and so on. How would people ever be able to vote to sustain a calling for me? I wished I had been kinder, more patient, more charitable, more like so many of you. (I also knew that I didn't have anything to wear and there was no way I could lose one hundred pounds in one week.) It was a tough day.

Later that afternoon I had the interview with President Faust. Some of it is a blur when it comes to remembering what I said, but I remember very well what he said. One thing that stands out for me was when he said, "Sister Thompson, we are all just ordinary people, called to do a work for the Lord for a season. Whom the Lord calls, the Lord qualifies." Then we just sat and cried together. He said he would pray for me if I would pray for him.

The week before general conference was one of the most difficult of my life. I could tell no one—not my sister, my father, no one. However, the Lord showed me His tender mercy by having my bishop call me shortly after I returned home from meeting with President Faust. He asked me if I needed to talk and if I needed a blessing. I needed both, and he came right over. I am so thankful for my priesthood leaders and that they are in tune with the Holy Spirit.

Sister Julie B. Beck told me I would receive tickets for my family to come to conference. One sister, to whom I am very close, lives in Virginia. One brother travels frequently and is often out of town. Two days after my call, my stepmother, who had been ill and living in a care center for two years, passed away suddenly. It was a blessing for her to be released from the body that held her bound. It was also another tender mercy for me because my whole family was in town for the funeral that was held the day before conference. My dad and my brothers and sisters were all able to be with me as I was sustained in general conference.

Still, all of this was hard to take in. When President Thomas S. Monson read the names of the new Relief Society presidency, I remember thinking I would die if someone yelled out, "Not her!" As I walked up those steps to sit in the red seats, I wanted to just walk on by and sit with the Tabernacle Choir. I've always wanted to sing with the Choir and I think that was probably my only chance.

The week after general conference the sessions are replayed on BYU-TV. I watched that first session again and listened to the sustaining. Then I watched while the new people walked up to their seats and I said, "Yep, that's me."

Anyway, sisters, I don't understand the "whys" about this calling. There are so many capable, wonderful, dedicated women in this Church. But please know that I love the Lord and I love my sisters in the gospel. I also have a great love for Sister Beck and Sister Allred. It is amazing to me how quickly and firmly love grows as we serve together to build God's kingdom and serve His children.

It is so easy to recall many wonderful things that women have done for one another, for their families, and for the whole human race. From the minutes of the early meetings of Relief Society we learn what Emma Smith said: "We are going to do something extraordinary. When a boat is stuck on the rapids, with a multitude of Mormons on board, we shall consider that a loud call for relief—we expect extraordinary occasions and pressing calls."[1]

When the Prophet Joseph Smith organized the Relief Society he declared, "And I now turn the key in your behalf in the name of the Lord, and this Society shall rejoice, and knowledge and intelligence shall flow down from this time henceforth; this is the beginning of better days to the poor and needy."[2]

In one early meeting the secretary of the Relief Society wrote that "nearly all present arose and spoke, and the spirit of the Lord like a purifying stream, refreshed every heart."[3]

In another one of the early meetings of Relief Society, Joseph Smith said, "Men cannot steady the ark—my arm cannot do it—God must steady it. . . . Said Jesus, 'Ye shall do the work, which ye see me do.' These are the grand key-words for the society to act upon."[4]

Yes, I believe that the errand of angels is given to women. The song goes:

> *The errand of angels is given to women;*
> *And this is a gift that, as sisters, we claim:*
> *To do whatsoever is gentle and human,*
> *To cheer and to bless in humanity's name.*[5]

The Relief Society was organized by the Prophet Joseph Smith to bless the lives of women and families as we seek to come unto Christ. Relief Society was organized to provide relief to the poor and needy and to save souls. During the sesquicentennial of the Relief Society in 1992, thousands upon thousands of LDS women around the world participated in service and were on the errand of angels. The accounts received at headquarters were amazing.

Our wonderful Relief Society women, disciples of Jesus Christ, had cared for the sick, the poor, the needy. Hospitals were helped, food pantries were supplied, blankets and quilts were delivered by the thousands. Sisters aided the disabled and transformed homes needing repair. Women's shelters were build or remodeled, parks and community places were replenished and beautified, temple ordinances were performed for thousands of our deceased sisters, hygiene kits were assembled, literacy efforts blessed countless lives, and the list goes on and on.

Doctrine and Covenants 123:17 says: "Therefore, dearly beloved brethren [and sisters], let us cheerfully do all things that lie in our power; and then may we stand still, with the utmost assurance, to see the salvation of God, and for his arm to be revealed."

You are angels, daughters of God. It is my distinct honor and blessing to be among you and feel the warmth of your love and kindness. Thank you for all the good you do in this world. Thank you for blessing the lives of people all around you. Thank you for standing firm and believing that you are daughters of God.

NOTES

1. Relief Society Minutes, 17 March 1842; also in Jill Mulvay Derr, Janath Russell Cannon, and Maureen Ursenbach Beecher, *Women of Covenant*, (Salt Lake City: Deseret Book, 1992), 31.
2. Joseph Smith, *History of The Church of Jesus Christ of Latter-day Saints*, 7 vols., ed. B. H. Roberts, 2d ed. rev. (Salt Lake City: The Church of Jesus Christ of Latter-day Saints, 1932–51), 4:607.
3. Relief Society Minutes, 19 April 1842; also in Derr, Cannon, and Beecher, *Women of Covenant*, 36.
4. Smith, *History of the Church*, 5:20.
5. Emily H. Woodmansee, "As Sisters in Zion," in *Hymns of The Church of Jesus Christ of Latter-day Saints* (Salt Lake City: The Church of Jesus Christ of Latter-day Saints, 1985), no. 309.

A RECIPE FOR HAPPINESS

Vicki F. Matsumori

I have a confession. I am a "foodie." That means I love to eat. I also enjoy cooking, though not washing or cleaning up. I've taught cooking classes and taken cooking classes. And even though it's past my bedtime, I'll stay up to watch *The Ace of Cakes* on the Food Network.

Because of this love of food, I frequently examine other cooks' results. Have you ever done that—gone to a ward dinner or to a baby shower and looked at what someone has put on the table and wondered, "How did she manage that? My—fill in the blank here: cake, soup, salad, or whatever—doesn't look or taste like that. What is her secret?"

I have learned that many of the great dishes have special recipes, cooking tools, and methods. For example, nearly ten years ago in a cooking class in San Francisco, my daughter and I were introduced to silpat: a wonderful silicone product that is available everywhere now, but at that time could only be found in specialty stores. With it you can bake anything without having it stick to your pan. Those fancy, delicate, lacy cookies without a single cracked edge are possible because of this tool.

Here is the connection from cooking to our topic, and I hope this isn't too big of a leap—I realized that occasionally we look at other people and compare our lives to their lives. They seem to have a better final product

---

Vicki F. Matsumori serves as the second counselor in the Primary General Presidency. She has taught in junior high school and was an adjunct instructor at Salt Lake Community College. She and her husband, James, have three children.

than we do, although they have essentially the same life ingredients we have. What is their secret?

I wondered if they, too, like professional cooks, have special recipes or tools designed to help them. However, the truth of the matter is that we all have exactly the same things to have better lives. Those things are repentance, forgiveness, and the Atonement. So why do some seem happier or more at peace? I think it can be summed up in one word: attitude. This seems to be the difference.

When we are quick to repent or forgive, our lives come into harmony with Christ's teachings. It is the same attitude and understanding that Esther had—that through the Atonement, we can be instruments in God's hand "for such a time as this" (Esther 4:14).

Repentance

Elder Russell M. Nelson said: "While the Lord insists on our repentance, most people don't feel such a compelling need. They include themselves among those who try to be good. They have no evil intent. Yet the Lord is clear in His message that *all* need to repent."[1]

Those whose lives seem happiest understand that while they try to be good, they too need to repent and they need to do so immediately. The difference, then, is their attitude. They are not slow to use the tools of repentance or forgiveness, but are quick to try to follow the Savior's teachings.

Let me illustrate. Elder Jeffrey R. Holland relates a story that took place when he and Sister Patricia T. Holland were living in New England and he was attending graduate school. Sister Holland was the ward Relief Society president, Elder Holland was in the stake presidency, and they had two small children.

He says: "One evening I came home from long hours at school, feeling the proverbial weight of the world on my shoulders. . . . Then, as I walked into our small student apartment, there was an unusual silence in the room.

"'What's the trouble?' I asked.

"'Matthew has something he wants to tell you,' Pat said.

"'Matt, what do you have to tell me?' He was quietly playing with his toys in the corner of the room, trying very hard not to hear me. 'Matt,' I said a little louder, 'do you have something to tell me?'

"He stopped playing, but for a moment he didn't look up. Then two enormous, tear-filled brown eyes turned toward me, and . . . he said, 'I didn't mind Mommy tonight, and I spoke back to her.' With that he burst into tears, and his entire body shook with grief. A childish indiscretion had been noted, a painful confession had been offered. . . .

"Everything might have been just terrific—except for me. . . . I lost my temper. It wasn't that I lost it with Matt—it was with a hundred and one other things on my mind. But he didn't know that. . . .

"I told him how disappointed I was and how much more I . . . expected from him. . . . Then I did what I had never done before in his life: I told him that he was to go straight to bed and that I would not be in to say his prayers with him or to tell him a bedtime story. Muffling his sobs, he obediently went to his bedside, where he knelt—alone—to say his prayers. . . .

" . . . Pat did not say a word. She didn't have to. I felt terrible!

"Later, as we knelt by our own bed, my feeble prayer for blessings upon my family fell back on my ears with a horrible, hollow ring. I wanted to get up off my knees right then and go to Matt and ask his forgiveness, but he was long since peacefully asleep.

"My own relief was not so soon coming, but finally I fell asleep and began to dream, which I seldom do. I dreamed Matt and I were packing two cars for a move. . . . As we finished I turned to him and said, 'Okay, Matt, you drive one car and I'll drive the other.'

"This five-year-old very obediently crawled up on the seat and tried to grasp the massive steering wheel. I walked over to the other car and started the motor. . . . As I pulled away, he cried out, 'Daddy, don't leave me. I don't know how to do it. I'm too little.' And I drove away.

"A short time later, driving down that desert road in my dream, I suddenly realized . . . what I had done. I slammed my car to a stop, threw open the door, and started to run as fast as I could. . . . [T]ears blinded my straining effort to see this child somewhere on the horizon. I kept running, praying, pleading to be forgiven and to find my boy safe and secure.

"As I rounded a curve . . . I saw the unfamiliar car I had left Matt to drive. It was pulled carefully off to the side of the road, and he was laughing and playing nearby. An older man was with him, playing and responding to his games. Matt saw me and cried out something like, 'Hi, Dad. We're having fun.' Obviously he had already forgiven and forgotten my terrible transgression against him.

"But I dreaded the older man's gaze, which followed my every move. I tried to say 'Thank you,' but his eyes were filled with sorrow and disappointment. I muttered an awkward apology and the stranger said simply, 'You should not have left him alone to do this difficult thing. It would not have been asked of you.'

"With that, the dream ended, and I shot upright in bed. . . . I threw off the covers and ran to the little metal camp cot that was my son's bed. There on my knees and through my tears I cradled him in my arms and spoke to him while he slept. I told him that every dad makes mistakes but that they don't mean to. I told him it wasn't his fault I had a bad day. I told him that when boys are five or fifteen, dads sometimes forget and think they are fifty. . . . I told him that never again would I withhold my affection or my forgiveness from him, and never, I prayed, would he withhold them from me."[2]

Elder Holland understood the importance of making use of the tools of repentance and forgiveness immediately. It is the same with us. It is our desire and attitude to bring our lives immediately into line with the Savior's that will help us develop better lives and "end products."

FORGIVENESS

I have been impressed by the number of people who have this same attitude of forgiveness. They understand the importance of bringing their lives into harmony with the Savior's teachings. Recently my local newspaper has been full of stories about them.

"Grief, forgiveness" was the headline in February 2007. The article described the feelings of a father who lost his pregnant wife and two of his children to an alleged drunk driver. The father openly forgave the teenage driver and asked fellow church members to pray for the driver.[3] Truly, it is through forgiveness that the healing process begins.

"Ellis would forgive shooter, husband says." Later that same month, a gunman entered a shopping area in downtown Salt Lake City and took the lives of five people, including a young woman. At the funeral, her husband said, "I forgive the guy who shot and killed those people. . . . We don't know what he was thinking. . . . But we can all forgive."[4]

President James E. Faust spoke about an incident that took place in an Amish community when a milkman entered their schoolhouse and shot and killed some of the girls. Speaking of them, President Faust said, "This shocking violence caused great anguish among the Amish but no anger. There was hurt but no hate. Their forgiveness was immediate."[5]

CONSEQUENCES OF AN UNFORGIVING ATTITUDE

However, the headline that I cannot forget appeared before these terrible February tragedies. It reads, "I'm past forgiveness." The article tells of a young woman who was kidnapped by her parents and refers to her own inability to forgive them.[6] Without knowing or understanding all of the facts from either side, I have had great concern for the young woman. Her attitude of nonforgiveness is in direct conflict with modern-day scripture: "Wherefore, I say unto you, that ye ought to forgive one another; for he that forgiveth not his brother his trespasses standeth condemned before the Lord; for there remaineth in him the greater sin" (D&C 64:9).

President Faust explains one of the consequences that occurs when we do not forgive. He said: "We can find all manner of reasons for postponing forgiveness. One of these reasons is waiting for the wrongdoers to repent before we forgive them. Yet such a delay causes us to forfeit the peace and happiness that could be ours."[7] Lack of peace and happiness is the cost of being "past forgiveness."

Let me share a familiar story that illustrates what happens when someone has an unforgiving attitude. In the early days of the Church, when Thomas B. Marsh was the President of the Quorum of the Twelve Apostles, his wife and another woman decided to exchange the milk and the strippings so they could make a little larger cheese than they otherwise could.

While Mrs. Harris was faithful to the agreement, Mrs. Marsh, wishing to make extra good cheese, saved a pint of strippings from each cow. As we might expect, a fight arose, and the matter was taken to the First

Presidency. They agreed that Mrs. Marsh was guilty of failure to keep her agreement.

And then with an unforgiving attitude, Thomas B. Marsh "went before a magistrate and swore that the 'Mormons' were hostile towards the State of Missouri." The result was the "exterminating order, which drove some 15,000 Saints from their homes."[8]

Thomas B. Marsh "lost his standing in the Church. He lost his testimony of the gospel. For nineteen years he walked in poverty and darkness and bitterness, experiencing illness, and loneliness. . . . Finally, like the prodigal son in the parable of the Savior (see Luke 15:11–32), he recognized his foolishness and painfully made his way to . . . [ask] Brigham Young to forgive him and permit his rebaptism into the Church. He had been the first President of the Council of the Twelve, loved, respected. . . . Now he asked only that he might be ordained a deacon and become a doorkeeper in the house of the Lord."[9]

Forgiveness of offenses is not easy. It is difficult in any situation, but it is possible. I have a friend who has taught me a great deal about forgiveness. Those who meet her think she has lived a life free of adversity, but as a child she lived in a dysfunctional family where hurt came from those who should have loved and protected her the most. She has remained positive in her attitude and has freely forgiven them for wrongs that were admitted, as well as for offenses that to this day have never been acknowledged.

As a mother of adult children, she has now experienced the heartache of a child lost to drug addiction. She deals daily with those consequences. Yet if you saw her, you would be struck by her bright countenance and peace with the world.

I once asked her how this is possible. And not surprisingly, once again it boils down to attitude. This is the story she told me: She was born with a hole in her heart. Because of that, she was always tired and subject to illness. She says she learned at a very young age to conserve her energy for the things that mattered most and that she wanted to do.

For example, her best friends knew that she could not make it through one entire rope-jumping song (you know, "Teddy bear, teddy bear, touch the ground, teddy bear, teddy bear, turn around"). She would take a nap on the day they planned to play in order to save her energy. Once they arrived, she would play with them and take her turn jumping rope as long as she could. When she got tired, she would lie down on the cement and immediately fall asleep. Fifteen minutes later she would get up and finish the rope-jumping song. Because of this experience, she says she knew she could not afford to waste any energy harboring grudges or hurt.

President Faust said: "It is not easy to let go and empty our hearts of festering resentment. The Savior has offered to all of us a precious peace through His Atonement, but this can come only as we are willing to cast out negative feelings of anger, spite, or revenge. For all of us who forgive 'those who trespass against us' (Joseph Smith Translation, Matthew 6:13), even those who have committed serious crimes, the Atonement brings a measure of peace and comfort."[10]

THE ATONEMENT

It is the Atonement that makes the tools of repentance and forgiveness effective in our lives. It is our faith in the Savior, our trust in His teachings and in His ability to overcome our transgressions, that allows His Atonement to help change our hearts. It is the Lord who provides the way for each of us to pay our debt. It is through His sacrifice that we are allowed to return to Heavenly Father, contingent upon our willingness to follow Him in faith.

After all we can do, the Atonement also makes it possible for us to forgive even when we feel like we are past forgiveness. Let me illustrate: A woman we'll call Sister Smith lives in a town not far from here. She struggled with feelings of anger and hurt when her son-in-law was unfaithful to her daughter. The result of his infidelity was a broken marriage. Her daughter was devastated and struggling with feelings of low self-esteem. Her now single-parent status made day-to-day living seem impossible.

Sister Smith knew that the animosity she felt towards her former son-in-law was affecting everything and everyone around her. The anger she felt was all-consuming. Moreover, she knew the doctrine of the kingdom. Although he had never come to ask for forgiveness, she knew that she was required to forgive her son-in-law and that she needed to remove this hatred from her heart.

She did all that she knew to do. She prayed to have a forgiving heart.

She went to the temple. She asked for a blessing from her husband. Yet the anger and hurt persisted day after day and week after week.

One day, as she was driving in her car, these familiar unkind feelings for her son-in-law welled up inside her. Once again she prayed for a forgiving heart. And suddenly the load was lifted from her. She says she cannot describe the peace that filled her as she realized she had truly forgiven her son-in-law.

President Faust explained that "the Atonement not only benefits the sinner but also benefits those sinned against—that is, the victims. By forgiving 'those who trespass against us' (Joseph Smith Translation, Matthew 6:13) the Atonement brings a measure of peace and comfort to those who have been innocently victimized by the sins of others. The basic source for the healing of the soul is the Atonement of Jesus Christ."[11]

CONCLUSION

I think we all have the desire for a great "end product": a life filled with peace and happiness, a life free from the burden that accompanies transgression, and a life released of unkind feelings that harbor unforgiving attitudes. That life is available to all of us because of the tools of repentance, forgiveness, and the Atonement. It is our attitude that makes the difference.

I am reminded of a poem by Marguerite Stewart called "Forgiveness Flour."[12] It describes the kind of attitude that does make the difference.

Forgiveness Flour

When I went to the door, at the whisper of knocking,
I saw Simeon Gantner's daughter, Kathleen, standing
There, in her shawl and her shame, sent to ask
"Forgiveness Flour" for her bread. "Forgiveness Flour,"
We call it in our corner. If one has erred, one
Is sent to ask for flour of his neighbors. If they loan it
To him, that means he can stay, but if they refuse, he had
Best take himself off. I looked at Kathleen . . .
What a jewel of a daughter, though not much like her

Father, more's the pity. "I'll give you flour," I
Said, and went to measure it. Measuring was the rub.
If I gave too much, neighbors would think I made sin
Easy, but if I gave too little, they would label me
"Close." While I stood measuring, Joel, my husband
Came in from the mill, a great bag of flour on his
Shoulder, and seeing her there, shrinking in the
Doorway, he tossed the bag at her feet. "Here, take
All of it." And so she had flour for many loaves,
While I stood measuring.

May each of us be quick in our desire to repent and be free in our distribution of forgiveness. May we understand that it is through the Atonement of our Savior, Jesus Christ, that we can have a life filled with peace and joy.

NOTES

1. Russell M. Nelson, "Repentance and Conversion," *Ensign*, May 2007, 103; emphasis in original.
2. Jeffrey R. Holland and Patricia T. Holland, *On Earth As It Is in Heaven* (Salt Lake City: Deseret Book, 1989), 165–68.
3. "Grief, Forgiveness," *Deseret Morning News*, 12 February 2007, B1.
4. "Ellis Would Forgive Shooter, Husband Says," *Deseret Morning News*, 17 February 2007, A14.
5. James E. Faust, "The Healing Power of Forgiveness," *Ensign*, May 2007, 67.
6. "'I'm Past Forgiveness,' Bride Says," *Deseret Morning News*, 19 January 2007, A1.
7. Faust, "Healing Power of Forgiveness," 68.
8. George A. Smith, in *Journal of Discourses*, 26 vols. (London: Latter-day Saints' Book Depot, 1854–86), 3:283–84.
9. Gordon B. Hinckley, "Small Acts Lead to Great Consequences," *Ensign*, May 1984, 83.
10. Faust, "Healing Power of Forgiveness," 69.
11. James E. Faust, "The Atonement: Our Greatest Hope," *Ensign*, November 2001, 20.
12. Marguerite Stewart, "Forgiveness Flour," *Religious Studies Center Newsletter* 7, no. 3 (May 1993): 1; as quoted by Madison U. Sowell, "On Measuring Flour and Forgiveness," *BYU Speeches 1996–97*, 22 October 1996, 10.

WINNING ISN'T EVERYTHING

Dean Hughes

I used to be competitive, but I've improved a lot lately. I have three children and nine grandchildren who are all smarter than I am and a wife who's more important. I'm losing my speed, my athleticism, my balance, my mental sharpness, and a certain amount of bladder control. When a guy can't win, competition loses some of its appeal.

Well, that's all absurd, of course, but isn't it interesting how our minds work? Why do we automatically think everything is a competition? Who makes the rules around here, anyway? Who decided life was a contest?

What is it we tell young people? You've gotta have a dream! You've got to go out there and win the game of life! That sounds like great advice. And maybe, at some level, it is a good thing to tell them, but how easily we pervert that kind of thinking into something not just ugly, but dangerous. In the great arsenal of satanic weapons, I think maybe the glorification of competition has become a weapon of mass destruction. And we are the victims, along with our kids.

I realized when I was young that I wanted to be *somebody*. I grew up in Ogden, and I came from the wrong side of town. I think that's why I felt a need to do something big with my life. By junior high I had decided I was going to be a writer. I guess I supposed that writers were rich and famous

---

Dean Hughes holds a bachelor's degree from Weber State College and master's and PhD degrees from the University of Washington. He teaches creative writing classes at Brigham Young University. He and his wife, Kathleen, have three children.

and important. And that was being *somebody*. By the time I graduated from high school, I wanted *more than anything* to be a published author.

Yes. I just said "more than anything," and that suggests the core of the problem.

It took me seventeen years to get my first book published, and when I finally did, I basked in the glory—but for some reason, that first acceptance just wasn't quite as wonderful as I had expected. I always wanted more: more publications, bigger sales, better reviews, more sense that I was now important. I was doing what I had set out to do, but for some reason, I still didn't feel like I was *somebody*.

Do you hear what I'm saying? Does anyone out there recognize the thought process I'm describing? Have any of you spent your lives trying to convince yourself you have worth? Do you feel ecstatic when you win and worthless when you lose? Do you win a little glory and think you'll never doubt yourself again, and then find that the joy only lasts a few days? Then you need a new dose?

Is there any chance we're chasing the wrong prize?

Christ tells me I don't have to win anything to win His love. But the world whispers to me, "No one will ever study *your* books in a literature class. You better write something better before your time runs out."

Or what about this form of competition? "If I can save up just a little, I could buy a beautiful widget. And if I had me a really nice widget, made out of quality plastic, *and fancier than my neighbor's widget,* I think I could be satisfied."

So you get yourself a nice widget—a big screen, high-speed, digitized, space-age widget—and you feel great for a while. But you find yourself longing for more things—bigger widgets, fancier widgets. And when you go to your class reunion, you worry that all your old friends have collected more widgets than you have.

The worst thing is, you keep telling yourself, "Money can't buy happiness. What really matters to me is family, Church, and friends." And you believe it. But, oh, those widgets. They have siren voices, and they call to you as you drive past the mall. You know they're in there, and if you don't get them—on sale—someone else will.

American life: Americans have two value systems. Most of us are religious, and many profess to believe in Jesus Christ, but we're also capitalists. And that tempts us to be materialists. We give honor to both philosophies, and we never seem to notice that in some ways they contradict one another.

We believe in a competitive market. It's designed to bring the best out of us and to produce the best products for the best price. It's a great concept.

But why is it we feel so uneasy about the free market system every year at Christmas? Suddenly we get uncomfortable and we blame our problem on the stores. "Free enterprise" turns into that great evil, "commercialism." So we buy a turkey for a family that doesn't have one. We prove to ourselves that we're on Cratchet's side, not Scrooge's, and we feel better about ourselves. Then January comes, and the contest starts over.

I've been working with a humanitarian group called Hope Projects. We're working to get clean water, schools, greenhouses, medical clinics, and flush toilets to some of the poorest people in the world, in the high Andes of Peru. These are simple people, and they have nothing. When we go into their villages, we take solution to blow bubbles, and when we blow those bubbles, the kids think it's miraculous. They run and jump to catch the bubbles, their faces full of delight. It always bring tears to my eyes to watch them. Then I think of my grandkids in their beautiful, carpeted rooms with all their toys and electronic entertainment, and I wonder which children are happier.

The people in those villages are amazingly cooperative. They understand that to survive in such difficult circumstances, farming on the sides of precarious mountains, getting through the dry season and the wet season, they have to help each other.

I suppose we need to teach these people to be more advanced. They usually have two shirts, if they're lucky—one to wear and one to wash. Someday, maybe they'll become like us. They'll have one to wear and three dozen to wash. And they'll learn that a person should never wear the same shirt two days in a row. Won't that improve their lives!

When they become advanced, they won't just play soccer as a community, getting up games with old and young, laughing and forgetting to keep score. They'll form leagues, and they'll argue with the referees about every call. Maybe we can even teach them Church ball, when they're *really* advanced.

Or maybe we can teach them that when one team gets well ahead with time running out, that team's fans have the right to sing, "Na, na, na, na, na, na. Hey, hey, hey, goodbye." They'll learn there just isn't anything better than to beat your opponent and then taunt him.

What's happened to us? Isn't it possible to compete and be kind at the same time? There's a name for that. It's called sportsmanship. I used to hear a lot about that. Another thing I hear a lot is, "Winning isn't everything; it's the only thing." Do we believe that?

Or a better question: Is that what Christ believes?

If life isn't a contest, what is it?

Three years ago I went to see my family doctor. He told me my PSA was high, and after he talked for a time, I said to him, "Are you trying to tell me I have cancer?"

He said, "Yes, I think you probably do." And then he said that we had probably found the cancer early, and chances were ninety percent that I would be fine. I got in my car and started home. I was doing fairly well at first, but I kept thinking, "We *probably* got it early." "Ninety percent chance." Uncomfortable thoughts kept intruding themselves: What if we *hadn't* gotten it early? What about that ten percent? I asked myself how I felt about dying soon, and that set off an interesting response. I thought, "I still haven't written a *great* book. I wanted to do that." I guess I was saying to myself, "I'm still not *somebody*. And I want to *be somebody* before I die."

I thought I'd outgrown that kid from the wrong side of Ogden, but clearly, I hadn't.

As I reached Heber Valley, I picked up my cell phone to call Kathy. And suddenly it hit me. I was about to call my wife to tell her I probably had cancer, and I was worrying about my *writing career*. It was like my blinders had finally been ripped off. I've known for a long time that my writing is not really important—not like being a fine human being, a good husband, father, and grandfather. I've known it, but that other thing was still there. I still wanted "more than anything" to be a great writer.

If you weren't shocked when I said that the first time, I hope you are now.

In the months and now years that have followed that day, I have thought a great deal, and I started to imagine myself facing the Lord. Do you think He cares about my writing career? In one sense, yes. He cares *what* I write, whether I use what talent I have to do something worthwhile. But does He care whether the world thinks I'm important? Does He rely on the judgment of the reading public? Does He read reviews and check best-seller lists?

What the Lord clearly knows is what I've been trying to learn all my life. I *am* important. I'm important to *Him*. And that makes me inherently important. I'm exactly as important as you are. And you are exactly as important as I am. We *are not* in competition with one another. The lion's share of what we long for, fight for, compete for in this world really doesn't matter.

Some of you probably had "bigger plans" in your life. As a child, you were given a formula for success: Have a dream, work for it with all your heart, and you will be . . . what? Happy? Important? Famous? Rich? Wealthy? What is it we wanted?

Maybe you wanted to be the CEO of your own company, or a ballerina, a senator, or an attorney, a fashion model, or an artist. And maybe that's what you're doing. But maybe some of you met a guy, got married, and started having children. And maybe the dream got lost or postponed. And for some of you, maybe there's still this nagging feeling that you didn't do what you set out to do. You didn't become important.

Supposing you're raising kids right now. That's all. You're just a plain old mom. But here's a hypothetical. What if the Lord thinks that being a parent is the single greatest, most *important,* job in the world? Is it possible that all you moms who are going nuts trying to deal with diapers and soccer leagues and belligerent teenagers—maybe all at the same time—and giving it your best shot will all finish in a tie for first? Or is it possible there is no first, no contest at all? Is it possible you have nothing to prove to each other? That you can support and help each other, not feel that your kids have to win every prize to make *you* worthwhile?

And if that's what we should teach our children, is it wrong to teach them to do their best, their very best? It's what President Gordon B. Hinckley has asked of us. Is it wrong to ask them to lengthen their stride? It's what President Spencer W. Kimball taught. Excellence is not wrong. Magnifying our gifts, our talents—that's a good thing. Becoming more like God—that's what life is all about. But our goal is not to win some game the world has invented.

Who are the happiest people on this earth? How many so-called successful people have become so devoted to their dreams that they've lost track of what really matters? How many superstars have ruined their lives with all the forms of self-indulgence and self-destruction?

The Lord teaches us that the *meek* will inherit the earth. I wonder, do we actually believe in meekness? I know the Lord does, but do we? The world offers almost no rewards to the meek; only God does. But if we chase the world's rewards, perhaps we'll never learn that it's a broken heart and contrite spirit that the Lord loves most.

As it turned out, I did have cancer. I also had surgery, and I'm okay. The cancer is gone. But I'm trying harder now to find my way toward a Christlike life, and it isn't easy. I still experience those moments when I long to be more important—*somebody*. But a friend of mine showed me a scripture recently that I'm trying to keep in mind all the time. It's Moroni 8:25–26.

Notice the steps in this process: When we repent we receive a remission of our sins. When our sins are forgiven, we become meek and lowly of heart (grateful?). And when we are meek, we are visited by the Holy Ghost. Then under the influence of the Holy Ghost, we can learn perfect love and hope. We can keep that perfect love through *prayer* (meekness), and if we keep our perfect love, we will dwell with God.

I don't even like to think of life as a competition with myself. When I *strive* to be righteous, I seem to rise and fall. I'd like to think I can repent enough, humble myself enough to attain perfect love—something I feel at times but still can't hold. But I want to pray for it and keep it. That's what life is for. That's what we're here on earth to do: to acquire the traits of godliness.

We need to get out of the game, the world's game. We need to find our joy in supporting one another, thinking the best of each other, noticing what's good about each other, taking joy in each other's successes, and lifting arms when they hang down. It feels good; it feels right when we live that way, doesn't it? Cooperating instead of competing—you know the joy.

And here's what I have to say to you and to me. We're *somebody*. We're God's children. How can we be any more important than that?

I bear my testimony that Christ loves all of us, but not just all of us—each of us. He loves you so much that He suffered and died for you—not just for all of us but for *you*. He knows your name. We please Him most when we love one another, when we love our family, and when we feed His sheep. I know this. You know it. We just have to remember it even when the world screams in our ears that other things matter more.

The world honors the aggressive, even the greedy, but Christ loves meekness. He grants us His Spirit when we're open to it. We don't have to win championships to impress Him; we only have to become more like Him.

RESISTING THE URGE TO
BE OFFENDED

Nancy N. Allen

I once attended a musical production of one of my favorite stories, *Little Women.* You probably know the story, with Marmie the mother and her four girls, Meg, Jo, Beth, and Amy. They are a family living life, loving one another, and working together to achieve their hopes and dreams. The youngest sister, Amy, wants more than anything to have what Jo has, to do what Jo does, to wear the pretty dress, to dance at the ball. So, when Jo is invited to the big party and Amy is not, Amy gives way to her anger and throws Jo's precious manuscript, her life's literary work, into the fire. In return, Jo explodes at Amy's childish act and gives way to her temper, unleashing cruel and cutting words, and exclaims, "I'll never forgive you as long as I live." Later that night, Marmie, the wise and valiant mother, takes Jo in her arms and lovingly says: "My dear, don't let the sun go down upon your anger. Forgive each other, help each other, and begin again tomorrow."[1]

Elder Neal A. Maxwell helped us understand why Jo and Amy—and all of us—struggle to love and to forgive. He said: "The reality [is] that in the kingdom we are each other's clinical material; the Lord allows us to practice on each other, even in our imperfections. And each of us knows what it is like to be worked on by a 'student' rather than a senior surgeon.

Nancy N. Allen serves as a member of the Primary General Board. She has also served with her husband, Rex, and their children in the Switzerland Geneva Mission. Life's joys come from her callings as a wife, mother, and grandmother.

Each of us, however unintentionally, has also inflicted some pain. . . . Unsurprisingly, therefore, we do notice each other's weaknesses. But we should not celebrate them."[2]

How do *we* respond when we are offended? How do *we* react when we are misunderstood, treated unkindly, or abused—in small or even devastating ways?

I wish to share two ways to resist being offended and a true way to find peace.

THE CHOICE IS OURS

My dear cousin was unable to have any children for many years. Finally, she and her husband adopted three beautiful babies. Then, surprise, surprise, she gave birth to a beautiful daughter, and then another, and yet another! Her children were the joy of her life until one bleak day, through the fault of another, her two youngest daughters were killed in an accident. She describes her anguish and her pain as if her heart had literally broken in two. She could have hated the person responsible. She could have "cursed God" and died in her soul. But instead, she turned *to* the Lord and His plan, forgave, and went forward—serving and lifting others. Then some years later came another terrible blow when her husband unexpectedly took his own life. With this indescribable pain came unending complications and implications. Now, some said, surely she could give in to despair, anger toward her companion, and anguish and alienation from God. Yet she knew taking offense would bring only further pain for her *and* for her family. Each time I ask how she is coping, she says firmly, "Life is about choice. And I'm choosing to turn to God for strength and trust in His plan for me." She refuses to be offended. She is daily choosing peace.

Elder David A. Bednar taught in the October 2006 General Conference:

"It ultimately is impossible for another person to offend you or to offend me. Indeed, believing that another person offended us is fundamentally false. To be offended is a *choice* we make; it is not a *condition* imposed upon us by someone or something else.

". . . To believe that someone or something can *make* us feel offended, angry, hurt, or bitter diminishes our moral agency and transforms us into objects to be acted upon. As agents, however, you and I have the power to act and to choose how we will respond to an offensive or hurtful situation."[3]

Do you remember the story of revenge and the rattlesnake by Bishop H. Burke Peterson? A group of teenagers were playing in the Arizona desert. Without warning, one of the girls was struck on the ankle by a large rattlesnake. The deadly poison raced into her bloodstream. Bishop Peterson explained, "This very moment was a time of critical decision." He described how they could immediately help their companion, or they could chase the snake and destroy it. Unfortunately, they chose revenge, the venom took its toll, and despite later efforts, this young woman eventually lost her leg. Bishop Peterson summarized the terrible lesson: "It was a senseless sacrifice, this price of revenge. . . . There are those today who have been bitten—or offended, if you will—by others. . . . What will you do when hurt by another? The safe way . . . is to look inward and immediately start the cleansing process. . . . The longer the poison of resentment and unforgiveness stays in a body, the greater and longer lasting is its destructive effect."[4]

I loved what President James E. Faust taught us in April 2007 General Conference about forgiveness: There may be "anguish . . . but no anger. There [can be] hurt but no hate." When we have "faith in God and trust in His word" such that it becomes a "part of [our] inner beings," or heart, forgiveness can be immediate.[5]

We can also learn much from Pahoran, leader of the Nephites in the Book of Mormon, about trusting motives and resisting the urge to be offended. It was a time of war. Captain Moroni led the fight, but his soldiers were tired and starved, bleeding out their lives (see Alma 60:9). No provisions came from the government. Finally he wrote a stinging rebuke to his leader, Pahoran. Was he asleep? Uncaring? Unfaithful? What Moroni did not know was that Pahoran had been driven out of the capital and nearly killed.

In Pahoran's shoes, how might we receive such a rebuke? Would we blame, become defensive, or return rebuke for rebuke? To Pahoran's great credit, he looked beyond Moroni's harsh words to the "greatness of [his] heart." Pahoran refused to be offended for a word, and simply said, "it mattereth not" (Alma 61:9).

What can we learn from Pahoran when a Church leader or coworker speaks sharply, when a family member bristles, or when we are accused of something we did not do?

How many of us, or our children, wear a CTR ring? It's a great reminder to "Choose the Right." We know we can *choose* to have peace and happiness. And when we do, we are worthy to enjoy the Holy Spirit and we are blessed with more energy to serve others. We can be as Esther, prepared to "come to the kingdom for such a time as this" (Esther 4:14).

However, sometimes I'm afraid we wear a CTP ring—"Choose the Pain"! When we choose to be offended, we no longer have peace, we waste precious life wallowing in anger or even hatred. It diverts our talents from doing things we were born to do.

How can we "Choose the Right" rather than "Choose the Pain"?

"Forgiveness is not always instantaneous," President Faust taught. "When innocent children have been molested or killed, most of us do not think first about forgiveness. Our natural response is anger. . . .

"Most of us need time to work through pain and loss. We can find all manner of reasons for postponing forgiveness. One of these reasons is waiting for the wrongdoers to repent before we forgive them. Yet such a delay causes us to forfeit the peace and happiness that could be ours. The folly of rehashing long-past hurts does not bring happiness."[6]

Can you think right now of a situation where someone has done something to you that could be potentially offensive? What choice are we making—CTR or CTP? It is ours to choose. It is our choice. I invite us to choose today to resist the urge to be offended.

Now, I know we will all want to make the right choice, but at times it can seem impossible. Where do we find the *strength* to forgive, to let it go, to choose peace? This brings me to my second point.

THE STRENGTH TO MAKE THE RIGHT CHOICE COMES THROUGH JESUS CHRIST

The life of another close friend was shattered when her husband left her and their temple covenants, seeking pleasure elsewhere. She said the following: "My prayer is that through this whole thing, I will not become bitter. I know that it will only ruin my life as well as the lives of my children. I pray for Christlike love and strength each and every day."

This saintly sister understood.

The strength to *let go* comes as we "lay hold" on Jesus Christ. We do this by first repenting—repenting for our failing to forgive. Repentance means "turning," looking inward and cleansing the soul. The Bible Dictionary describes it as finding "a fresh view about God, about oneself, and about the world."[7] That fresh view can bring freedom and strength.

As we repent and seek to understand the Atonement, we come to realize that Jesus Christ has already paid the price for our sins, as well as for the sins and mistakes of everyone, *including* those whom we feel have offended us. The Savior asks that we repent and forgive for our sakes—our sakes—so that we might not suffer as He did (see D&C 19:15–17).

Jesus taught, "I, the Lord, will forgive whom I will forgive, but of you it is required to forgive all men" (D&C 64:10). He can say that because He paid the full price and fully understands. When we choose to remain offended, are we saying that we will not accept His sacrifice for someone else? In Matthew we read, "But if ye forgive not men their trespasses, neither will your Father forgive your trespasses" (Matthew 6:15).

Mercy can be fully extended only to those who are willing to extend it to others. We *all* need the mercy that the Atonement provides. "It is by grace that we are saved, after all we can do" (2 Nephi 25:23). And one thing we must do is repent for our failing to forgive.

Let us seek the Lord's strength to allow the Atonement to apply to others. With the strength of Christ, we can just "let it go" as my friends have done!

With our repenting, we can also pray for charity for those who have offended us. The Savior taught, "But I say unto you which hear, Love your enemies, do good to them which hate you, bless them that curse you, and pray for them which despitefully use you." And then this startling scripture continues: "But love ye your enemies, and do good, and lend, hoping for nothing again; and your reward shall be great, and ye shall be the children of the Highest" (Luke 6:27–28, 35).

Charity is a gift from the Lord that we must earnestly seek. Mormon taught: "And charity suffereth long, and is kind, and envieth not, and is not puffed up, seeketh not her own, is not easily provoked, thinketh no evil, and rejoiceth not in iniquity but rejoiceth in the truth, beareth all things, believeth all things, hopeth all things, endureth all things. . . . Wherefore, my beloved brethren, pray unto the Father with all the energy of heart, that ye may be filled with this love, which he hath bestowed upon all who are true followers of his Son, Jesus Christ" (Moroni 7:45, 48).

"Perhaps the greatest charity comes when we are kind to each other," taught Elder Marvin J. Ashton, "when we don't judge or categorize someone else, when we simply give each other the benefit of the doubt or remain quiet. Charity is accepting someone's differences, weaknesses, and shortcomings; having patience with someone who has let us down; or resisting the impulse to become offended when someone doesn't handle something the way we might have hoped. . . . Charity is expecting the best of each other."[8]

"Real charity is not something you give away; it is something that you acquire and make a part of yourself. And when the virtue of charity becomes implanted in your heart, you are never the same again."[9]

Let us pray for charity, the pure love of Christ. How can we not love others when Christ Himself has shown perfect love for us, even in our weaknesses and sins? "Who am I to judge another / When I walk imperfectly?"[10]

LET US MAKE THE RIGHT CHOICE TODAY

We started with Marmie, Jo, and Amy and the walls we can build that cause such pain. We learned from the Brethren, from the scriptures, and from my friends the importance of choosing the *right* and how to avoid choosing the *pain. It is a choice, dear sisters! And the strength to make that choice can only come from our Redeemer as we repent and pray for charity.* I invite us all to begin today to forgive others, love as Jesus loves, and find true peace in life.

I would like to share one more story. I know something of this process myself. Many years ago, I struggled with deep hurt and anguish as a result of another's choices and actions. It was an extremely difficult time. My pain was deep. I felt justified in feeling angry. This went on for many years until through personal scripture study, and with help from a Relief Society lesson, I realized that even though I did not cause this tragedy, I still needed to forgive—the Savior had already paid the price for all sin. But how could I do it? It was too big for me. I prayed and prayed to find the way, to find a place in my heart to let go, to find forgiveness. I also prayed for charity, as I knew this was a gift that I needed more than ever before.

After some time, I came to desire forgiveness for my own unforgiving heart. Praying hard for strength and sincerity, I sought out the person involved. It is hard for me to describe what happened when we spoke. From the top of my head to the ends of my toes, I felt a cleansing, an enveloping spirit of peace like nothing I had felt before. In an instant, I was relieved of my hurt and pain as well as my anger and bitterness. I only felt love for this person, complete Christlike love. It was a gift. It was *the* gift. It has now been years since I had that experience, but the feelings of peace and love remain. I testify that the Atonement of Jesus Christ is real. There is a power in Him to which we can turn for strength. I was a different person after that experience. Our Savior Jesus Christ healed my heart.

> I stand all amazed at the love Jesus offers me,
> Confused at the grace that so fully he proffers me.
> I tremble to know that for me he was crucified,
> That for me, a sinner, he suffered, he bled and died.
> . . . .
> I think of his hands pierced and bleeding to pay the debt!
> Such mercy, such love, and devotion can I forget?[11]

No, dear sisters, we will not forget! We can choose! We can remember the price Jesus Christ paid to bring us everlasting peace. We can seek and gain His strength to resist the urge to be offended and to forgive and let go.

> Oh, it is wonderful that he should care for me
> Enough to die for me!
> Oh, it is wonderful, wonderful to me![12]

NOTES

1. Louisa May Alcott, *Little Women* (Ann Arbor, Mich.: Ann Arbor Media Group, 2006), 77–78, 74–76; see also Allen Knee, *Little Women, the Musical* (New York: Cherry Lane Music, 2005).

2. Neal A. Maxwell, "A Brother Offended," *Ensign*, May 1982, 38–39.
3. David A. Bednar, "And Nothing Shall Offend Them," *Ensign*, November 2006, 90; emphasis in original.
4. H. Burke Peterson, "Removing the Poison of an Unforgiving Spirit," *Ensign*, November 1983, 59.
5. James E. Faust, "The Healing Power of Forgiveness," *Ensign*, May 2007, 67.
6. Faust, "Healing Power of Forgiveness," 68.
7. Bible Dictionary, s.v. "repentance."
8. Marvin J. Ashton, "The Tongue Can Be a Sharp Sword," *Ensign*, May 1992, 19.
9. Ashton, "Tongue Can Be a Sharp Sword," 19.
10. Susan Evans McCloud, "Lord, I Would Follow Thee," in *Hymns of The Church of Jesus Christ of Latter-day Saints* (Salt Lake City: The Church of Jesus Christ of Latter-day Saints, 1985), no. 220.
11. Charles H. Gabriel, "I Stand All Amazed," in *Hymns*, no. 193.
12. Gabriel, "I Stand All Amazed," in *Hymns*, no. 193.

Righteous Routines and Holy Habits

Margaret D. Nadauld

Whenever Mother's Day comes around, I'm reminded of a Mother's Day when all seven of our sons were little boys. I came downstairs on that Sunday morning, alone because my husband had left already for his early morning Church meetings and the children were not stirring yet.

I was basking in the beauty of a clean, uncluttered, orderly home. For this moment there were no toys out of place, no cookie crumbs on the countertops. It made me so glad. I'd worked hard at my Saturday routines so that all would be in order for Sunday. I had to give a Mother's Day talk in sacrament meeting, and our extended family was coming for dinner later on.

As I stood in the family room, the sun streamed in through the east windows and I thought how peaceful it all was. Suddenly the peace was shattered as seven little heads popped up from behind the couch and yelled out, "Surprise! Happy Mother's Day!" as they threw macaroni with wild enthusiasm into the air and all over me and my nice clean room! They hadn't been able to find rice so they threw macaroni instead (confusing Mother's Day with a wedding)! After hugging and laughing and overcoming the surprise, it was time to get in gear and clean up.

So much for the efforts of my Saturday routine.

Margaret D. Nadauld has served as the Young Women General President. She has also served as president of the Utah chapter of the Freedoms Foundation at Valley Forge and as vice president of the Utah chapter of American Mothers, Inc. She and her husband, Stephen, have seven sons.

Much of our life is based on routine, and so is nature.

Many weeks ago as I was preparing for this conference, I looked up from my desk to see a breathtaking array of blossoms that covered the trees, where just the week before they were laden in snow. The elegant pink blossom of the weeping cherry was in contrast to the full white blossoms of the flowering pear. The yellow forsythia bush and the color of spring's tulips, hyacinths, and daffodils created an exquisite scene from my window. It was a rich display of something that happens routinely every spring. It happens in so many parts of the world. The beautiful, routine events of spring are greatly anticipated by all of us who have been through winter. And thankfully, right on schedule, it happens every year, though the seeming suddenness of it catches me off guard somehow. I'm thankful for the routines that God created in nature in this part of His world. There is something very comforting, encouraging, and even exhilarating about that.

The routines of nature set an example for us.

We could consider the routines of our lives. What do they consist of? We have recently returned from serving in Geneva, Switzerland, where my husband was the mission president. For three years we were immersed in the daily routines of mission life, making it second nature. But helping missionaries adjust to this rigorous routine was not always easy. In fact, I remember thinking to myself that my friend was so right when she said while on her mission, "The trouble with this life is that it is so *daily!*" However, once a missionary commits to the required and righteous routines prescribed by mission rules, he begins to be blessed with the power to do the holy, hard work he came to do.

The routines that families have can likewise be a source of power.

Some of the important routines of life center around the heart of the home—the kitchen. This is such a special room, for in this very room can be found nourishment for the spirit as well as nourishment for the body.

On one occasion I happened to be in the home of one of our Apostles about the time school let out. I was impressed with what I saw in the orderly kitchen. There on the table were two glasses of milk and homemade cookies in anticipation of the arrival of their two children from school. It just seemed so welcoming, so pleasant, so tempting! Wouldn't you like to come home from a hard day at school to see that someone cared for you and thought about you?

There is even something therapeutic about time spent in the kitchen routines. While the mother is puttering around, scouring the sink, chopping vegetables, stirring the soup, wiping the counter, the daughter is mumbling about "that cute boy" or "you will never believe what happened at lunch today" or "my algebra class is so . . ." You are there to just listen while you're working away.

One time one of the boys came home for lunch with a couple of friends. They were chattering about something that was going on that they never would have sat down and described to me face to face, but there I was in the kitchen with my back to them as I was scouring the sink, then shining the taps and faucet. By the time they left that area was so shiny and bright, it had never looked so good. And in the process I had learned a variety of useful things about what was going on in their lives and about the way boys think and communicate!

A major routine of the kitchen is, of course, meal preparation. I have to admit it is a fairly daunting task to prepare meals regularly for a family, and the larger and older the family becomes the more is required, like the scripture that states "unto whom much is given much is required" (D&C 82:3). But there is great reward for fulfilling and magnifying your calling in this regard. As important as weekly family home evening is, I have no idea how one can raise a strong healthy family by only getting together for an hour once a week for family night.

From years of personal experience, I can't emphasize enough the importance of the regular, daily practice of gathering the family around the dinner table to eat a balanced, nutritious meal together. There is such strength derived as a family gathers with all their feet under the same table. And the good news is that your family can do it! I promise that if you cook it, they will come. I don't know how, but it happens. It's like magic! It's kind of like the blessings that come when you do any worthy thing. Keep the time consistent, set the table, fix the food, ring the dinner bell, and in due time magic will begin to happen in your family. Be sure that your children get to take turns setting the table and helping you cook and that the whole family helps with the clean up. That makes it go quickly, and it's a great way to bond!

Dinnertime could be a good time to place scriptures to the side of each place setting and read together before or after dinner. Think of it as an hour with meatloaf and Moroni. It's also a wonderful time to discuss the events of the day—you know, who lost their tooth during circle time or the newest joke (you know, don't you, that laughter helps in the digestive process?). The Kennedy family used to discuss world affairs and current events, and they raised a president of the United States and two U.S. senators. I know of some families who learn a new vocabulary word each day at dinner; others look at the world map on the kitchen wall and discuss faraway places with strange-sounding names. Some learn about ancestors as they look at the family tree on the wall. Mainly, mealtime can be filling and pleasant and happy and bonding.

Noted and inspiring historical author David McCullough speaks of the importance of learning from history. He said, "Bring back the dinner table, bring back dinner talk—bring back dinner!"[1] I couldn't agree more! The routine of family dinner hour yields many benefits that could even make your home a more holy place.

In the kitchen of my mother's home there is a comfortable green couch next to the table. It is a most inviting place to sit and chat a while. While Mother was busy doing routine things with dough in her special corner of the kitchen, we were there solving all the problems of the world as we gathered on and around the green couch nearby. Looking back, we now think of those times as sacred "kitchen councils." You've had them too. If a record had been kept of those kitchen councils it would reveal the cycles of life. Our topics were like the ones you discuss: how to know if you have received an answer to your prayers, or if the boy you are dating is "the right one"; planning weddings; sharing recipes; menus for two; the effects of pregnancy; the experiences of delivery; dealing with the sleep habits of infants; toilet training toddlers; effective budgeting; effective diet tips; how to motivate children to pick up socks, make beds, do their chores, do their homework; menu ideas for families; sharing ideas for teaching Relief Society; the care and raising of teenagers; gospel doctrine; planting of perennials; dealing with arthritis; planning funerals; menus for one.

The righteous routine of one very special little mother, working in her corner of the kitchen doing things with dough, provided a setting where generations gathered to discuss important matters and encourage one another in the establishment of holy habits designed to bless their families not just momentarily but eternally. Kitchen connections!

Mothers' routines can have a profound influence.

As a young boy, the Prophet Joseph Smith was influenced by the routines of his mother. He was an observant child as she studied the scriptures in search of religious truth, and surely he watched her as she went into the woods to pray about the concerns of her heart. It is little wonder that when he himself began to have questions about religion that he would in turn follow the righteous routines he had observed his mother practice. He too turned to the Bible to find an answer to his burning question about which of all the churches was true. There he learned that he must ask God for the answer. It is no surprise that he felt it natural to go into the woods to pray. He found a quiet grove of trees, a sacred spot where he knelt and offered a humble, honest boy's prayer to God. Indeed, he "opened up the heavens with his faith."[2] What a blessed event resulted. I thank God for Joseph's holy habit of prayer, learned in the home of humble parents and by their righteous routines.

I remember visiting with a stake president about the practice of prayer in our lives. He paused in our conversation and became slightly emotional and then recalled to me how he still remembers kneeling in his crib as his mother taught him to pray. It was a regular routine they shared as he prepared for bed each night, and it became a holy habit that blesses his life now and will do so forever.

Consider the little child who is in the habit of kneeling at his mother's knee and repeating after her the words of his own personal prayers. By this tender tutoring routine, a child is taught the sacred language of prayer, the reverence of prayer, and the reality of a kind Heavenly Father who listens as we pray to Him. Soon a child is able to express the feelings of her heart without the help of Mother. A child learns to pray the same way she learned to walk and talk on her own, and the sooner learned the greater the blessing. Of all the strengthening, powerful teachings about prayer, it is this personal, one-on-one kneeling humbly before God to thank Him and seek His help, this holy habit, that will bless a child's life daily and constantly. You can give a child no greater gift. Mothers be thanked for teaching a child to pray.

A little boy, only seventeen months old, fell asleep on his parents' bed one night. They roused him and helped him to his own bed in his groggy state. When he reached there, before getting in, he automatically knelt down at his bedside, as he had been taught to do, to say his prayers—a holy habit born of a righteous bedtime routine.

Family prayer is important. Prophets counsel us to hold family prayer. Family prayer is not enough. Every individual needs the enabling power that comes through personal, private prayer.

I know one man who didn't have such a blessing in the home of his youth. But the time came in his young life when he was taught to pray at church. So as a young man, he knelt by his bed and began to pray because a teacher had showed him the way. His youthful prayers, he testifies today, are the thing that kept him from evil forces among his neighborhood friends and other associations and experiences of youth. Later on, it was through an answer to prayer that he gained the courage to ask his parents' permission to serve a mission.

There are many like him who have been able to access the power that prayer offers because they were taught to pray by missionaries or Primary teachers or others important in their lives. On one of my first assignments after being called as Young Women General President, I was sent to the Philippines. I will always remember the time in one of the meetings there when an older brother stood at the pulpit to offer the opening prayer. I still remember the strength of his spirit as he prayed, acting as voice for the congregation. In the middle of his prayer he paused a moment, and then he said, "Heavenly Father, please bless our prophet, President Gordon Bitner Hinckley." The way he said it, the humility with which he prayed, and the respectful language of prayer that he used left a lasting impression on me. Knowing that this man was a first-generation member of the Church, having been baptized when he was an adult, I realized that he had been taught to pray by missionaries.

In 2006 a movie was produced with a Church theme where two teenage boys are at the age to serve missions. The one decides to go, and the other decides to enter skateboard competitions, to buy a bigger skateboard, and even to buy a truck. When the first boy is leaving to go to the Missionary Training Center he stops by the home of his friend to say good-bye and they have a serious conversation. The skateboarder asks his friend how he knew he should go on a mission. The missionary says that he knelt on the hard floor and prayed.[4]

Teaching someone to pray and to have private, personal prayer is a sacred assignment. I believe that it is an assignment from heaven. Whether you are a visiting teacher, a teacher of children or youth, a missionary, or a mother and you have the sweet opportunity to teach someone to pray, you have an opportunity to bless the life of an individual forever, as well as the countless others for whom she will pray and in turn teach to pray.

Think of a husband and wife kneeling together at their bedside, just the two of them together, holding hands, to humbly seek the Lord through sincere prayer. A wife loves to hear her husband pray, and she's happy to take her turn the next night. It is a unifying moment where husband and wife remember that their marriage has a third partner—and He is God. They report to Him. They thank Him. They seek His divine assistance. They need Him. Oh, they need Him. Every hour they need Him[4] as they pray over their household, their crops and flocks and fields, against the power of their enemies (see Alma 34:18–27). Following the prayer as a couple, the day is not complete until each individual then goes before the Lord alone in the attitude of humble, private, personal prayer.

It is in the prayerful moments that we accept the Lord's invitation extended in Moses 6 to "walk with me" (verse 34). As we pray, we show our Father in Heaven that we need Him and we trust Him to "lead [us] by the hand, and give [us] answer to [our] prayers" (D&C 112:10). When we kneel to pray we show our humility. When we kneel to pray we follow the pattern of the Savior. Some prayers, of course, are offered as we meet the experiences of the day and are unable to kneel, but we love knowing that we can come to Him without appointment. We can come as we are. He is always there for us. That is His holy habit.

I am grateful for the knowledge that we have a loving Heavenly Father. I am grateful to be able to count on the order and routine of His kingdom. Many of the blossoms of spring that I enjoyed so much as I prepared this message have given way to the leaves of early summer. That is part of the routine of nature. We can count on it happening every year. It is my prayer that we will have the desire to take joy from this divine pattern of righteous routine in our lives. I know that when we do that we will be blessed by forming holy habits that will give us strength and patience and hope and courage and power in the dailiness of our lives.

NOTES

1. David McCullough, as quoted in "Author Offers Wise Words on History," *Deseret Morning News*, 27 March 2007, A12.
2. Janice Kapp Perry, "A Young Boy Prayed," 1977, in Janice Kapp Perry, *Songs from My Heart: The Stories behind the Songs* (Salt Lake City: Sounds of Zion, 2000), 28.
3. Annie S. Hawkes, "I Need Thee Every Hour," *Hymns of The Church of Jesus Christ of Latter-day Saints* (Salt Lake City: The Church of Jesus Christ of Latter-day Saints, 1985), no. 98.
4. *Money or Mission*, motion picture, directed by John Lyde, 2006.

MAKING THE HOME A MISSIONARY TRAINING CENTER

Silvia H. Allred

My husband was called to preside over the Missionary Training Center in Santo Domingo, Dominican Republic, and that's where we were when I received the call to serve as first counselor in the Relief Society General Presidency. Because of this recent experience working with missionaries and helping them become true representatives of Christ to do His work, I would like to recognize and celebrate the small things that you faithful women do in your homes every day to rear righteous children, preparing them to become missionaries. This is an errand of angels given to women.

I will begin by comparing the Missionary Training Center to the house of God.

Once a week we and all the missionaries go to a session in the temple. It gives us an opportunity to reflect on the covenants we have made. It helps us keep focused on the purpose of our existence, our mission on earth, and the worth of each soul.

In Doctrine and Covenants 88:119, the Lord is speaking about establishing a house of God—a temple. I will liken it to a Missionary Training Center. He said:

Silvia H. Allred, first counselor in the Relief Society General Presidency, previously served in the Dominican Republic, where her husband, Jeffry, presided over the Missionary Training Center. A native of El Salvador, Sister Allred is the mother of eight children.

"Organize yourselves; prepare every needful thing; and establish a house, even a house of prayer"—A day at the MTC always begins and ends with prayer. Prayers are offered during personal and companion study time, in district meetings, before meals, in classes, and in every meeting. It really is a house of prayer.

"A house of fasting"—At the MTC missionaries learn and practice the true law of the fast. They know that fasting and prayer go together and that when they fast and pray with faith, they will be more open to receiving answers to their prayers and blessings and guidance from the Lord.

"A house of faith"—Missionaries strengthen their faith in Jesus Christ and His atoning sacrifice as they study the scriptures, understand the doctrine, and obey with exactness. They exercise their faith as they rely on the Holy Ghost to teach them and to help them learn.

"A house of learning"—A lot of time is spent in classrooms with instructors who teach language, culture, teaching skills, doctrine, and Christlike attributes.

"A house of glory"—We hold worship services, devotionals, and firesides. We sing hymns. Every missionary prepares a talk each week, and they bear testimony.

"A house of order"—They learn to plan and use their time wisely. They also help keep their rooms and facilities clean, and they do their own laundry.

"A house of God"—In an atmosphere of love, respect, trust, and confidence, they become true representatives of Christ and share the gospel with others. There is a special feeling at the MTC. You feel the Spirit. It is a house of God.

When a young man or woman enters the MTC, he or she will not suddenly transform into a well-prepared and obedient missionary. That preparation must begin years before, in his or her home. Mothers play an important role in this preparation. Elder David A. Bednar of the Quorum of the Twelve stated, "The single most important thing you can do to prepare for a call to serve is to *become* a missionary long before you *go* on a mission."[1]

To do that, it helps to live in a home where the gospel is at the center. Missionary spirit develops in a home where parents and children share the gospel with one another. Missionaries need to know the doctrine; they need to know how to pray with real intent. They need to know how to invite the Spirit into their lives. These things will give them the confidence, the strength, and the power to go and teach.

Some missionaries shared with me their feelings of gratitude to their mothers for helping them learn to love the scriptures, for teaching them to pray, and for always making the effort to hold family home evening and ensure that they had a gospel discussion as part of it. An elder told me that his mother had served a mission and she always shared her mission experiences with him, which made him want to serve a mission. Another sister said her mother would invite nonmember friends into their home, and she would share her testimony with them. This sister missionary became very accepting of members of other faiths and felt comfortable sharing her beliefs with them.

These missionaries bring to mind the story of two thousand stripling warriors in the Book of Mormon. Helaman describes the faith, courage, and integrity of these young men:

"And they were all young men, and they were exceedingly valiant for courage, and also for strength and activity; but behold, this was not all— they were men who were true at all times in whatsoever thing they were entrusted.

"Yea, they were men of truth and soberness, for they had been taught to keep the commandments of God and to walk uprightly before him" (Alma 53:20–21).

"Yea, they had been taught by their mothers, that if they did not doubt, God would deliver them.

"And they rehearsed unto me the words of their mothers, saying: We do not doubt our mothers knew it" (Alma 56:47–48).

"Yea, and they did obey and observe to perform every word of command with exactness; yea, and even according to their faith it was done unto them; and I did remember the words which they said unto me that their mothers had taught them. . . .

"Now this was the faith of these of whom I have spoken; they are young, and their minds are firm, and they do put their trust in God continually" (Alma 57:21, 27).

What we learn from our mothers comprises our core values. A woman who patiently teaches a young child to pray, who makes time to read the scriptures, who teaches how to dress appropriately for worship services, who helps prepare talks and family home evening lessons, is helping prepare a son or daughter to become a missionary. There are many other values, good habits, and skills that are taught in the home that help prepare our youth to become effective missionaries: learning how to study, doing assigned tasks well, finding joy in a job well done, assuming responsibilities, expressing gratitude, maintaining personal cleanliness, acquiring basic cooking skills, treating others with courtesy and respect, getting up on time, being obedient, giving service, being self-reliant; the list goes on and on.

When our eight children were young, I never thought that our home was also a missionary training center, but in a real sense, it was. Our two boys served missions, and three of our six girls also found great joy in serving missions. "Out of small things proceedeth that which is great," we are told in Doctrine and Covenants 64:33.

I am grateful for the mothers who taught and prepared the two missionaries who knocked on my door forty-seven years ago, bringing the news of the restored gospel of Jesus Christ.

I am grateful for all the small things the noble women of the Church are doing to prepare the next generation of missionaries. They understand the significance of mothers getting their children where they need to be; they sense that mothers are the anchor of the good things that happen, the predominant figure in the righteousness of youth. My plea to you is to keep doing it and not give up—you are laying the foundation of a great work, and the Lord is on your side. He will bless you, and your children will thank you for it.

I have a firm testimony of the divinity of Jesus Christ. He is our Savior and Redeemer, the Son of God. He loves us and has entrusted to us the important errand of teaching and setting standards in our homes. I pray that the Lord will continue blessing you as you prepare the next generation of great missionaries.

NOTE

1. David A. Bednar, "Becoming a Missionary," *Ensign*, November 2005, 45; emphasis in original.

GETTING THE WORDS OF CHRIST INTO THE HEARTS OF OUR CHILDREN

Terry B. Ball

As Nephi finished writing on the small plates, he recorded a final admonition to his brethren. He pleaded with them to "feast upon the words of Christ" and promised them that "the words of Christ will tell you all things what ye should do" (2 Nephi 32:3; see also 2 Nephi 31:20). That promise holds true for a latter-day covenant people as well. That God has preserved the words of Christ through the scriptures, and made them available to us today, is one of the marvelous manifestations of His love for us. What a blessing to know that as we face the challenges of mortality in this very troubled world, God has not left us without direction. Our responsibility, like that of Nephi's brethren of old, is to learn how to effectively access that direction—how to "feast" upon the words of Christ. I would like to share a few ideas about how to feast upon the words of Christ. They are really simple ideas, but they have blessed my life and may be of some value to you.

A practice common to our Jewish brothers and sisters can teach us much about feasting upon the word. If you have visited a typical Jewish home, you may have noticed a small rectangular or cylindrical container attached to right-side doorposts. Perhaps you noticed the home's occupants acknowledge the container with a look, a nod, or a touch as they

---

Terry B. Ball is the dean of religious education and a professor of ancient scripture at Brigham Young University. A former seminary and institute teacher, he has also served as a bishop and is a husband and father.

passed through the door. You may know that as they do so, it is not the container itself they are reverencing but what is inside it. If you open the container you will find a mezuzah, a parchment upon which is written several passages from the book of Deuteronomy. These passages remind them of their commitment to love and serve God.

I especially appreciate the passage of the mezuzah taken from Deuteronomy 6:4–9. These verses were spoken by Moses shortly before he finished his mortal ministry. I love these words. I love the way they make me feel and the insight that they give me into the way our Father in Heaven wants us to feast upon the scriptures. It reads:

"Hear, O Israel: The Lord our God is one Lord;

"And thou shalt love the Lord thy God with all thine heart, and with all thy soul, and with all thy might.

"And these words [I think it is helpful to substitute the word *scriptures* here for *words*—And these scriptures] . . . shall be in thine heart" (verses 4–6).

It is helpful to note that the passage does not say the scriptures are to be in your head—rather they are to be in your heart. To the Old Testament people to whom this instruction was first given, the heart was the seat of values. It dictated what was important to them and how they saw and perceived the world. It is one thing to merely know the words in your head. It is quite another for them to be in your heart. If they are in your heart then they influence the way you see the world, what you value, and how you think.

Moses' admonition recorded in Deuteronomy then goes on to teach how you get the scriptures into your heart, and particularly how parents can get the scriptures into the hearts of their children. In verse 7 he instructs, "And thou shalt teach them [the scriptures] diligently unto thy children." That's an important adverb—diligently. We do not get the scriptures into the hearts of our children if we only teach them occasionally, haphazardly, or reluctantly, but rather diligently. The verse continues, "And [thou] shalt talk of them when thou sittest in thine house, and when thou walkest by the way, and when thou liest down, and when thou risest up." Moses seems to be inviting us to make sure that the scriptures influence all of our conversations and actions.

To make the point even more poignant, he continues, "And thou shalt bind them [the scriptures] for a sign upon thine hand." I think the imagery suggests that the scriptures should influence everything you do. You bind them on your hands. Moses then instructs, "And they [the scriptures] shall be as frontlets between thine eyes" (verse 8). Thus he teaches that the scriptures need to influence and dictate not only all we do with our hands, but also all we see and all we think as well. Many of our observant Jewish brothers and sisters take this counsel very literally. Often when they worship they will tie to their left arm and their forehead a small cube-shaped box known as a tefillin. Inside the box will be a parchment upon which is written this passage, along with other verses, that remind them of their obligations to God and His words.

In Deuteronomy 6:9, Moses further instructs, "And thou shalt write them [the scriptures] upon the posts of thy house." The Hebrew word translated here as "posts" is mezuzot, the singular form of which is mezuzah. From this admonition of Moses comes the Jewish practice of placing what is now called a mezuzah upon the doorposts of their homes. It serves to remind them that in all their comings and goings the influence and teachings of the scriptures are to go with them—they are to be a part of everything that happens in their lives.

This is the ideal—to diligently teach the scriptures to our children so that the way they see the world; the things that they value; the way they make decisions; and their conversations, thoughts, actions, comings, and goings are all flavored, enhanced, even dictated by words of God that have found a way into their hearts. It is the job of mothers and fathers to teach their children in such a way that the scriptures are in their hearts. Doing so requires you to feast upon the words of God yourself. The scriptures must find a way into your hearts too.

I would like to share four specific things we can do, ways that we can feast upon the words of God, that I believe will help the scriptures have access to the hearts of our children and to our own hearts.

First, it is important and helpful for us to use the scriptures to validate life's successes. Let me illustrate what I mean with a personal experience.

I taught seminary for some time in a little town in Idaho. While there I taught one particular student four years in a row (it was a one-man seminary). Every day for those four years when he showed up for class, we went through the same routine. He would come in and sit down at his desk without getting his scriptures out of his storage compartment at the back of the room. I would then go back to the compartment, pull his scriptures out, bring them to his desk, and set them on the front right corner, where they would sit untouched for the remainder of the class. When the class was over, he would get up and leave. I would then go to his desk, get his scriptures, and dutifully put them back in his box.

In spite of this awkward situation we were good friends. On one occasion when we were discussing our routine I asked him why he would not even touch the scriptures. He told me that he did not care much for them. That was obvious, but I wondered why, considering he came from a faithful family that was committed to living the gospel. I asked him if his family read and used the scriptures in their home. With a roll of his eyes he moaned, "Oooh, yes." Upon further inquiry I learned that it was his perception that every time he did something wrong, his parents would use the scriptures to chastise him. Can you see why he had a negative association with the words of Christ? To him they were a club that was used to beat him into submission.

I think I may understand why his parents used the scriptures in that way. They likely had been taught and believed that the scriptures contain solutions to life's problems, so naturally they turned to the scriptures to correct problems. I believe this is correct reasoning, but it is not complete reasoning. If we only use the scriptures to correct problems we miss one of the most beautiful aspects of the sacred words, for the scriptures contain not only solutions to life's problems, but also validations for life's successes. I have since thought how different it could have been for the boy if his well-meaning parents had not only used the scriptures every time they caught their son being bad, but also, and perhaps much more often, used the scriptures to reward the young man every time they caught him being good.

Such a habit would have blessed this boy and his parents. It can help you too. For example, perhaps you have a daughter who is getting ostracized and losing opportunities and friends because she chooses not to wear some of the immodest fashions of the day. You could put your arm around her and say, "Sweetheart, what a great decision you are making. You know, you are just like Joseph. Do you know that when Joseph was sold into Egypt he made some good choices and there were some immediate negative consequences? You're just like him. You're doing what's right even though the consequences may be uncomfortable for a time. Sweetheart, you just keep making good choices. Who knows, someday you may be the prime minister of Egypt!"

Or what about your twelve-year-old deacon son who volunteers to do an extra fast-offering route on the Sabbath day. When he comes home late, you ask him why and he tells you. You could put your arm around him and hug him and say, "You know, son, you're just like King Benjamin. King Benjamin understood the principle of servant leadership. He taught us that one of the best ways to serve God is to serve others. Son, you just keep making these kinds of choices. Perhaps someday you'll build a tower and sing the song of redeeming love and people will come to listen."

Think what could happen if we knew the scriptures so well that we talked about them and used them often in such ways to reward our children when we caught them being good. We would raise children that love the scriptures. They would think in their hearts, "I love the scriptures because they make me feel good. They tell me when I am doing right. They validate life's successes." Children with such feelings in their hearts always get their scriptures out in seminary class!

A second simple way we can feast upon the words of Christ and help them enter our children's hearts is to help our children memorize favorite passages. Have you noticed that when you memorize scriptures you begin to think in scriptural language? The phrases and passages come into your mind at those times when you need faith, strength, or direction. You probably memorized some passages in seminary, but it helps children to begin memorizing before they reach seminary age. Have you memorized some scriptures? Let's do a test. I'll start a scriptural passage. See if you can finish it.

"I will go and . . ." (1 Nephi 3:7).

"I, the Lord, will forgive whom . . ." (D&C 64:10).

"A new commandment I give unto you, that ye . . ." (John 13:34).

"Be ye therefore . . ." (Matthew 5:48).

"For behold, this is my work and my glory—to . . ." (Moses 1:39).

"And it came to pass . . ."

I am teasing with the last example, but aren't you glad you've memorized some scriptures? Doesn't it make you feel good to think and say the words? Do you find that the words echo in your mind in your desperate hours or in times when you need faith or strength? Helping our children learn and memorize such powerful passages of scripture is one way we help them put on the armor of God. I hope that you will often share your favorite passages of scripture with your children and help them memorize the words, even while they are young. Teach them with the passion, the faith, and the love that you feel for the words. They will share it and take it into their hearts.

Next, we can help the scriptures enter the hearts of our children if we help them find their heroes in the scriptures. How sad it would be if our children's only heroes were comic book superheroes or pop music stars. How much better it would be if their heroes were people from the scriptures. What if, instead of wanting to be Wonder Woman, your daughters wanted to be like Ruth? What if they grew up knowing that it is okay to have faith and that we should have faith even if it means we may have hardships, maybe a lifetime of hardships ahead of us? What if, instead of idolizing some morally challenged movie star, your children wanted to be like Jacob, who went five hundred miles to find someone in the faith to date?

What if, instead of idolizing Michael Jordan, your sons wanted to be like Joseph? What they didn't want to be "like Mike" but wanted to be "like Joseph"—like Joseph, who refused the advances of Potiphar's wife? Who, when the temptation came, said, "How then can I do this great wickedness, and sin against God?" (Genesis 39:9). What a wonderful thing.

Think how exciting it would be if, while you were washing your dishes, you looked out the kitchen window and instead of seeing the children playing Superman they were playing Samuel the Lamanite or Daniel in the lions' den. What if your daughters grew up wanting to marry someone like Hezekiah instead of a movie star? Oh, what a remarkable man Hezekiah was! I tell the young coeds in my classes that if they meet a man like Hezekiah they should marry him. If he is not interested in them I tell them to flirt with him until he is. I tell them, "You just chase him and chase him and chase him until he catches you."

A fourth thing we can do to help the scriptures find their way into the hearts of our children, and into our own hearts, is to develop the ability to use what I call a "sermon in a sentence." That phrase is not my cre-ation, but I like it: "A sermon in a sentence." There are certain principles taught in the scriptures that can be summarized in a word or sentence from the scripture. Using those "sermons in a sentence" in our conversa-tions, in our language with our children, can help them remember those principles and values and give them special meaning. Let me offer a cou-ple of examples.

Let's start with Exodus 19. In this chapter the eighty-year-old Moses has just brought the children of Israel out of Egypt and led them to the foot of Mount Sinai—the very mount where he received his call to return to Egypt and lead Israel out of bondage. Once at Sinai I suspect that Moses might have thought, "I'm done. I've got them here." Then Moses climbed the mountain, perhaps to report to the Lord. On that occasion the Lord instructed Moses to return to the people and say to them: "Ye have seen what I did unto the Egyptians, and how I bare you on eagles' wings, and brought you unto myself. Now therefore, if ye will obey my voice indeed, and keep my covenant, then ye shall be a peculiar treasure unto me above all people: for all the earth is mine" (Exodus 19:4–5). Thus God offered Israel the opportunity to enter into a wonderful relationship with Him. If they would keep His covenants and commandments they would be His peculiar treasure. The term translated as "peculiar treasure" in this passage is actually one word in Hebrew, the word *segullah*. I love the word *segullah*. What does it mean to be *segullah*—to be a peculiar treasure?

Verse 6 gives an explanation that I think has special meaning to Latter-day Saints: "And ye [meaning the people] shall be unto me a king-dom of priests, and an holy nation." A *segullah* people then are a kingdom of priests, a holy nation (holy meaning sanctified, set apart, special). In ancient Israel a priest was one who was allowed to enter into the house of the Lord and perform temple ordinances. What then was the Lord offer-ing Israel at Sinai? If they would accept the covenant and the command-ments, then the whole nation or kingdom, all the people, would have access to the temple and its blessings and covenants.

After Israel expressed their desire to enter into this covenant to become *segullah* (Exodus 19:7–9), the Lord further instructed Moses to tell them that they had three days to get ready to make the covenant. At the end of those three days the Lord declared He would "come down in the sight of all the people" to put them under the covenant (verse 11). The next three days were likely full of anticipation for the children of Israel, but unfortunately, as we read in Doctrine and Covenants 84, they failed to adequately prepare, for they "hardened their hearts and could not endure his [God's] presence" (verse 24). On that third day, rather than coming "down in the sight of all the people," the Lord called Moses alone to the top of the mount and explained to him that the people were not yet ready (Exodus 19:20–24). The decisions the Israelites made then and over the ensuing weeks ultimately resulted in their receiving a lesser law and covenant than that initially offered (see D&C 84:23–27). We know the lesser law as the Mosaic Law. Under this law they would not be a "kingdom of priests." Rather, only a select few, the priests chosen from among the tribe of Levi, would be allowed to enter the temple and do temple ordinances. What a tragic missed opportunity (compare Hebrews 3:10–4:11).

This is one of the great differences between the lower law and the higher law. Under the lower law, only a select few represent the people as priests. Under the higher law, all, upon conditions of righteousness, can have access to the most sacred ordinances in the house of the Lord. All can be *segullah*. To be *segullah*, then, can mean you are special, chosen, and set apart. You are determined to keep the commandments of the Lord and live a better life because you are *segullah*. What a wonderful concept to teach your children, that they can be *segullah*—that they can succeed where the ancient children of Israel failed. *Segullah* is a sermon in a sentence. Think what could happen if you taught this concept to your children and then used the word often in your conversations with them.

Simply saying the word would remind them of a complex and inspiring set of principles. For example, imagine what your daughter will think after bearing her testimony in sacrament meeting when you put your arm around her and whisper in her ear, "*Segullah*." Or what if you came home one day to find that, miracle of miracles, your son has taken the trash out without being asked! What will he remember if you give him a big hug and whisper in his ear, "*Segullah*." Or maybe one Sabbath you see some children being irreverent in the church foyer and your child being tempted to join them. You could help him make the right choice by smiling as you say to him, "Remember *segullah*." In fact, when your daughter goes out on her first date, you do not have to embarrass her by yelling out, "Remember who you are!" as she heads out the door. Rather, you can just say *segullah*. She will know what you mean. Perhaps her boyfriend will ask, "What does that mean?" What a wonderful way to start off the date—your daughter teaching the young man this beautiful idea of *segullah*. Think what kind of influence that discussion could have on their evening activities!

Now let's look at another sermon in a sentence. I love the writings of Isaiah. In the last chapters of Isaiah, the prophet writes especially to teach his people of the greatness of God and His plans to redeem them. As he does so, Isaiah frequently contrasts the marvelous agency and power the Lord has to the impotence of idols. In the middle of Isaiah 44, the prophet poignantly exposes the foolishness of worshipping idols. He ridicules the idolaters' practice of making their idols out of wood from trees that they have cut down. He describes a man who raises a tree, cuts it down, and then uses it for various purposes, including making something to worship.

"Then shall it [the tree] be for the man to burn; for he will take thereof, and warm himself; yea, he kindleth it, and baketh bread; yea, he maketh a god, and worshippeth it; he maketh it a graven image, and falleth down thereto" (Isaiah 44:15).

Can you see how absurd this sounds to Isaiah? Isaiah cannot understand how a thinking person could cut down a tree, use part of it to light a fire for heat, use part of it to cook with, and then worship the rest—to make a god out of a chunk of wood. To highlight the foolishness of the practice, Isaiah describes it two more times:

"He burneth part thereof in the fire; with part thereof he eateth flesh; he roasteth roast, and is satisfied: yea, he warmeth himself, and saith, Aha, I am warm, I have seen the fire:

"And the residue thereof he maketh a god, even his graven image: he falleth down unto it, and worshippeth it, and prayeth unto it, and saith, Deliver me; for thou art my god.

"They have not known nor understood: for he hath shut their eyes, that they cannot see; and their hearts, that they cannot understand.

"And none considereth in his heart, neither is there knowledge nor understanding to say, I have burned part of it in the fire; yea, also I have baked bread upon the coals thereof; I have roasted flesh, and eaten it: and shall I make the residue thereof an abomination? Shall I fall down to the stock of a tree?" (Isaiah 44:16–19).

Can you see how silly that sounds to Isaiah? And it will sound silly to your children, too. Perhaps they will say, "Those people sure weren't very smart! We are not foolish enough to worship idols!" At that point you will likely explain to them that idolatry can be a problem today also. You will tell them an idol is anything that you make more important than God. And you'll list some examples like cars, jobs, or their body, or their boyfriend, or their video game, or their computer terminal, or . . . You will observe, "What a foolish thing it is indeed if we give more of our devotion and time to something other than God."

I like the sermon in the sentence that Isaiah gives in the next verse of this discussion. As he speaks of such a foolish idolater he says, "He feedeth on ashes: a deceived heart hath turned him aside, that he cannot deliver his soul, nor say, Is there not a lie in my right hand?" (Isaiah 44:20). The imagery is provocative and begs the question, "How is the worshipping of idols like eating ashes?" Imagine you are hungry. In your right hand, the hand with which you eat, you have a pile of ashes. For some reason you have been led to believe a lie, that eating the ashes will satisfy your body's need for nourishment. If you eat the ashes will your hunger be satiated? You might be able to eat enough to reach the point where the hunger pangs go away. You might even think, "I'm so full I couldn't eat another ash." But have you been nourished? Would it be possible to have a belly full of ashes and still die of malnutrition? The answer is obviously yes, for there is no nutrition in the ashes. Although you have eaten the ashes and gone through all the actions required to nourish your body, you have believed a lie and given your time and energy to indulging in something of no real value or substance. So it is with individuals who give their best time and devotion to something other than God. They are "feeding on ashes"—trying to satisfy a hunger with something of no eternal value or substance.

Think of the many ways you could use this sermon in a sentence. Imagine that you walk into your TV room and your children are watching an advertisement for a movie that is not wholesome. What would you communicate to them by saying, "He feedeth on ashes! Who would want to eat those ashes?" They will know just what you mean by that sermon in a sentence. Perhaps your daughter will learn this sermon in a sentence so well that when her date wants to take her to see that inappropriate movie, or another like it, she will say, "I don't want to see that." When asked why, she will respond, "Because he feedeth on ashes." Her date will say, "What do you mean?" Perhaps she will say, "Let's to go my house and study Isaiah instead. I'll teach you all about it." Now that would be a better date!

As you carefully feast upon the words found in the scriptures you will discover your own favorite "sermons in a sentence." What a blessing your discoveries can be if you will share the sermons with your children and use the words and phrases often as you teach, reward, and direct them.

These are only a few simple examples of how you can help the words of Christ find passage into the hearts of your children and into your own as well. I invite you to try them. May you use the scriptures to validate life's successes with your children and loved ones. May you help them memorize passages that can bless them and direct their thoughts. May you help them find their heroes in the scriptures and in the stories that are found therein. May you help them identify and use the sermons in a sentence that can inform their decisions and actions. Doing so requires you to feast upon the words of Christ regularly. If you feast with the idea in mind that you are doing so to enable you to diligently teach your children, it will add an exciting dimension to your scripture study. May the Lord bless you in that effort.

"We Do Not Doubt Our Mothers Knew It"

Becky Nelson

"O that I were an angel, and could have the wish of my heart, that I might go forth and speak with the trump of God" (Alma 29:1). My heart is full, and I do feel as Alma, not that I "glory of myself" (Alma 29:9), but I glory in that which I have been asked to do: to bear witness and testify of our divine calling and role as mothers in these latter days and how we might educate ourselves in fulfilling this most sacred of responsibilities.

A few Saturdays ago I was driving down the highway, having just dropped our youngest child off at a friend's, her fourteen-year-old laughter still ringing in the air. Golden sunlight shimmered across the sky as the sun set deeper in the west. A team of little leaguers and their cheering parents caught my eye in the distance, and a flood of memories came rushing through my mind. Weren't we just there with our own little boys? That same weekend I'd been tending our seventeen-month-old granddaughter while her parents were out of town. It was as if we had our own little daughter back, her smiles and laughter so characteristic of her mother twenty-four years earlier. How did those years go so fast? I longed to trade places with Emily in Thornton Wilder's play *Our Town* and relive just one day in my young motherhood life!

I would choose a chaotic day, with little ones running through the

---

Becky Nelson, a wife, mother, and grandmother, was a substitute seminary teacher for many years and is a graduate of Brigham Young University. She is grateful for life, her family, and the gospel of Jesus Christ.

house, green sweatpants and red tennis shoes, baseball bats and soccer balls lying in the yard, chattering voices and squeals at the dinner table, spilled milk and evening baths—and I would stand in the middle of it all and take it all in! I would gaze into their trusting faces and sparkling, dancing eyes. I would listen to the stories, and who hit what home run, and I would treasure every moment—even the one when I found out from a neighbor that our five-year-old daughter and a friend were standing on the corner of the entrance to our neighborhood holding a large sign that read Will Werk for Food!

I rejoice with Jane Clayson, when she said at the 2006 Conference on the Family: "Motherhood is surely the highest and holiest of assignments. I believe it is . . . 'the noblest office or calling in the world.'"[1] As mothers our sacred responsibility is to carefully teach our children to have faith in the Lord Jesus Christ and to be strong, contributing members of the family. How can we educate ourselves to teach, train, discipline, and care for our children? How can we teach so that they will be able to say, "We do not doubt our mothers knew it"? (Alma 56:48).

To instill such faith in the hearts of our children, we must first have an unwavering testimony of who we are and what our mission is— "Beloved spirit daughters of God, whose lives have meaning, purpose, and direction"—as stated in our Relief Society declaration. Once empowered with this conviction, we can more fully educate ourselves to teach, in partnership with God, His beloved children on this earth. I believe there are four steps that are essential in this education process.

1. KNOW THE ENVIRONMENT

We must understand the conditions of where we will teach and the environment of those we will be teaching. President Boyd K. Packer told BYU students in January 2007 that they live in a time of war—a spiritual war that will never end. He said that "largely because of television, instead of looking over into that spacious building [spoken of in Lehi's dream], we are, in effect, living inside of it."[2] President Spencer W. Kimball said in 1980, "The time will come when only those who believe deeply and actively in the family will be able to preserve their families in the midst of the gathering evil around us."[3] Our beloved prophet, President Gordon B.

Hinckley, confirmed that to be true when he stated in 2004: "I do not know that things were worse in the times of Sodom and Gomorrah. . . . We see similar conditions today."[4] Do we understand the challenges, temptations, and outside environment that our children live in?

As a people, we go to great lengths educating society, and those we are responsible for, on the calamities that may confront us. We make and review evacuation plans and prepare for fires, floods, and famines.

There isn't one reading this who would not call out to her children in times of danger, putting her child's safety ahead of her own. But what of the spiritually destructive firestorms that rage all about us now, invisible though they are, but deadly just the same? Have we educated ourselves as mothers to know what the dangers are, where the storms rage, and how close our children are to those paths of destruction?

2. Seek Spiritual Knowledge

We can seek spiritual knowledge through the gift of wisdom. In talking with my young married daughter, I asked her, "Jenny, how would you go about educating yourself to teach your children to have faith in the Lord Jesus Christ?" She said, "Well, it's certainly not something I would Google—you have to be in tune." I am confident that she did not mean "in tune" with surfing the Web or all of the many technological search engines that are at our fingertips but "in tune" with a much higher power.

We are so richly blessed to live in a day where knowledge and opportunities for education are greater than ever before in the history of the world. We are encouraged to get an education and rightly so, but in all of our getting, let us not be guilty of—as Paul warned Timothy about those in our day—"ever learning, and never able to come to the knowledge of the truth" (2 Timothy 3:7). In Proverbs we read that "wisdom is the principal thing; therefore get wisdom: and with all thy getting get understanding" (Proverbs 4:7). Wisdom is understanding that comes *through the Spirit* and *verifies truth*.

How can we possibly underestimate the power of spiritual knowledge and wisdom in our education process? Do you remember hearing the story of the Haun's Mill massacre, when Sister Amanda Smith recounts going into the blacksmith shop after the horrible attack on the Saints, only to find her husband and young son dead? How grateful she was to find Alma, her six-year-old, yet alive, but wounded badly. She knelt down and pleaded with the Lord for help. She said, "Oh my Heavenly Father, what shall I do? Thou seest my poor wounded boy and knowest my inexperience. Oh, Heavenly Father, direct me what to do!" She was "directed as by a voice" instructing her to make a slippery elm poultice and fill the horrible wound in his hip. After five weeks of laying face down, a flexible gristle grew in place of the missing joint and socket.[5]

How many of us have faithfully pleaded with our Father in Heaven in like manner, that despite our inadequacies, He would instruct us in how to minister to the wounds of our children's souls—that spiritual gristle could grow in their place, that they may "run and not be weary, and . . . walk and not faint" (D&C 89:20).

In the Doctrine and Covenants we read, "Let him that is ignorant learn wisdom by humbling himself and calling upon the Lord his God, that his eyes may be opened that he may see, and his ears opened that he may hear" (136:32).

3. Search, Ponder, and Pray

How important it is in this education process that we combine humbly calling upon our Heavenly Father, searching the scriptures, and taking the time to ponder the thoughts and feelings that come into our hearts and minds; however, taking the time to do so can be a challenge. In the past, simply praying and getting my scripture reading done for the day was my goal, but I have found later in life that there were hidden blessings in seeking the Lord early. Now this searching time has come in the quiet morning hours, when the phone is not ringing, the home is still, and I can come in humble supplication to a loving Father in Heaven before I begin my day. I have found that taking this time was not something I was doing for the Lord, but rather a priceless gift He sought to give me—a looked-forward-to and treasured time when I can read, ponder, and discuss with my Father in Heaven those things that are a concern to me. It has brought peace, increased knowledge and understanding, testimony, and direction to my life—the Spirit on call throughout my day.

Camille Fronk Olsen, in her book *Mary, Martha, and Me*, has said,

"When God comes first in our lives, . . . whatever comes second will always be right. . . . Putting God first supplies direction to our quest for balance, for finding the One Needful Thing whose gifts cannot be taken from us."[6]

As we take the time to search, ponder, and pray, we learn and understand the doctrine of Jesus Christ that will in turn bless and guide our families through these latter days. Consider this thought from Elder Henry B. Eyring:

"A wise parent would never miss a chance to gather children together to learn of the doctrine of Jesus Christ. Such moments are so rare in comparison with the efforts of the enemy. For every hour the power of doctrine is introduced into a child's life, there may be hundreds of hours of messages and images denying or ignoring the saving truths.

"The question should not be *whether we are too tired to prepare to teach doctrine* or whether it wouldn't be better to draw a child closer by just having fun or whether the child isn't beginning to think that we preach too much. The question must be, 'With so little time and so few opportunities, what words of doctrine from me will fortify them against the attacks on their faith which are sure to come?'"[7]

The scriptures are the greatest parenting manual ever written, and when combined with prayer and contemplation they can greatly increase our learning!

4. Claim Our Blessings

How essential it is that we exercise *faith* in the Lord Jesus Christ and claim the blessings and privileges that come through the Holy Ghost. I rejoice to live in this dispensation, the fulness of times, when the power of God is unrestrained on this earth. But, do we have faith in that power and use it to its full capacity in our homes and with our families? In our Saturday evening session of stake conference in August 2006, President Packer told us, "We live far beneath our privilege, because we do not understand the power that comes from the gift of the Holy Ghost." He cited 3 Nephi 9:20: "And ye shall offer for a sacrifice unto me a broken heart and a contrite spirit. And whoso cometh unto me with a broken heart and a contrite spirit, him will I baptize with fire and with the Holy

Ghost, even as the Lamanites, because of their *faith* in me at the time of their conversion" (emphasis added).

The Lamanites referred to were the people of Ammon—the mothers and fathers of the two thousand stripling warriors. They are described as being "firm in the faith of Christ, even unto the end" (Alma 27:27).

How is our faith? Do we understand that the privileges associated with the gift of the Holy Ghost are God's power from on high given to us if we are worthy and *exercise our faith in that power*? Are we calling upon those privileges? Do we seek priesthood counsel and blessings from husbands, fathers, brothers, home teachers, and bishops? Are we fasting, with faith and trust in the Lord, for blessings and understanding that He seeks to give us? Are we attending the temple, where possible, on a regular basis and claiming the blessings that come from within? Do we seek by faith to understand and apply the amazing gift of the Atonement? As we do this we've been promised that we shall "feast upon this fruit [of our faith] even until [we] are filled"! (Alma 32:42).

How Do We Teach?

I am surrounded by valiant mothers, sisters, teachers, and friends who with their unconditional love and faith in the Lord Jesus Christ have taught me great lessons. I think of my own mother and father, who had such a gift for sensing and taking the teaching moments. Together they instilled in me from a young age a desire to know and understand my Heavenly Father's plan. I don't remember the furnishings that adorned our home or the color of the paint on the wall—I just remember that it was the most wonderful place in the world, a place where I felt safe and loved and important. Their faith and testimony of the Savior, Jesus Christ, was an anchor to me in those impressionable years, and their love and guidance was a firm foundation on which I could build my own individual worth and testimony.

I've thought about the things I would change in preparing to teach our children if I could go back. First, I would somehow give myself permission and find a way to take that precious morning time to put God first in prayer, scripture study, and contemplation, even amidst the long list of "to dos" that scream at me from my planner. And second, I would make sure to get one-on-one time with each of our children on a regular basis. Why? you may ask.

As we spend time with our children we come to know them and understand their needs; as we spend time with the Lord we come to know and understand the solutions and answers to those needs. And I believe something else miraculous happens. We begin to feel His unconditional love for us and our children—the pure love of Christ. Even as it is important for us to know and feel our Heavenly Father's love for us, it is just as important for our children to know and feel His love for them and our love for them. It comes down to time and it comes down to love in how we teach our children.

The first ten minutes after children or teenagers walk through the door are so vitally important in gleaning what's on their mind and how they are feeling. We can learn more in those ten minutes than we can even an hour later, for they are off and on to other things. As we *take time to sense* the teaching moments and know when to put aside our other activities to be with them, inspire them, and help them to see that which is right; as we *discipline by teaching* the whys and wherefores of important principles, and *help them face consequences* for poor choices rather than punishment for bad actions; as we *encourage* more than we criticize and *share* feelings, frustrations, joys, and sorrows, our eyes become open to their souls, and they will begin to feel our genuine interest and love for them, as well as to increase in their own knowledge and understanding. This kind of love and teaching will last long after the isolation or scolding or hurried answer. It is an unconditional love.

How do we inherit unconditional love? Years ago, when I was a young wife, my husband and I were having a little discussion—in fact, I was quite bothered and indignant that he could actually feel the way he did and not see my point of view. I have long since forgotten the issue we were discussing, but I will never forget the lesson taught by a loving Heavenly Father. As I lay on my side of the bed, feeling frustrated and justified, my husband having fallen asleep long before, I knew I must get on my knees and pray for peace and comfort. As I knelt to pray, a scripture reference came to my mind. I was anxious to read it, thinking it would bring the validation and comfort that I needed, but when I picked up my scriptures to read, instead I received loving counsel that I have never forgotten.

"And charity suffereth long, and is kind, and envieth not, and is not puffed up, seeketh not her own, is not easily provoked, thinketh no evil, and rejoiceth not in iniquity but rejoiceth in the truth, beareth all things, believeth all things, hopeth all things, endureth all things." It was as if He was saying to me, "Wherefore, my beloved [daughter], if ye have not charity, ye are nothing, for charity never faileth. Wherefore, cleave unto charity, which is the greatest of all. . . . Charity is the pure love of Christ, and it endureth forever" (Moroni 7:45–47).

My son and his friends were once joking about the fine line that runs between my "mother bear instinct" and my charitable love for him. His laughter turned immediately solemn as he whispered in hushed tones, "Oh, the mother bear instinct—that scares me more than anything!" You see, in times of temptation and moments of nurturing he has seen that mother bear in my eyes, that look that says, "I will protect you above all else; I will stand at the very jaws of the adversary before I will let Satan take you into his grasp." He knows that I know that Satan is real and wants to do anything he can to rob my son of his happiness and divine birthright. But it was Satan who wanted to take away choice, and it was a loving Father, who, offering all, gave us the gift of agency. Yet even with choices that have taken loved ones miles away spiritually, the testimony and faith of a loving family can be the magnet that draws them back again.

I have been moved to the depths of my very soul as I have witnessed a dear friend—struggling with the challenges of a beloved daughter who has not yet caught the vision of who she is—be led prayerfully, instinctively, step by step, in the very hour and moment to needed answers and help. I have no doubt that the day will come when that precious daughter will bear witness that she did not doubt her mother knew that "God [c]ould deliver" her (Alma 56:47). Her mother has humbly testified that it is the power of the Atonement that allows us to "bear all things" and love unconditionally. If we will teach and bear testimony to our children of a loving Heavenly Father and the Savior Jesus Christ, pray with them, and love them with the kind of love that is His love, I believe that miracles can come.

As we develop this love, enriching it with faith in the Savior Jesus Christ, I believe we come to see more clearly our children as God sees them and to love them as He loves them. We will come to see each other as God sees us. We will feel of His love for us, and the more we feel of that love, the more we will want to share it with others—no matter who they are. It is the love that miracles are made of. It is the pure love of Christ—the greatest life-changing power on the earth. It is the love that, if bestowed upon our children by teachers, parents, grandparents, and loved ones, will keep them safe amidst the armies of the adversary, even if they fall. It will be this love that brings them to their feet again.

On the wall in our bedroom hang the pictures of our children when they were very young. Below them is the inscription "Behold Your Little Ones," reminiscent of the Savior's words to the Nephite people when He took their little children *one by one* and blessed them. It is a reminder to me of the sacred trust and responsibility that has been bestowed upon us as their parents. I treasure the years we have had to nurture, love, and grow with them. I can't go back and relive those days as Emily did in *Our Town*, but I rejoice in looking forward! The basement where teenagers gathered and root beer floats were served is a little more quiet now—instead, toys from days gone by have come out of the closets and into the small hands of a second generation. I thrill in the opportunity to share our love and testimony with them. I reverence their parents—our children—as they take their turn to teach, and I pray that we can be a blessing and support to them as they do so. In a talk entitled "The Golden Years," President Packer encourages us to "keep the fire of [our] testimony of the restored gospel and [our] witness of our Redeemer burning so brightly that our children can warm their hands by the fire of [our] faith."[8]

I know that our Heavenly Father and Savior live, that they love us and want to bless us with their comfort, peace, and power. As we seek to educate ourselves in teaching our children, may we come to reverence and honor the sacred calling of motherhood; may we understand the conditions where we teach and immerse ourselves in the scriptures, thoughtful meditation, and humble prayer. May we seek spiritual knowledge through wisdom and exercise faith in the Lord to claim the privileges and blessings that can come through the power of the Holy Ghost.

As we take time with our children to love and teach as the Savior does, with His pure and honest love, I bear solemn testimony that we will witness miracles. We have been called to the kingdom for such a time as this—to teach our children, grandchildren, and those within our influence so that they will not doubt our firm and anchored faith in the Savior Jesus Christ, nor our love for and faith in them.

NOTES

1. Jane Clayson, "I Am a Mother," 2006 Conference on the Family sponsored by The Church of Jesus Christ of Latter-day Saints, Salt Lake City, September 9, 2006.
2. Boyd K. Packer, "Lehi's Dream and You," BYU devotional address, 16 January 2007.
3. Spencer W. Kimball, "Families Can Be Eternal," *Ensign*, November 1980, 4.
4. Gordon B. Hinckley, "Standing Strong and Immovable," *Worldwide Leadership Training Meeting*, 10 January 2004, 20.
5. *Our Heritage: A Brief History of The Church of Jesus Christ of Latter-day Saints* (Salt Lake City: The Church of Jesus Christ of Latter-day Saints, 1996), 47.
6. Camille Fronk Olson, *Mary, Martha, and Me* (Salt Lake City: Deseret Book, 2006), 106.
7. Henry B. Eyring, "The Power of Teaching Doctrine," *Ensign*, May 1999, 74; emphasis added.
8. Boyd K. Packer, "The Golden Years," *Ensign*, May 2003, 84.

"SEASONED TO PERFECTION"

Mary Ellen Edmunds

Before my father went home (at age ninety-five), I watched him go through many seasons. While some were exceedingly challenging, he seemed committed to doing his best, no matter what his circumstance. Towards the end, I began having the feeling that my dad had been "seasoned to perfection." I love that phrase, and I chose it as the title for what I want to share. I'll tell you the title I *really* wanted to use, though: "Wisdom Comes with Age—Sometimes Age Comes Alone."

Life has a lot of seasons, doesn't it? I love the changes from winter to spring, from summer to fall. I like having all four seasons, with the promise of the next one in the current one. When I was little, my favorite months all had the letter *u* in them: June, July, August. I loved summers. But I've changed. Now all my favorite months have *r* in them, starting with September.

Our lives have seasons, and as with the weather, there are some which seem more enjoyable, productive, interesting, beautiful, or whatever. If our whole life were our favorite season, we likely wouldn't learn or grow as much. It might even get boring.

If my mother had allowed me to eat only my favorite food (macaroni

---

Mary Ellen Edmunds served as a director of training at the Missionary Training Center in Provo, Utah, and as a member of the Relief Society General Board. She served full-time proselyting and welfare missions in Asia and Africa. Sister Edmunds is a well-known author and popular speaker.

and cheese) through all my growing-up years, I might look even worse today than I do! Speaking of my mother, she was going to be my visual aid today. I wanted to show you beauty, humor, and enthusiasm at almost ninety-three. She decided it was too far from there to here. But I hope I can age as gracefully and naturally as my parents, enjoying life every bit as much.

How about *your* life—what have your seasons been like so far? Do any of you feel like you're getting close to season one hundred? Not that you're one hundred years old—you could be only thirty and feel like you've had one hundred seasons.

Maybe you're raising children, doing your best to make sure they're happy and healthy, clothed and fed, bright and well-mannered, and so on. Do you receive a lot of advice about how to make it through this season? I hope you have more people who genuinely help, rather than just evaluate and judge what and how you're doing.

Maybe this is your season for a demanding Church calling, and if it were the only thing you had to do in your life you could really "do a number" on it. But you're doing well—you're praying, studying, preparing, and giving your best. And you're somehow keeping up with all the other things in your life most of the time.

Perhaps you sometimes feel lonely, abandoned, not needed. If that is a season you're experiencing, I pray it won't last long.

Maybe you're in school, and you wonder if you'll ever be finished with tests, and papers to write, and pages to read, and lectures to comprehend. Do you wonder if there will ever be a time when you can read for pleasure again?

Maybe you're serving as a missionary, either as a young person or as a senior missionary. For many, this particular season seems like an oasis—challenging, but beautiful. It might be hard to say yes to a mission, but oh, the incredible experience of representing Jesus Christ wherever He sends you!

Maybe your season is closer to being like my mother's. She says she is so far over the hill she thinks she only dreamed about it! "Sunrise, sunset—swiftly fly the years."[1] Mom had a stroke when she was seventy-eight and highly recommends that if you're going to have one of those you should not wait too long. She feels she would have enjoyed her stroke so much more if she'd been younger.

She realizes there are things she used to do which she just can't do anymore. (You don't have to be past ninety before you realize there are things you can no longer do.) Driving a car is one of the most difficult things she had to let go of, and it was the same for my father. Maybe for you it will be square dancing or skydiving. Maybe you'll miss being in the rodeo or taking long walks.

My mother lives with my younger brother John; his wife, Melanie; and their six children. Melanie's parents also live there for much of the year, so it's a full and busy household. There are many experiences and sweet blessings that come from having three generations living together.

This family has had, for several years, a little Pug dog named Ivan. In early March, Ivan was very sick and had to be put to sleep. This was a very difficult thing for the family, especially my mother, who loved the dog and enjoyed the companionship so much. It was also a very difficult thing for nine-year-old Jill. She wrote her feelings down a little while after Ivan died. I share them without having made any corrections.

"IVAN . . . I miss Ivan. He was my best friend. He was my favorite pet of those 7 years.

"He was my favorite pug dog. He had to get put to sleep Mar. 3, 2007 because all his muscles in his body started to hurt each second. There was no medication we could give him to save him from this illness. We couldn't just leave him like this . . . So we had to put him to sleep.

"So far it has been the most difficult thing so far in my life. I loved him with all my heart.

"If I had the choice I would of taken his spot to die. I hope that the angels are taking good care of him. I love Ivan and miss him, that's all I got to say."

A little child sharing a sense of loss with her grandmother is a precious, holy thing.

My mother looks back on many interesting seasons—a mother of eight with many grandchildren and great-grandchildren, a nurse, Silver Beaver, self-taught farmer and vet, exceptional cook and gardener, Relief Society president, camp director, and so on.

Your list is just as amazing.

Maybe your season is similar in some ways to mine. (Although I realize that we're never in *exactly* the same circumstance as anyone else). I'm retired, but I'm as busy as I ever was. Inside I feel like I could still leap tall buildings, but in reality I can hardly leap dust balls. I say silly things like, "I'm not as young as I used to be." Duh!

There's that phrase from the book of Luke, describing some of us as "stricken in years" (Luke 1:7). I think my mother and I (and maybe many of you as well) feel the same way as expressed by a man when he turned 85: "Old age is always fifteen years older than I am."[2]

I don't remember when I first discovered that I could no longer take the stairs two or three at a time or run without getting tired. Or run at all. Now I get out of breath just hauling the garbage can out to the street. And it's so much harder these days to get in and out of my pup tent! Am I really the same person who was voted best female athlete in my high school a hundred years ago?

One thing that has changed is my hearing. I take after my dad rather than my mother in that department. A couple of years ago I was on a flight from Salt Lake City to Oakland, California. A man sat beside me who looked like he was a frequent flyer.

So when he got seated I asked, "Do you fly a lot?"

"I sure do."

I asked what business he was in, and he said, "Books." Oh, that was an easy one to respond to! I went on and on about some books I had read recently, telling him how much I'd enjoyed them. Then I asked if he thought people read as much as they used to, and he said he thought they probably did.

I then asked, "When you travel, are you selling books?"

He looked at me with a bit of humor mixed with a sigh and said, "Boats . . . b-o-a-t-s . . . boats."

"Oh."

I told the stake Relief Society president and her husband about this experience, and the next day when they took me back to the airport we crossed over the Golden Gate Bridge and went down near the bay. There were some beautiful boats out on the water, and one was really huge. The husband said, "Wow, that's a pretty big book!"

It wasn't long after that trip that I got my hearing aids.

I never thought it would be my turn to notice these little surprises of nature—these saggings and malfunctions, the slowing down and suchlike. These days it takes twice as long to look half as good. I find myself humming, "Have I done any good in the world today?"[3] a little more often than I used to. I'm still looking forward most of the time, but I also find I look back more than I did when I was twenty or thirty.

I'm never bored, and I feel thankful for that. I'm also very grateful that I tend to be happy and cheerful most of the time. (But I have my moments! I'm normal!)

We've all been changing since the day we were born, haven't we?

As I've been thinking about all of this, I've decided that many seasons overlap. Several might descend on us at once. We think spring has come, but there's another "cold snap." We think summer will be long and hot, and all of a sudden it's time to harvest the apples, roll up the hoses, and carve the pumpkins.

Each age, each season, has lessons and satisfaction which can be known only by experience. What have your seasons taught you? Have they helped to bring insight, compassion, faith, patience, perspective, and other qualities of soul? Are we getting all we can out of each of our seasons?

Sometimes we try to deny our age or to mask the signs of aging. Many observers feel that this is a great obstacle to aging gracefully. There are challenges in growing older, yes, but there are also many benefits.

Here are some perks of being over sixty-five:

- Kidnappers are not very interested in you.
- There is nothing left to learn the hard way.
- Most things you buy now won't wear out.
- You can quit trying to hold your stomach in.
- Your investment in health insurance is actually beginning to pay off.
- Your supply of brain cells is finally down to a manageable size.

Other benefits of growing older include increased wisdom, a wonderful depth of character, a collection of extraordinary memories, letting go of things that don't matter, and focusing on things that matter most. And you can finally let go of activities more suited to younger bodies. As Golda Meir said, "Being seventy is not a sin."

Think of the average age of the fifteen men whom we sustain as prophets, seers, and revelators! I'm not a math major, but I figure it's somewhere around seventy-six. President Gordon B. Hinckley, at almost ninety-seven, really affects those numbers, doesn't he? These fifteen men have around 1,163 combined years of life experience. We are in good hands!

Aging is not a sudden event; it's a process. And there just is not a way to grow younger, is there? The fountain of youth is a myth, except that I think I found a recipe that comes pretty close:

"For the natural man is an enemy to God, and has been from the fall of Adam, and will be, forever and ever, unless he yields to the enticings of the Holy Spirit, and putteth off the natural man and becometh a saint through the atonement of Christ the Lord, and becometh as a child, submissive, meek, humble, patient, full of love, willing to submit to all things which the Lord seeth fit to inflict upon him, even as a child doth submit to his father" (Mosiah 3:19).

We mortals will all eventually die. The goal isn't to live forever—the goal is to create and invest in something that will! And along the way we need to value each other not just for what we can do, but for who we are.

I've interviewed several women to get their take on this whole issue of aging. Very interesting! This may surprise you, but I got an e-mail from Mary Methuselah. (Write that in your journal: "Edmunds got an e-mail from Methuselah's wife!") Her friends called her Muffy. Here are some excerpts from her e-mail:

"So you're talking about aging, are you? Well, I lived almost thirty years after my husband died (at age 969), so that takes me pretty near having lived 1,000 years. And you think 100 years is a big deal! Ha ha. Trying adding another zero! You think you're old? My husband was a 'boy' of 100 when Adam himself ordained him to the priesthood. Did you know my husband was an astronomer? Lots of people don't know that. By the way, his nickname was 'Meth,' and I think he'd have had to change it if he lived now. Life on earth was pretty interesting for me. We didn't worry about things like cholesterol or road rage, nor did we have manicures, Botox, or tummy tucks. Those I don't think I'd have missed even if I'd have known about them, but oh, to have indoor plumbing and electricity! I have to say that I really loved my father-in-law, Enoch, even though it took me a few days to get over being left behind when he and his city were taken to heaven. My husband helped me realize that it was on purpose—that he and I both needed to keep teaching what our parents had taught. Our grandson Noah became quite famous—you've probably heard of him. He only lived to be 950. And did you know he was around 600 years old when he finished building the ark? And you think you're too old to be a Scout leader or a Laurel adviser! Can you imagine being 500 years old before you have a mid-life crisis?? So don't talk to any of us about getting old. Just enjoy your experiences, and do your best."

I'm so grateful to Muffy Methuselah for this wonderful e-mail.

A thought often attributed to General Douglas MacArthur is one you've likely heard:

"Nobody grows old by merely living a number of years; people grow old by deserting their ideals.

"Years may wrinkle the skin, but to give up enthusiasm wrinkles the soul. . . .

"You are as young as your faith, as old as your doubt; as young as your self-confidence, as old as your fear; as young as your hope, as old as your despair."[4]

To me, there is a difference between aging (a very natural phenomenon which happens to all of us) and growing old. Thus, I have come up with some alternatives to growing old:

- Growing happy and grateful and content.
- Growing wise and kind and endurable—yes, endurable, able to endure to the end! (It kind of sounds like adorable, and that's another good alternative to growing old—growing adorable!)

Some who reach retirement age seem to feel, "I've done my share. Now it's someone else's turn." But withdrawing can actually hasten the aging process. What if President Hinckley had decided to "retire" at age sixty-five, or seventy-five, or even eighty-five or ninety-five! Thank goodness he didn't! Just think, if he had retired at age sixty-five, we'd have missed over thirty years of his goodness, his leadership, his humor, his faith, and his counsel.

The Savior "increased in wisdom and stature, and in favour with God and man" (Luke 2:52), and so can we. We still have a lot of living to do.

You're never too old and it's never too late to *keep learning*. My friend Florence Richards used to choose one new thing to learn each year. One year it was how to play the accordion. She told me she found someone in the ward who had one in their attic. By Christmastime she could play "Lady of Spain" pretty well.

What is it you do to keep learning, to keep your mind active and busy? Maybe you work on crafts or crossword puzzles. Maybe you read or keep a journal. Some aging people challenge themselves with trying to remember the names of their children and grandchildren, or they go overboard and try to remember spouses *and* birthdays! That'll keep your brain busy!

You're never too old and it's never too late to *live each day with purpose and enthusiasm.* I love seeing older people who still have passion for the things which matter most to them. (And by this time they should have a pretty good idea of what matters most!)

It's never too late to *give things away.* Do this while you can still remember why you've saved some of your treasures—why they mean so much—and you can explain that as you give these treasures to someone you love.

You're never too old to *dream dreams, to serve, to remember, to be cheerful, to do some exercising of both body and mind.*

You're never too old to *reach out to those in need, to smile, to be a happifier.*

You're never too old to *keep covenants, to communicate openly and honestly with Heavenly Father, to become more Christlike and Godlike.*

President Hinckley shared the following:

"To you older women and men who are widows and widowers, how precious you are. You have lived long and had much of experience. You have tasted the bitter and the sweet. You have known much of pain and sorrow and loneliness and fear. But you also carry in your hearts a sweet and sublime assurance that God our Father will not fail us in our hour of need. May the years that lie ahead be kind to you. May heaven smile upon you. May you draw comfort and strength from your memories. And may you, with your mature kindness and love, reach out to help those in distress wherever you find them."[5]

That's beautiful, isn't it? (I think of him when I read it.)

Some of us may have feelings similar to what is recorded in Psalm 71: "I am as a wonder unto many; but thou art my strong refuge. . . .

"Cast me not off in the time of old age; forsake me not when my strength faileth" (Psalm 71:7, 9).

There will never come a time when your Heavenly Father forgets about you. There's not some policy in heaven where you turn seventy and they "turn you loose." "She can't move fast enough anymore to get into trouble, so focus on the young 'uns." I share again a phrase from the quote I read from President Hinckley: "You also carry in your hearts a sweet and sublime assurance that God our Father will not fail us in our hour of need."

> *E'en down to old age, all my people shall prove*
> *My sov'reign, eternal, unchangeable love;*
> *And then, when gray hair shall their temples adorn,*
> *Like lambs shall they still in my bosom be borne.*[6]

May the years that lie ahead be kind to you. May heaven smile upon you.

NOTES

1. Sheldon Harnick, "Sunrise, Sunset," in Jerry Bock, *Fiddler on the Roof* (New York: Pocket Books, 1966).
2. Bernard Baruch, in *Observer* (London), 21 August 1955.
3. Will L. Thompson, "Have I Done Any Good?" in *Hymns of The Church of Jesus Christ of Latter-day Saints* (Salt Lake City: The Church of Jesus Christ of Latter-day Saints, 1985), no. 223.
4. The poem "Youth" by Samuel Ullman was quoted by General Douglas MacArthur without attribution on his seventy-fifth birthday, in a speech to the Los Angeles County Council, American Legion, Los Angeles, California, January 26, 1955. http://www.bartleby.com/73/2099.html. Accessed 6 November 2007.
5. Gordon B. Hinckley, "A Conversation with Single Adults," *Ensign*, March 1997, 63.
6. Attributed to Robert Keen, "How Firm a Foundation," in *Hymns*, no. 85.

Light Cleaveth unto Light

Allison Warner

Not only am I grateful to be married but I am grateful for the way it came into my life. For a while I did not always see the hand of the Lord as I was on the path to marriage, but I see now that His plan for me was carefully orchestrated to bless me in profound ways.

Perhaps some of you are not presently married and are wondering if my remarks will apply to you. I certainly hope so, because establishing an enduring marriage relationship begins long before we enter into a marriage covenant. My friend Barbara Lockhart, who is in her sixties and not yet married, responds to questions about whether she is discouraged about her marital status by saying, "Oh no, because every day when I wake up I am one day closer to being married." She knows that in the eternal scheme of things each day is a preparation for a promised blessing that will be bestowed on all who qualify themselves through righteous living.

My earthly preparation for marriage began on July 31, 1951, when I was born into a home where, as my patriarchal blessing later confirmed, I was loved and taught the truth. I was subsequently baptized and given the gift of the Holy Ghost. Each week as our family participated in various Church meetings, including Primary, Sunday School, Young Women, and especially sacrament meeting, when we renewed our baptismal covenants, my testimony grew.

Allison Warner is a wife and mother who has previously served as a ward Young Women president, counselor in a ward Relief Society, and Gospel Doctrine teacher.

182

While in high school, I received my patriarchal blessing and was promised that I would find a husband and rear children, in the due time of the Lord. Also in high school, I took a class called Family Living in which we were given an assignment to plan our wedding, detailing all the elements and costs associated with that event. By my calculations I could do it for $850. I was set!

Within two years of graduation, I was a bridesmaid at my two best friends' weddings and I knew mine couldn't be far behind. I continued my education at Brigham Young University. When I was twenty-two, I met a friend in one of my classes who hadn't been married until she was twenty-four. Twenty-four! I thought that was very old, and I couldn't possibly wait any longer than that. So I set my deadline to be married by twenty-four.

At twenty-seven and still unmarried, I began my first real job, and with my first paycheck I bought a ring and a set of china dishes, which I stored with other items I had collected in anticipation of being married.

I had a wide circle of friends whom I had met in college, and we engaged in lots of fun activities. I was now thirty, and in my heart I knew that if I were to realize my dreams of being a wife and a mother, I had to leave my circle of friends, some not focused on marriage, and some losing interest in the Church. It was a lonely time for me. I was now not only unmarried but without the social interactions I was used to.

I moved home for a time and was accepted with open arms into my home ward and given opportunities to serve, which helped fill the void I felt in my life. My testimony grew, I began to rely on the Lord more fully, and blessings began to flow. When I was thirty-two, I received my endowment in the temple and felt strengthened by the covenants I made there. In all this, I was learning what it meant to wait for the due time of the Lord.

When I was growing up, something of supreme importance happened in my life, although I did not recognize it at the time. My parents decided to remodel their existing house instead of building on the lot they owned directly across the street from our home. Right around the corner on Maple Lane, the Warner family was living in a house that was becoming cramped for their growing family. My parents offered to sell their lot to the Warners. The Warners took so long to respond that my mother wondered if they should tell them they would come down a little on the asking price.

My dad thought the price was fair, but they both decided that they would rather pick their neighbors than have the money. So they made another offer, the Warners accepted, and the deal was sealed. They built their house, and our families grew up happily across the street from each other keeping up a constant flow between our two houses.

The Warners' oldest son, David, was between the ages of two of my younger sisters. At this point in the story I am reminded of a phrase my mother used to use: "Once out of the burning shed." As a girl, Mother went to the movies on Saturday afternoons, and sometimes in the weekly serial that was shown before the main feature, the villain would tie up the hero, lock him in a shed, and then set fire to it. The serial would end, leaving you in suspense, to be continued the next week. When you returned the next week, the serial began with these words appearing on the screen: "Once out of the burning shed . . ." The hero, miraculously unscathed, would proceed to apprehend the villain and set the world right. Knowing that I'm leaving out some important details in my story, let me just say, "once out of the burning shed" and one month shy of my thirty-seventh birthday, David and I were married in the Salt Lake Temple.

We had known each other so long and so well before we were married that we were sure we would be spared many of the adjustments other newly married couples had to make. We smile now when we think of that, because marriage requires everyone, including us, to adjust, to adapt, to grow, and to change. And thankfully so!

One thing was certain: I began to see evidences in my life of something the Lord has taught us in the Book of Mormon. In Ether 12:27 He says, "I give unto men weakness": weakness or, in other words, susceptibility to sin and temptation, a consequence of living on this earth in a body of flesh and blood.

"What kind of a gift is that?!" I've asked myself. I have lots of things on my personal wish list, and weakness is not among them. I have never considered weakness anything but unwanted interruption to the achievement of my goals. No one has ever complimented me on my weakness. No one has told me to keep up my weakness or that they admire me because of the things I can't do.

But nonetheless, I have been given weaknesses. And because the

Lord is no respecter of persons, there is a good chance my spouse has been given some too. It seems paradoxical that in order to receive the highest degree in the celestial kingdom, a man and a woman, both of whom battle weakness, and who by design are fundamentally different from each other, must be joined together in marriage.

We can gain some understanding when we read the whole verse in Ether: "And if men come unto me I will show them their weakness. I give unto men weakness that they may be humble; and my grace is sufficient for all men that humble themselves before me; for if they humble themselves before me, and have faith in me, then will I make weak things become strong unto them" (Ether 12:27).

Interesting, isn't it, that the antidote for weakness is humility? To many in the world today humility is a sign of weakness, not the path to becoming strong. So the first step to becoming strong is to humbly accept the Lord's invitation to come unto Him so that He can show us our weakness.

The Lord tells Moroni, "Because thou hast seen thy weakness thou shalt be made strong, even unto the sitting down in the place which I have prepared in the mansions of my Father" (Ether 12:37). It is in seeing our weakness and our profound need for forgiveness and redemption that we open ourselves to strengthening, that we seek it and make place for it. Seeing clearly, honestly, then, is essential.

In William Shakespeare's play *King Lear*, as Lear in a rage prepares to banish his youngest daughter, Cordelia, the Duke of Kent implores him, "See better, Lear."[1] Any spouse in any marriage can tell you of times when "seeing better" has healed and strengthened their marriage relationship.

I have heard the advice to keep your eyes wide open before you get married and then keep them half-closed afterwards. How can the Lord help us "see better" in our relationships if our eyes are half-closed? How can He "show" us the truth about ourselves and our relationship to the person to whom we are joined?

We need help. We need insight, and we need light. Consider the sun and its many properties. Among other things it has the ability to warm, nourish, illuminate, and purify. Likewise, the light we receive from our Father in Heaven through His Son, Jesus Christ, has the ability to warm, nourish, illuminate, and purify our spirits. It is His light that will allow us to "see better" when we look at our spouses and ourselves.

His light is not only in us, but also all around us. In D&C 88:11 and 13 we learn that "the light which shineth, which giveth you light, is through him who enlighteneth your eyes, which is the same light that quickeneth your understandings; . . . the light which is in all things, which giveth life to all things." He is in the very middle of our lives, inside and out. His light is always available to us if we will but turn to it, live in it, bask in its warmth, and see by it.

We are taught that "light cleaveth unto light" (D&C 88:40). To cleave means to cling closely, steadfastly, or faithfully to something or somebody. When light is clinging to light it is impossible to tell where one source of light begins or the other one ends. It becomes all one light.

I think it is no accident that the very same word, *cleave,* is used in a comprehensive commandment about the marital relationship. In Moses 3:22–24 we read: "And the rib which I, the Lord God, had taken from man, made I a woman, and brought her unto the man. And Adam said: This I know now is bone of my bones, and flesh of my flesh; she shall be called Woman, because she was taken out of man. Therefore shall a man leave his father and his mother, and shall cleave unto his wife; and they shall be one flesh." We are not only to cleave to the light of the Lord but also to cleave unto our spouse. The woman was made a separate entity from the man, and then both the man and the woman were instructed to become one.

I am grateful that the Lord allows me to demonstrate my love for my husband by cleaving to him and striving to become one with him. Now, becoming one does not mean that I am trying to become like my husband or that he is trying to become like me. Together, we are both trying to become like our Father in Heaven, full of His light and one with Him. For in Jacob we are instructed to "cleave unto God as he cleaveth unto you" (6:5).

The instruction to cleave unto God is further illuminated in the Doctrine and Covenants where the Lord tells Emma Smith to "cleave unto the covenants which thou hast made" (25:13). Cleave, hang on fiercely with all your energy, with each act, thought, intuition, or desire. We must cleave to all our covenants—cleave to our baptismal covenants, cleave to the personal covenants we make when we are endowed, and, ultimately, cleave to the covenants we make when we are sealed to our spouse.

The scriptures are replete with examples of ways to use our physical bodies to cleave to our spouse. They come in the form of admonitions, commandments, invitations, and even warnings. Let me offer a few examples.

We have talked about light and its influence on us. In Matthew we learn that "the light of the body is the eye" (6:22). When your eyes meet your husband's, what does he see there? Does he see your faith in him, your love for him, your admiration of him, your enjoyment in him? Does he see the Savior's light spilling forth? If so, chances are good that you will see the same things reflected back to you in his eyes. "And if your eye be single to my glory, your whole bodies shall be filled with light, and there shall be no darkness in you; and that body which is filled with light comprehendeth [or seeth] all things" (D&C 88:67).

A powerful image comes into my mind when I read in Proverbs 2:2, "Incline thine ear unto wisdom, and apply thine heart to understanding." When I am inclining my ear to my husband I have to be in close proximity to him, leaning toward him to hear the words he is saying. To apply my heart to understanding, it has to be drawn out to him trying to comprehend the meaning of what he is saying. To comprehend something means to grasp the meaning or nature of it or to include one thing as a part of another. So when I incline my ear and apply my heart, I can learn something new about the very nature of my husband, and I can include his view as part of my own.

Again from Proverbs comes another lesson for all of us: "Who can find a virtuous woman? for her price is far above rubies. . . . She openeth her mouth with wisdom; and in her tongue is the law of kindness" (31:10, 26). I had an experience once that drew me up short. One day, while having a conversation with one of my sons about a certain behavior he was struggling with, I asked, "How are you going to remember not to repeat what happened today?" He thought for a moment and answered, "You know that voice you use when you're really mad? I'll just think about that, and I'll remember not to do it anymore for sure." I was chastised and vowed to let the law of kindness govern my tongue more often.

Our daily activities are designed to give us opportunities to cleave to each other. During the day, when I have ironed my husband's shirt, or cooked a meal for him, or picked his socks up off the floor—as I have encountered these tokens of his life—impressions have come to me of specific ways to help him. Prayers in his behalf have formed in my mind, and my heart has been drawn out to him and his needs. I find myself looking forward to his return and the feeling in our home when he is there. I long to cleave more earnestly, more steadfastly, and more faithfully to him when he is brought to my remembrance through these simple routine acts of service.

The most powerful way to remedy the challenges we face in our marriages is to live our lives so that we can be filled with the light of the Savior and then to cleave to one another by the power of His light.

The scripture that tells us "light cleaveth unto light" is not so much a commandment as it is a statement. Light is drawn to light; it inclines toward light; it is attracted to light, until it becomes all one light, indistinguishable from its source. Light cleaveth unto light—perhaps there is no more powerful recipe for a great marriage in all of scripture.

Some time ago some very dear friends of ours found themselves on the brink of divorce. One of them moved out of the house, taking one child, and one stayed in the house with the other child. Things of a very serious nature had escalated, and there was, to any reasonable onlooker, sufficient reason to divorce.

Our interactions with each of them were wrenching. The pain of the things they had and were experiencing were evident on their faces. Although they were not members of the Church, each sought priesthood blessings. I was present at one of those blessings when the Spirit of the Lord was poured out abundantly. The presence of the Holy Ghost filled the room, and from that moment despair and darkness began to be dispelled. A few weeks after the blessing I received a phone call asking me if I would like to meet both of them for breakfast. I dropped everything, hurried to the restaurant, and found them sitting across the table holding hands, their countenances filled with light. As we talked, one of them said, "The only way we could have come back together is by the Spirit. Christ is in our marriage now." The light, which had been impossible to light by themselves, had been rekindled by the Source of all light, the Savior Himself. They had humbly come to the Lord and had seen their weaknesses through the light of His love. Now, full of His light, they were cleaving to each other and becoming strong because of it.

Every day we have experiences that can help us. A few weeks ago one of our sons was struggling to control his behavior in school. Finally one day he came home from school to report he had had a perfect day. We tried some positive reinforcement, and the next day he came home with a perfect report again. I asked him how he did it. He said, "Mom, I retraced my steps."

What a great insight! When we are struggling and have lost our way and can't quite seem to get our ourselves back on track, we can retrace our steps. Retrace the steps that led you to fall in love with your husband. Retrace your steps through the scriptures that have brought you comfort or given you new insights. Retrace your steps through prayers you have offered and answers you have received. Retrace your steps by renewing your baptismal covenants as you partake of the sacrament each week. Retrace your steps as you attend the temple, where you made your own covenants and where you have received peace and guidance.

"We go to the temple to make covenants, but we go home to keep the covenants that we have made,"[2] Elder J Ballard Washburn taught in general conference a few years ago. A friend of mine and her husband attended the temple, and at the conclusion of the endowment session they asked if there was a private place in the temple where they could pray together. They were told that was the purpose of their home.

Surely our homes have the potential to be as holy as our temples when they are inhabited by husbands and wives who honor their covenants. This lesson was taught to me on Christmas Eve a couple of years ago. My mother had gone to my sister's home to celebrate Christmas. I went to pick up something at my mother's house. I stood in her kitchen alone retracing in my mind the Christmas Eves that had come before. Each Christmas Eve as I was growing up, we gathered as a family in the living room and my father would read the Christmas story found in Luke and then bear his testimony. That was the moment each year that Christmas truly began for me, the moment when we as a family would consider the miracle of the birth of the Savior and the promised miracle of His Atonement and Resurrection. At those moments contention, unkindness, and strife had no hold on any of us. We were united in love, filled with His Spirit, our hearts turned to each other.

I realize now that part of the feeling I felt on past Christmas Eves was a direct result of my parents' baptismal and temple covenants. Because they cleaved to their covenants, they were entitled to lay claim to the blessings promised to Abraham. They had accepted the gospel themselves and taught their posterity of Jesus Christ. Our home was hallowed by those covenants. Standing alone in my parent's kitchen I felt the same feelings I had felt on those Christmas Eves as strongly as if the house were filled with each member of my family. I knew I stood on holy ground, ground made holy because my parents honored their covenants by cleaving to the Savior and, consequently, to each other. How grateful I am for the example of righteous parents.

I began to feel the power of the covenants that David and I made in the temple not long after we were married. My father was the director of the newly constructed BYU Jerusalem Center. My parents came home for my wedding and then returned to Jerusalem. A few months later, David's mother and his sister Alice and I went to Jerusalem to visit them, leaving David behind to finish spring semester at school. It was our first prolonged separation since we had been married.

On the plane on the way home I wrote this in my journal: "This morning as I was packing and wishing the hours away until I was home with David I told Alice, 'This trip has been too long!' I don't know if it really had been or if I had measured out the time in my mind and was running out of whatever it takes to be separated from my husband. In any case, I felt such a longing to be with him again and hence wished the next few hours away. The wishing only seemed to make them longer. This was the first time I had left my parents behind since being married. And while I felt sadness at being separated from them and associating with them, I truly felt that I was going home—to our home, David's and mine, and I couldn't wait." The sealing power is real, and I was feeling its effects sitting on an airplane ten thousand miles away from my husband. Already we had begun the journey toward becoming one. And although we had only been married a few months, already I felt incomplete without him.

We are still on that journey. And although that journey is fraught with the challenges that naturally come to all of us, I have always found that as we together seek for Heavenly Father's light, and cleave to it, our weakness is made strong and we become sanctified. "Therefore, sanctify yourselves that your minds become single to God, and the days will come that you shall see him; for he will unveil his face unto you" (D&C 88:68). When we have become one, and are sanctified, and the Lord unveils His face to us, we will recognize Him in part because we will have already seen Him reflected time and again in the faces of our spouses.

NOTES

1. William Shakespeare, *King Lear,* act 1, scene 1, line 166.
2. J Ballard Washburn, "The Temple Is a Family Affair," *Ensign,* May 1995, 12.

MAKING COURSE CORRECTIONS IN LIFE'S VOYAGES

Kristin Trussel

I love the gospel of Jesus Christ. The gospel brings peace, hope, direction, and promise to my life. My greatest desire is to return to live with my Heavenly Father along with the people that I love. I sometimes feel like holding up a big sign that says Celestial Kingdom or Bust!

We learn in the Pearl of Great Price that the return of each one of us is also God's greatest desire. Moses 1:39 reads, "For behold, this is my work and my glory—to bring to pass the immortality and eternal life of man." He wants us all to be on a Celestial Kingdom or Bust journey in this life.

The Prophet Joseph Smith said, "A very large ship is benefited very much by a very small helm in the time of a storm" (D&C 123:16).

Now, I have never had the experience of navigating a very large ship in the time of a storm, but I do have an SUV with power steering. Isn't it amazing that with just a few fingers and a thumb, I can maneuver two tons of vehicle through traffic? Power steering does not require monumental strength or determination to completely change the direction your car is going. Likewise, our efforts to change or correct our course do not always have to be monumental. Small adjustments in our thoughts, words, and

---

Kristin Trussel loves being a wife, the mother of five children, and a homemaker. She served a mission in Peru and has served in leadership positions in ward Young Women, Relief Society, and Primary presidencies. Whether it is with Sunbeams, Gospel Doctrine, or the Laurels, one thing that brings her true joy is teaching the gospel of Jesus Christ.

actions can produce powerful change in getting us or keeping us on the course back to our Heavenly Father. Small and simple steps are the power steering in our life's voyages. Or, "by small and simple things are great things brought to pass" (Alma 37:6).

I am going to share with you three basic navigational tools our Heavenly Father has given us to help us chart our course back to Him.

1. HUMBLY TRUST IN OUR LOVING HEAVENLY FATHER

Proverbs 3:5–6 reads: "Trust in the Lord with all thine heart; and lean not unto thine own understanding. In all thy ways acknowledge him, and he shall direct thy paths."

We all have been given the same potential destination, but we each have been given our own individual path or route to reach that destination. I had the sweet opportunity of serving a mission in South America. I love Peru and the wonderful people I met there. I especially loved my first companion, Hermana Cruz. Her childhood and youth had been completely different than mine. She lived in extreme poverty; I was blessed with an overabundance of temporal blessings. Her father was an alcoholic and left her mother to raise her large family; I was blessed with parents, grandparents, and a large extended family who I know love me and always support me. She was a convert to the Church of just a few years; my genealogy has pioneer roots. One day she asked me, "Why do you think you were so lucky to be born in the United States and in the gospel?" After some sweet discussion, the Spirit bore witness to both of us that with an eternal perspective it doesn't really matter where we have been or where we are. What matters is where we are headed.

Having the humility to trust and accept our Father in Heaven's life choice for us—with gratitude, regardless of the detours, bumpy roads, and sometimes boring scenery—will provide peace and happiness on our journey.

I was blessed with a mother who trusted in the Lord and humbly accepted the journey our Heavenly Father chose for her. Shortly after my mother married her high school sweetheart and had me, her only child, she was diagnosed with Hodgkin's lymphoma. When I was just an infant, the doctors told her she would most likely have only six months to live.

Despite the physical decline of her body, and the heartache I know she must have felt facing the thought of leaving her precious family, she did not complain or murmur about her stormy voyage. I treasure a recording made of a talk she gave at a Relief Society meeting shortly before she died. These are her words as she testifies of her trust in the Lord:

"I know this church is true, and I am so grateful for that extra day I have each morning to maybe be of service to others. I know my Heavenly Father knows me; with all the fasting and prayers on my behalf and my constant nagging at Him, He knows me. And if He does take me, it will be for some purpose, and I will feel it a privilege to maybe be able to serve others somewhere else if this is what He has in store for me. I hope that He will let me stay here with the people that I love. But I have a testimony that He will do those things that are best for me. I love the gospel; my life would be nothing without it. I leave you with my testimony and hope that you will take your testimonies to those that need you."

I am so grateful Heavenly Father blessed me with a righteous mother and that he allowed her to live eight years and not just those six months the doctors promised. Throughout those years, as her physical body weakened, her spirit grew stronger and her determination to stay on course steadier.

She did this through small and simple things such as:
- being grateful for each day,
- looking for and speaking of the blessings she had instead of dwelling on the adversity in her life,
- and looking to the gospel plan for hope and promise.

2. Pray Sincerely and Often

In Numbers 21, we read that when the Israelites were bitten by fiery serpents they cried to Moses to please ask the Lord to help them. The Lord told Moses to make a serpent of brass, and if the Israelites would look upon the serpent they would be healed. In Alma 33, we read that many of these Israelites did look and did live. But there were many whose hearts were hardened; because of the easiness of the way and because they did not believe in such a simple thing, they perished. I have often asked myself, "Why did they not look? It seems so simple." But may I suggest that prayer may be just like looking to the serpent. It is so simple—maybe even easier than looking at a serpent because when we pray within our hearts, we don't even have to move a muscle. We can pray at any time, in any place, and in any situation. Nobody but ourselves can prevent us from praying. Heavenly Father has made it very easy to communicate with Him. Yet how often do we seek out our friends and family with our concerns and our joys without even considering conversing with the Lord in prayer about the matter?

I have struggled with this dilemma, and I am trying harder to seek out the Lord more. Sometimes I have had to pray just to feel the desire to pray.

I have prayed during a heated conversation that I might be humble enough to say something that could diffuse the situation.

I have prayed to know how to implement morning family prayer. Praying together in the evening after family scripture study is not usually a problem for my family. But with my daughter starting early-morning seminary, each member of my family has a radically different morning schedule, and praying together in the morning was proving to be a challenge. My seminary student gets up at 5 A.M., and my second daughter gets up an hour after that for junior high and leaves just right before my two elementary girls need to get up. And because I have a very dear and hard-working husband who has a radical travel schedule and is sleep deprived most of the time, waking everyone up at 5:30 A.M. was not going to work. I prayed over this and felt impressed that for our morning family prayer it would be acceptable to my Heavenly Father if I prayed with each family member individually as they woke up. I would be the string that links our morning family prayer together. My family has been blessed because of my seeking out the Lord about this. I have felt an increase in love, communication, and kindness with each of my five children as I have begun to kneel individually with them each morning for our "family prayer."

I have prayed over the phone with a dear friend as her ship was going through her own tremendous personal storm. I was too far away from her to put my arms around her or do anything to help, so I told her I was going to say a prayer right then. As we prayed, I felt her strength increase.

I have prayed a few months after the birth of my third child. I was struggling with self-doubt and insecurities. I felt overwhelmed and dissatisfied with my abilities to mother a newborn and two preschool girls, keep house, be a loving and supportive wife to my husband, and so on. After several tearful days in my pajamas, I was at the bottom of the barrel. I put a video in for my three- and four-year-olds, went to my room two levels above the girls, shut the door, and fell to my knees in despair. I cried to my Heavenly Father that I did not feel fit to raise these precious girls. I couldn't do it all and they deserved better than my mothering skills and example of housekeeping. And I was sure He had made a mistake sending me any of His children at all. I pleaded for help, for strength, and for reassurance. Just at that moment, and long before their video had ended, my two little girls crept up those two flights of stairs to my room, opened the door, and quietly came in. Right in the middle of my prayer, I felt sweet little hands rubbing my back and a sweet little voice saying, "It's okay, Mommy, I love you. Be happy!"

I know that our Heavenly Father does hear and answer our prayers.

But I also know, because I learned at a young age, that sometimes His answer is not what we hope for, but that a loving Heavenly Father will always provide for us what we need. The last night my mother was in our home was a calm and sweet one. I did not know as I went to bed that it would be the last night I would see her. Sometime in the night I was awakened with the news that my mother was going to the hospital. This was not the first hospital trip she had made in the night. Going to the doctor and the hospital was a usual occurrence, and being so young, I usually would have taken news like that in stride. However, this night I sensed that something was different.

I remember feeling panicked, frightened, and desperate. For the first time in my eight-year-old life, I realized that my mother was indeed going to die. I remember jumping out of my bed and kneeling and praying intently to Heavenly Father that He would allow my mother to live. I remember crying and trying to bargain with Him that if she had to die, would He please at least keep her alive until I was married and had a child of my own? As I was kneeling, crying, and pleading in prayer, I came to know, in a very personal and real sense, why the Holy Ghost is called the Comforter. As I prayed I felt a sweet peace surround me, a peace so real and abundant that I quickly quit crying and was able to climb back into bed and fall fast asleep. My Father in Heaven did not grant the pleas of my prayer that night that my mother would live, but He did provide for me. He sent the Holy Ghost to calm my troubled heart and replace the panic and fear with peace. I testify to you that He did answer my prayer that night. I am so grateful for that experience! Since I was eight years old there has never been a doubt in my mind that there is a God who watches over us and loves us. That night, prayer was the small helm that steered me through a great storm in my voyage.

3. Continually Nourish Our Souls

I did not have a lot of experience with the scriptures as a child. My father joined the Church when I was four years old. After my mother died, life was difficult for my father and me. We both were doing the best we could just to survive emotionally. We didn't understand the strength the scriptures could bring. However, after a lifetime of small and simple steps, I now understand the strength of the scriptures. I love the scriptures! Let me share with you some of those small and simple steps that helped me gain such a great love for the scriptures.

My first step was in a Sunday School class when I was young. We had a returned missionary for a teacher. I don't remember his name or even his face, but I remember how I felt as he testified that the Book of Mormon was the most correct book ever on the earth and that it contained all the answers to obtain happiness in this life. It was a brief encounter, but I felt something—small and simple steps.

As a teenager, I was sleeping at a friend's house. We were leaving very early in the morning to go to a camp. As teenage girls do, my friend and I stayed up way too late talking and chatting. Finally, when it looked like we would get just a few hours of sleep, we decided to go to bed. I was going to sleep in the spare room next to hers. I was so tired, all I wanted to do was fall on the bed and sleep in a heap. But I had the thought, *Is there an alarm clock set?* I shuffled back to her room expecting to see my friend asleep, just as I wished to be. Instead, as I pushed open her door, there was a light still on in her room, and she was there reading her scriptures. As I looked at her, I felt that familiar feeling and I felt a desire to be like her. I knew it was a good thing—small and simple steps.

As a Laurel I was blessed to have an angel here on earth as a Young Women president. She loved the scriptures and bore very sweet and powerful testimony of them. I felt that feeling again and again in her lessons and whenever I was blessed to be with her.

She played the guitar and knew I had a desire to learn to play also. She invited me to experiment upon the word by telling me she would give me guitar lessons if I would read the Book of Mormon as payment. A deal was made, and I started opening and reading my scriptures. I have to tell you I don't remember understanding or feeling anything as I read the first 427 pages. I was pretty much just moving my eyes and turning pages and checking off my chart until page 427, 3 Nephi 11. As I read those pages I could see Christ appearing to the Nephites in my mind, and I felt a familiar, very good feeling in my room. I wanted to keep reading more than my daily goal of check marks on the chart. I read the whole account of Christ's ministry to the Nephites before putting my book away that night. Unfortunately, after Christ's ministry in 3 Nephi, I went back to moving my eyes, turning pages, and checking off my chart. But for one night I felt something reading the scriptures—small and simple steps.

Wonderfully, as a young adult, I had an amazing friend as a roommate. She knew of my inexperience with the scriptures and asked me if I wanted to read them together. As we read the Book of Mormon together, she had a gift for making the prophets and stories come alive and helped me see how we can liken the scriptures to our lives and how to use them for spiritual strength. I will always be grateful to my Heavenly Father for those precious months I had as her roommate. That small step of reading nightly with my friend set me on a course to serve a mission. "By small and simple [steps] are great things brought to pass."

While serving that mission, the studying and teaching and testifying from the scriptures every day cemented the testimony and passion I feel for the scriptures now. It was such a blessing to immerse myself in the scriptures by reading, teaching, and testifying of them every day. I felt it was a privilege and honor to represent Jesus Christ and proclaim that the Book of Mormon is another testament of Him and the word of God.

Unfortunately, as a new bride and young mother, the time, passion, and energy I spent with the scriptures dwindled almost to a complete standstill. Apart from reading and preparing a lesson Saturday night, I was not nourishing my spirit, but more like keeping it on a diet. One day, I was blessed to have an *Ensign* article placed in my possession by that same friend who read with me before my mission. The article was about the ten virgins and the importance of filling our lamps with oil. I don't remember if the question was written in the article or not, but I felt the Spirit whisper to me, "Kristin, are you mostly polishing your lamp or filling it?" I then reflected on my days.

The fact was, I spent close to sixty minutes a day polishing my lamp with showering, blow drying my hair, and applying makeup. I thought of the time shopping for and caring for, washing and ironing and picking out what I and my little girls would wear in a day. Then there was all the cleaning and polishing and catalog perusing and shopping to find the perfect little "what not" for my home. I even thought of how much time I spent picking out just the perfect little outfits with cute little bows and matching little shoes for my two little girls. Yet I did not even spend five minutes a day in my scriptures—those same scriptures that I love and testified so strongly of on my mission.

I was ashamed and compelled to repent. I then made a commitment to myself that I would fill my lamp with oil, even if it was just a few drops, before any polishing was done. My friends know now that if they see me out in public with my baseball hat on and not necessarily smelling as fresh as a daisy that I had no time for my shower, but that I got carried away reading my scriptures and ran out of time to polish. The smallest thing of reading an *Ensign* article was a small helm steering me through my life's voyage.

I am so grateful the Lord provided us navigational tools to help us chart our course back to Him. I know that if we *humbly trust in our loving Heavenly Father,* He knows the course that is best for us. If we gratefully accept our journey, *pray sincerely and often,* and *continually nourish our souls* with the word of God, we will be on a course to return to our Heavenly Father. Through our small and simple steps coupled with the infinite and monumental step our Savior took for us through His Atonement, it is possible for all of us to reach our destination. For His willingness to suffer unimaginable pain and die for that purpose I give my eternal gratitude and love to our older brother, Jesus Christ. He is my king, my friend, and my Redeemer. I do love Him more than I could ever express. My testimony of the gospel of Jesus Christ is my most precious possession. I know that if we apply the principles Jesus Christ taught, along with the healing power of His Atonement, to our problems and pains and the messes we make in this life, they will be solved, healed, and made perfectly clean. I thank my Heavenly Father, who loves us so much He sent His Beloved Son.

I know Joseph Smith was a prophet of God. He was the one chosen to usher in the Restoration. One day I hope to throw my arms around him and thank him for his sacrifices. Because of his faith and courage, my life is blessed with

- the saving ordinances of the temple,
- the blessing of the priesthood power,
- continuing revelation through a prophet, Gordon B. Hinckley; and
- the Book of Mormon, the Pearl of Great Price, and the Doctrine and Covenants—more nourishment for my soul.

May God bless us to make small and simple steps and to remember that it's the Celestial Kingdom or Bust!

BE OF GOOD CHEER

Trenton Hickman

Many times in the scriptures, we see that the Savior counsels His prophets, apostles, and followers to "be of good cheer." Clearly, we choose to live an important aspect of the plan of salvation when we and our families find a way not just to be cheerful but to be cheered by Jesus and His role in helping us back to our Heavenly Father.

I'd like to discuss some of the different scriptural contexts for this phrase—"be of good cheer"—and explore a few ways that Jesus would have "us cheerfully do all things that lie in our power" so that we may "stand still, with the utmost assurance, to see the salvation of God, and for his arm to be revealed" (D&C 123:17).

BEING OF GOOD CHEER MEANS NOT FREAKING OUT

One of the first times in the New Testament record that we read of Jesus telling His disciples to "be of good cheer" can be read in Matthew 14:22–27 (and again in Mark 6:45–50). Jesus, having fed the five thousand, tells His apostles to set out by boat on the Sea of Galilee and to meet Him on the other side. While they head out by boat, Jesus retires to a

Trenton Hickman is an associate professor of English at Brigham Young University. He holds degrees from Brigham Young University and a PhD from the State University of New York at Stony Brook. He and his wife, Wendy, are the parents of three children.

nearby mountain to pray, and perhaps to find solace, because His cousin John the Baptist has just been beheaded and Jesus may have needed some time to be alone with the Spirit to think and to grieve. Shortly thereafter, the apostles encounter what the scriptures call a "contrary" wind and find themselves "tossed with waves"; Mark adds that they were "toiling in rowing" against this wind, one that clearly stood in the way of their arrival at the previously-agreed-upon destination where Jesus would be awaiting them. In the "fourth watch of the night," or between 3 A.M. and 6 A.M., the beleaguered apostles see Jesus walking upon the water to reach them and think that it is "a spirit, and [they cry] out in fear." Jesus, not wanting to scare the apostles, speaks unto them "straightway," or immediately, saying, "Be of good cheer; it is I; be not afraid."

How should we read Jesus' injunction to the apostles? Quite simply, Jesus is telling them to cheer up and not be scared, though he surely understands that seeing a figure walking on water in the early morning darkness would be enough to give anyone a fright. I wonder, though, if Jesus isn't also telling the apostles, if we were to translate it into more contemporary slang, "Don't freak out!" The apostles had no reason to fear— after all, they were doing exactly what Jesus had told them to do. Having been exactly obedient to Jesus' commands, why would the apostles worry that Jesus would fail them in their hour of need?

Even though we can likewise lay claim to the Savior's blessings, we all occasionally freak out. Not long ago, I sat in a large chapel in Puebla, Mexico, for sacrament meeting services. Three other LDS colleagues and I had escaped from our academic conference out to a nearby residential area where we'd located, with a taxi driver's help, one of the many LDS church buildings in the area. It was a bit warm in the chapel, but opened windows on either side of the room and a fleet of fans overhead moved the air around enough so that we could be comfortable.

Unfortunately, I wasn't nearly as comfortable sitting there as I should have been. The day before, when walking through the *zócalo*—the beautiful town square that is at the center of every colonial-era Mexican city— I hadn't been watching where I was going and had stepped into a narrow drainage hole, twisting my ankle, bloodying my shin, and soaking my foot in a pestilentially green pool of water at the bottom of the drain. Truth be told, the whole thing was hilarious, and even as I fell I could imagine how the whole thing looked to my group of friends and the shocked Mexicans spending an afternoon in the park with their families. If only there had been video footage of my pratfall, I'd have made it onto *America's Funniest Home Videos* for sure.

I slogged back to my hotel in my wet shoe and pants and surveyed the damage. I could already tell that things weren't going to be good. My leg and ankle were puffing up, and I was wary of the cuts on my leg and their immersion in the green slime. I showered, sizzled my cuts with the hand sanitizer that I'd brought with me to Mexico, and tried to prop my leg up on some pillows and rest. Despite all these efforts, by Sunday morning my lower shin, my ankle, and the top part of my foot had turned a blueberry purple. I could sense that nothing was broken, but my leg hurt, and the worrywart in me went into high gear. "How will I walk all over Puebla on my leg today?" I wondered. "What if I have to run through the airport in Mexico City tomorrow in order to make my connecting flight back to the States? What if my leg becomes infected before I get home and can get to my own doctor?" Though I had loved my stay in Mexico, I was in no mood to acquaint myself with the local medical system on the fly, but the prospect of hobbling around until I got home left my stomach churning.

These thoughts and more tossed in my head like a "contrary wind" as I sat waiting for sacrament meeting to start. Soon, however, the members of the Del Sol Ward came and greeted us—*poblano* men sharply dressed in white shirts and colorful ties, women anxious to present their shy sons and daughters, and others who wanted to shake the hands of the visiting *gringos*. After the initial press of friendly members returned to their seats to await the start of sacrament meeting, a white-haired grandmother with a wrinkled face and a few teeth missing in her smile inched over to us, her hand extended. I could see that her hands were gnarled and world-worn, her legs spidered with bulging veins, but she still made the effort to come over, shake my hand, and call me *hermano*.

At that moment, I realized that this was where I was supposed to be, my purple leg and foot notwithstanding, and that I'd be fine. I needed not to sit and stew but to "be of good cheer." Freaking out about my bruised leg—which probably wasn't as bad as my worried mind was making it out to be—wasn't going to do me any good right then, and fretting about my leg would keep me from this special opportunity to worship with these good people, many of whom were at church in spite of their own ailments, hunger, poverty, and other worldly cares.

In Doctrine and Covenants 61:36–37, we read: "And now, verily I say unto you, and what I say unto one I say unto all, be of good cheer, little children; for I am in your midst, and I have not forsaken you; and inasmuch as you have humbled yourselves before me, the blessings of the kingdom are yours." As we seek to obey our Heavenly Father and do our best to be of good cheer, we will be led along toward all the blessings that await us—blessings that we may not even have imagined could be ours. We would do well to remember that Jesus' walking on water was prelude to Peter being able to have the same wonderful experience, albeit for only a few seconds before Peter once again started to freak out and then found himself sputtering in the water. As we seek to "cheerfully do all things that lie in our power" and to keep from being afraid, who knows what wonderful things the Lord will be able to unfold in our lives and in the lives of our families?

Similarly, we need to not "freak out" when it comes to how we deal with each other in our families. Since we know that many of "the blessings of the kingdom" mentioned in Doctrine and Covenants 61 are tied to our eternal families, we would do well to pick our battles with one another as we go through family life together, for what will it profit us to flip out at every little thing that we don't like about members of our families or the choices that they make, only to find that we've lost in the process the very blessing we were seeking, that of having a loving relationship with them throughout the eternities? Sometimes making the choice to hold one's tongue with family members may feel like a miracle not unlike walking on water, but we surely don't want to forfeit eternal blessings for the immediate gratification of personal pride or because of disagreements that are petty when examined from a long-range view.

Being of Good Cheer Means That the Lord Will Cheer Us with His Spirit

In 2006, our second-oldest son, Jonah, turned eight and was baptized and confirmed. As part of the process of getting prepared to become an official member of the Church, Jonah began to think about what it meant to be baptized and specifically what it meant to receive the Holy Ghost in his life. "Dad," he asked me during one of our monthly father's interviews, "how will I know when the Holy Ghost is telling me to do something? Will I feel a warm feeling in my chest?" I told Jonah that sometimes we do feel a "burning in the bosom" when the Spirit speaks to us, but other times, the Spirit may communicate with us in more subtle ways that could even involve putting thoughts into our heads about things that we should do. "Sometimes, these thoughts will seem like they could be your own thoughts," I explained, "but you realize that they might be there because the Holy Ghost wants you to act on them."

A few weeks later, when it was Jonah's turn to choose our family home evening activity, he announced that he really wanted to take some cookies to Sister Beckstrand, an elderly sister in our ward whom I had home taught for several years. "Sounds great," I said. We love Sister Beckstrand, and I figured that whatever the reason that Jonah felt moved to deliver her some cookies, it was a great idea.

An hour or so later, Wendy and I waited with Noah and Jonah on Sister Beckstrand's doorstep. Jonah rang the bell, and Sister Beckstrand swept open her door with a wide smile. "Hello!" she said. "I see you've come to celebrate my birthday with me!" "Yes!" I answered, a shocked smile plastered on my face, and we entered her condo. At that moment, I felt like a huge loser of a home teacher. How could I have forgotten it was her birthday? We sat and ate cookies and milk with Sister Beckstrand, saw her birthday presents and cards, and enjoyed visiting together.

When we returned to our car to go home, Jonah piped up in back. "Dad, can I ask you a question?" he said.

"Sure," I answered.

"Did you know that it was Sister Beckstrand's birthday today?"

"No," I said, "I didn't."

Jonah thought about this for a minute. "But Heavenly Father knew it was Sister Beckstrand's birthday today, didn't he, Dad?"

I smiled. "Yes, Jonah, He did."

Imagine the cheer that Jonah felt when he realized that he'd followed some promptings from the Spirit that made someone else cheerful in turn!

One of the reasons we should be of good cheer is because we've been given access to the Spirit through the gift of the Holy Ghost, which we've been invited to receive. We also can access the Spirit through the revelation of God's will to our local Church leaders and to the Brethren. As we build into our lives a desire to receive the gift of the Holy Ghost and to maintain a personal and family lifestyle that aids in the Spirit being in our lives and homes, a great cheer will come as we hear the voice of the Lord in our small, everyday interactions. Is it any wonder that the prophets always return to the essentials of regular personal and family prayers, personal and family scripture study, family home evening, and so forth? All these activities invite the Spirit, and the Spirit brings us cheer.

Once, as I served in a bishopric in Orem, Utah, we were brainstorming ways to help members of the Church be more invested in studying the scriptures on a daily basis. I decided that I'd play devil's advocate a bit with the bishop, and I asked why, other than simply being obedient, members *should* read their scriptures daily. The bishop smiled, looked at me, and replied, "Oh, Brother Hickman, you've missed the point completely. We don't study the scriptures simply to master the information that's there. In fact, often when I study the scriptures I don't end up pondering those particular verses at all, but the feelings and impressions that the Spirit sends to me as part of my scripture study, impressions that may or may not have to do with the verses I'm reading. All I know is that I haven't found any surer way to invite the Spirit into my mind and heart than regular scripture study and prayer. Have you?" I had enough sense to smile and nod and not answer, since I too had experienced the good cheer that comes in such moments.

Being of Good Cheer Means Bringing Cheer to Others

In Acts 23, the Apostle Paul has been imprisoned in Jerusalem for preaching the gospel of Jesus Christ. There, he has been interrogated, smitten, and awaits death as a group plots how to kill him. But then the Lord appears to him in the jail and says to Paul in verse 11, "Be of good cheer, Paul: for as thou hast testified of me in Jerusalem, so must thou bear witness also at Rome." One wonders if Paul thought, "Oh, great! Just what I need! Out of the frying pan and into the fire!" What Paul may not have known is that he would have the chance to teach the gospel to many more important men in the Roman Empire before his death, and that even though it would take a shipwreck to do it, he would once again live a free man to continue the work he so loved to do.

Many years later, the same Jesus Christ would tell Orson Hyde in his ordination to "proclaim the everlasting gospel," to "be of good cheer, and do not fear, for I the Lord am with you, and will stand by you; and ye shall bear record of me, even Jesus Christ, that I am the Son of the living God, that I was, that I am, and that I am to come" (D&C 68:1, 6). Again, two forms of cheer work here. First, there is the pleasure of knowing that the Lord is with us, and will stand by us—how could that not cheer us up? Second, there is the cheer that bearing testimony of "the Son of the living God" brings. Missionary work—whether that is to unconverted or under-converted members of our own families or to friends and neighbors of other faiths—has its own unique type of cheer built in.

Over the course of my life, I've had several good friends become interested in the Church and want to take the missionary discussions. In every case, the act of being able to share my testimony and the deep feelings that I have for the gospel of Jesus Christ cheered me, even in the cases when my friends decided that they weren't interested in joining the Church. In the case of my good friend Mike who did choose to join the Church, my cheer has only increased as he served a mission, married in the temple, and now has had his first son be born in the covenant that he and his wife made with the Lord.

Bringing cheer to others isn't limited to missionary work, though. In fact, one of the best ways that we can make the gospel a reality is by actively working with our family to cement eternal relationships by creating good memories together. While family vacations and other once-in-a-lifetime activities with our families would fit into this category, I feel like it's the less-expensive, everyday sorts of activities that we engage in together that help us understand why we wanted to belong to a forever family in the first place.

For example, one of my best memories from my own family is a quirky activity that started as almost an afterthought one New Year's Eve and then evolved into a regular family activity in subsequent years. Wanting to celebrate New Year's Eve together without going out on the town, we decided to walk around the house gathering random items that would be divvied up as "props" to be used by two different "teams" that would make impromptu movies that the teams would have to conceive, plan, film, and present within the space of an hour or so. All of the props—however strange they might have been—needed to be used in the movies we would make, and every single person had to have some role in the film. The plots of these movies were crazy, even ridiculous—spies and intrigue, talk shows, the adventures of a misfit space crew on a strange planet where they crash-land—and trying to get the different scenes filmed in a single take was almost impossible because we'd burst out laughing. And what of the characters that we devised to fit these plots? With names like Nancy Ann Seancy, Pepe Bouffant, and Mad Cow Max, you probably get a sense of the insane range of possibilities.

By the time we'd made the movies, watched each other's over-the-top acting, and laughed at the improbable use of each prop, we had formed memories that would become the script for many of our future family interactions. To this day, some of the lines of dialogue from these movies have become sayings that we repeat to each other, and each time we share these off-the-wall lines, all those good feelings bubble back up all over again. While each of us has his or her favorite family movie, we all agree that none of these movies should go public anytime soon. In fact, a few years ago one of my sisters and her husband had their storage unit burglarized, and a copy of these family videos was among the stolen items. We were all sad for my sister and her husband's lost possessions, but we still can't help but crack up at the thought of the hapless thief trying to make sense out of these movies.

In December 2006, I sat in a sealing room in the Denver Colorado Temple with my youngest sister, Merideth, on her wedding day, and I looked around to see my mom and dad, my wife, and all my sisters there together. It was one of the best days of my life. To be sure, a significant part of cheer of that day came from knowing that all these special people in my life were worthy to be there; we gain happiness from knowing that we're keeping the covenants that we make with the Lord. But another important part of my cheer on that day had everything to do with our family movies and a thousand moments of family fun and closeness that I've stored up, one experience at a time, for all the years of our lives together. If through these sorts of experiences we can help our families to get a testimony of why we would want to live together forever, we have carried out some of the most important missionary work around.

BEING OF GOOD CHEER MEANS MAKING FULL USE OF THE ATONEMENT

In 3 Nephi 1, you'll recall that a day had been appointed when those who believed the words of Samuel the Lamanite regarding Christ's birth—and who were waiting for the signs of His first coming to the earth—would be put to death by the unbelievers. The prophet of that day, Nephi, decided that he'd approach the Lord in prayer. We read in verses 12 and 13: "And it came to pass that he cried mightily unto the Lord all that day; and behold, the voice of the Lord came unto him, saying: Lift up your head and be of good cheer; for behold, the time is at hand, and on this night shall the sign be given, and on the morrow come I into the world, to show unto the world that I will fulfil all that which I have caused to be spoken by the mouth of my holy prophets."

Though it's clear that the immediate source of cheer for Nephi and his people was to be their stay of execution—not a small prize, to be sure—the ultimate cheer referenced in the Lord's words is His birth, which would start the earthly phase of what we would know in its culmination as the Atonement, that great reconciliation between God and humankind for all of our sins and transgressions. We might consider as the other bookend of this scripture in 3 Nephi 1 the words that the Savior shares with His apostles in John 16:33 following His suffering, death, and resurrection: "These things I have spoken unto you, that in me ye might have peace. In the world ye shall have tribulation: but be of good cheer; I have overcome the world."

If there is only one cheer that we can instill in our own lives and in the lives of our friends and families, it should be that the Atonement of Jesus Christ gives us reason every day to find happiness, even under the bleakest of circumstances. Often, this cheer comes from the realization that the Atonement offers us a second chance to change our lives through repentance. Sometimes, though, the Atonement cheers us because it helps us see that Christ has perfect compassion for us in our moments of trial and stress, those times when we're really doing things mostly right but find ourselves down and out nonetheless.

Probably the first time that I really understood the capacity of the Atonement to help buoy up our spirits came during the first days of my mission in Venezuela. After a relatively comfortable night in the mission home and the last pancake breakfast I'd have for a great while, we met with the mission president to be told about our first companions. These companions arrived shortly thereafter to take us to our different areas across the Venezuelan countryside. My first area was only two hours from Caracas by bus, so my companion and I headed to the Nuevo Circo bus terminal in downtown Caracas—a bustling cacophony of a place, full of color and a sea of travelers. We purchased our fare and took my luggage to the bus.

After only a few minutes on the bus and only moments before our scheduled departure time, my companion abruptly told me, "Get off the bus. I think we need to check on your luggage." When we went around the back of the bus, two of my three pieces of luggage were missing. Before I knew it, my companion whisked me away and we ran through the congested parking lot where buses prepared to head to all corners of the country. Ahead of us, two Venezuelan men walked briskly away with my bags. My companion hollered something angry after them in Spanish—and I'm not sure I want to know what he said, but at the time I couldn't understand it. The men panicked and dropped one of the two stolen bags as they started to run. To this day, I regard with a strange admiration their ability to vault a tall chain-link fence with my heavy bag in their arms.

As we returned to the bus and started our ride to my first area, the realization of what had just happened set in, and I started to take a mental inventory of what I'd lost. My family pictures were gone. The patriarchal blessing I'd tucked away in the pages of my only set of English-language scriptures? Gone. Those special letters I'd saved that my mom and dad sent me while I was in the Missionary Training Center? All gone. A few hours later, my companion and I arrived at the apartment that we shared with another companionship of elders. They ruefully explained that they'd forgotten to pay the electricity bill, so I'd be unpacking by candlelight, and by the way, we didn't have a single investigator on our proselyting schedule because the missionaries had been feeling "a little under the weather lately and hadn't been able to get out much."

As I sat in the muggy darkness of my room putting my remaining belongings into a battered chest of drawers in the light of that single flickering flame, I reflected on all the homecoming talks I'd heard growing up in my ward in Boulder, Colorado. Best two years of my life. Loved the people. Wouldn't have changed anything. Sad to have to come home. I decided that there were two possibilities: either all those speakers had been lying through their teeth, or they'd decided to abandon the rigors of missionary work and be tourists instead, and heck, who wouldn't like an all-expenses-paid vacation for two years?

Then I was finished unpacking, and it came time to do what I'd done every day of my life—I'd say my evening prayer before going to bed. I'd had meaningful prayers before, but my prayers meant something different that night than they ever had before in my life. How could Heavenly Father have let all this happen to me on my first full day in the country? Was this supposed to be my auspicious introduction to "the field is white already to harvest"? (D&C 4:4).

I'm not going to lie and say that everything was better after that night—indeed, those first few weeks were very challenging ones. But that night I remembered a scripture that I had read but finally understood better than I ever had before: "Be still and know that I am God" (D&C 101:16). Heavenly Father hadn't forgotten me but was rather allowing me to learn a few things that I wouldn't be able to learn otherwise.

Though it seemed apocalyptic at the time, I've since learned that my first night in Venezuela was not one of the hardest things that I'd be asked to endure in my life. I'm sure that you can think of much bleaker days in your own life that seriously eclipse that one night that I suffered through in Maracay. Still, no matter the particulars or scale of the challenge, the lesson is the same: because of the Atonement of Jesus Christ, we can be of good cheer. Because of the Atonement of Jesus Christ, we can be still and know that God can cheer us through His Spirit, even in the darkest hours that we'll encounter in our lives.

Elder Neal A. Maxwell, himself one of the best examples I've encountered of one who was of good cheer even in the face of desperate odds, said: "Brothers and sisters, these are our days. This is *our time* on earth! These are *our tasks* to be done!

"And in these days, being of good cheer is part of being valiant in the testimony of Jesus. (See D&C 76:79; D&C 121:29.)

"Finally, in those moments when we feel the pain which is a necessary part of the plan of happiness, we can remember that there was an ancient time when that plan was first unveiled. Then the perceptive among us voted not secretly, but audibly—by shouting for joy! (See Job 38:7.) Let us not go back on those feelings now—for we saw more clearly then what we are experiencing now!"[1]

By not freaking out, by inviting the Spirit into our lives and the lives of our families, by bringing cheer to others, and by making full use of the Atonement of Jesus Christ, I testify to you that we can be of good cheer. Though our lives will include disappointment, sorrow, illness, and death, all of the suffering that we experience as human beings in this life has already been anticipated, experienced, and understood perfectly by our Savior Jesus Christ so that we can have a fulness of cheer in our lives on this earth and in the eternities to come.

NOTE

1. Neal A. Maxwell, "'Be of Good Cheer,'" *Ensign*, November 1982, 68; emphasis in original.

INDEX